EVENING PRAYERBOOK
Sunday Vespers
LITURGY OF THE HOURS

EVENING PRAYERBOOK

Sunday Vespers
LITURGY OF THE HOURS

PATMOS
TOOLS FOR WORSHIP

SHOHOLA, PA
IN ASSOCIATION WITH THE ST. THOMAS MORE
HOUSE OF PRAYER, CRANBERRY, PA

The English translation of the Introductory Verse, Antiphons, Responsories, Intercessions, Psalm-Prayers, Titles, Scripture and Patristic Sentences, Concluding Rite, and Canticle of the Lamb from The Liturgy of the Hours © 1974, 1975, 1976, International Committee on English in the Liturgy, Inc. (ICEL); the English translation of the Concluding Prayers from The Roman Missal © 1973, ICEL.
All rights reserved.

The Psalms: A New Translation © The Grail, (England) 1963.

The International Committee on English in the Liturgy, Inc. is grateful to the following for permission to reproduce copyright material:

Benedictine Nuns of Stanbrook Abbey, from Stanbrook Abbey Hymnal, "Unto Us a Child Is Given."

Church Hymnal Corporation, "Father We Thank Thee Who Hast Planted" © 1940, Church Pension Fund.

Geoffrey-Chapman Publishers for James Quinn, S.J., "May Flights of Angels Lead You On Your Way."

Faber Music Ltd., London from New Catholic Hymnal, © 1971 copyright by Faber Music Ltd., "At the Lamb's High Feast" (adapted by Geoffrey Laycock), "Christ Is Made the Sure Foundation" (adapted by Anthony G. Petti), "Christ Jesus Lay in Death's Strong Bands" (adapted by Anthony G. Petti).

G.I.A. Publications, Inc. Chicago, Illinois, from Worship © 1971 copyright by G.I.A. Publications, "Love Divine, All Loves Excelling."

Oxford University Press, London, for "When Mary Brought Her Treasure" by Jan Struther, 1901-1955, from Enlarged Songs of Praise, by permission of Oxford University Press.

Search Press, London, "Hail Redeemer, King Divine" by P. Brennan, C.S.S.R. from the Westminster Hymnal.

World Library Publications, Inc., 3825 North Willow Road, Schiller Park, Illinois 60176,: for Rev. M. Quinn, O.P., "O Christ You Are the Light and Day"; from Peoples Mass Book © 1971, copyright by World Library Publications, "Draw Near, O Lord," "O Sacred Head," "Sing praise to our Creator," "This is our accepted time."

English translation of the Gloria Patri, and the Magnificat by the International Consultation on English Texts.

New Testament Canticles (except the Magnificat) and Scripture readings in this work are taken from the New American Bible © 1970 Confraternity of Christian Doctrine, Washington, D.C. and are used by permission of the copyright owner. All Rights Reserved. No part of the New American Bible may be reproduced in any form without permission in writing from the copyright owner.

Cover art: "Sunset at Lavacourt," 1880, by Claude Monet; Musee du Petit Palais, Paris. Photo credit: Bridgeman-Giraudon/Art Resource, NY. Picture of book with hands is a detail from "Saint Cecilia," 1896, J. W. Waterhouse; The Andrew Lloyd Webber Art Foundation. "The Missal," 1902, J. W. Waterhouse; Unlocated. "Two Panels of a House Altar," 17th century, Stoganov School; "The Mother of God Hodegetria from Martvili, Georgian goldsmith's art, 10th century. Icon of Christ by Danaila Toneva of Bulgaria. Inside borders by Sister Anna Marie McCormick.

CONTENTS

Foreword

By Wayne Hepler

Rediscovery of the "value of Sunday" and the promotion of the Liturgy of the Hours as "the prayer of the whole people of God" are two pastoral initiatives that John Paul II has stressed repeatedly over the past few years of his pontificate. It is the purpose of this book to lend practical support to the Holy Father in the implementation of these initiatives in order that the Church might be renewed in her mission to make the face of Jesus Christ "shine before the generations of the new millennium."

"On Keeping the Lord's Day Holy"

The Lord's Day is lived well if it is marked from beginning to end by grateful and active remembrance of God's saving work...Even in lay life, when possible, why not make provision for special times of prayer—**especially the solemn celebration of Vespers**, for example . . . which on the eve of Sunday . . . might . . . complete the gift of the Eucharist in people's hearts? (Emphasis added.)

With these words from his Apostolic letter *Dies Domini* ("On Keeping the Lord's Day Holy"), the Holy Father in his characteristically gentle way reminds us that Sunday isn't over when Mass is over. How fitting it would be indeed if after Mass, the football game, naps, or visiting family, the faithful would come together with the whole Church throughout the world and complete their Sunday with the celebration of Sunday Vespers from the Liturgy of the Hours? This would in fact fulfill a specific directive that the Council Fathers at Vatican II expressed in the Constitution on the Sacred Liturgy: **"Pastors of souls should see to it that the chief hours, especially Vespers are celebrated in Church on Sundays and the more solemn feasts."** (Paragraph 100, emphasis added.)

"Promoting the Liturgy of the Hours as the prayer of the whole people of God"

In the Apostolic letter *Novo Millennio Ineunte* ("At the Beginning of the New Millennium") I expressed the hope that the Church would become more and more distinguished in the "art of prayer", learning it ever anew from the lips of the Divine Master. This effort must be expressed above all in the liturgy, the source and summit of ecclesial life. **Consequently, it is important to devote greater pastoral care to promoting the Liturgy of the Hours as a prayer of the whole people of God . . .** If, in fact, priests have a precise mandate to celebrate it, **it is also warmly recommended to lay people.** (Emphasis added.)

These words were spoken by John Paul II at his Wednesday General Audience March 28, 2001 to introduce his catechesis on the Psalms from the Liturgy of the Hours. They echo the words of paragraph 1175 from the Catechism of the Catholic Church: "The Liturgy of the Hours is intended to become the prayer of the whole people of God." They also express the desire of the Council Fathers at Vatican II who, forty years ago, wrote: **"And the laity, too, are encouraged to recite the Divine Office (The Liturgy of the Hours) either with priests, or among themselves or even individually."**

Why this renewed emphasis on the importance of the Liturgy of the Hours in the Church's life of prayer? A reading of the Constitution of the Sacred Liturgy, Chapter IV, *The Divine Office*, makes the reasons for this focus abundantly clear. **Simply stated, prayed in its approved form, there in no other prayer like the Liturgy of the Hours.** It is the official public prayer of the Church for every day of the liturgical year celebrating the life of Jesus Christ in its Seasons, Feasts and Saints—especially in the morning and evening. It is the "very prayer which Christ himself, together with his body addresses to the Father." It is an inseparable part of the whole Liturgy, an extension of the Holy Eucharist, and is devised so that the whole course of the day and night is made holy by the praises of God. To share in this prayer is the "greatest honor of Christ's spouse . . . standing before God's throne in the name of holy mother Church, praising the Lord and interceding for the salvation of the whole world." (SC ℭ 83-101.)

From a practical point of view the Liturgy of the Hours is a "source of piety and nourishment for personal prayer." Indeed it has been called a "school of prayer." In this "school" Christians learn that prayer is expressed "not just in imploring help but also in thanksgiving, praise, adoration, contemplation, listening, and ardent devotion, until the heart truly falls in love." (NMI 33.) Over fifty years ago, in the Year of Jubilee 1950, when the Liturgy of the Hours was first published in English, Francis Cardinal Spellmen of New York wrote an article entitled "An Incentive to Prayer" in which he said "any earnest soul who looks about for helps in his life of prayer . . . need look no further." Extolling the significance of the translation of the Prayer Book into English, the Cardinal predicted that the Breviary would "more than likely become the *Vade Mecum* (companion prayer book) of the man in the street." This hope obviously has not yet materialized and even though after the Second Vatican Council the Prayer Book was revised to make it more accessible to the laity, the Liturgy of the Hours has remained the forgotten part of Church's public prayer. However, with the Holy Father's exhortation not to be content with the "minimum", we are convinced that the time is right to "dare" to introduce the faithful to the celebration of the Liturgy of the Hours. (*Spirtus et Sponsa*, № 14.)

Providentially, my wife and I were introduced to praying the Liturgy of the Hours in the mid 1980's, soon after our conversion to the Catholic Church. For years we prayed Evening Prayer just once a week together with another couple who were familiar with the format of the Office. This was surely a small beginning, but in praying this one "Hour" once a week we became familiar with the rubrics of the prayer and learned how to find our way through the Prayer Book. Slowly we added other Hours to our prayer discipline and began to use the Office as a resource for family prayer. As we gained confidence in praying the Hours, we began to introduce the Liturgy of the Hours to our friends, which eventually led to the building of the St. Thomas More House of Prayer to pray and promote the Liturgy of the Hours among the laity.

To these ends, then, **that the Lord's Day be lived well** and that the Liturgy of the Hours become what it is intended to be, **"the prayer of the whole people of God,"** we have published this volume *Evening Prayerbook: Sunday Vespers*. It takes the one "Hour" targeted by the Council Fathers, Sunday Evening Prayer (Vespers) and makes it completely accessible to those inspired to pray with the Church. Included is a tutorial clearly delineating the rubrics and flow of the prayer. There are cross-references to Christian Prayer (the Liturgy of the Hours in the single volume) and a supplement illustrating the organizational structure of the Prayer Book to facilitate taking the next step in learning to pray the Hours.

In whatever ways this volume is used by the laity, whether "with the priests, or among themselves, or even individually," from our experience, we are confident that praying just this one Hour regularly will be the introduction into the love affair of a lifetime, an **"eternal lifetime"** in fact!

How to Use This Book

For those of you new to praying the Liturgy of the Hours, we have included the following tutorial for Sunday Evening Prayer. As you learn about the various parts of this prayer, you will also be learning how to pray the other Hours of prayer as found in the book of *Christian Prayer*. Be aware that the rubrics will vary from place to place. This tutorial is meant to be a guide, but not an absolute rule. To determine what feast to pray, please see the liturgical calendar beginning on page 147.

1 **Begin with the Introductory Rite.** Make the sign of the cross when you see the red symbol ✠ (in Latin, red translates as "rubric"). When there are two or more people praying together, one person recites the line following the red ℣ (= verse). All others present respond with the line following the red ℟ (= response).

Rubrics in brackets are optional, but are normally done when praying with a group.

If "Glory to the Father" is abbreviated, the complete text may be found on the front flap of this book.

2 **Begin praying the hymn.** The green dot (✦) marks off alternating strophes for when two or more people are praying together. The first person or group should pray the first strophe, and the second should follow, continuing to alternate throughout the hymn, changing at every green dot (✦).

3 **Begin each psalm or canticle with an antiphon** (noted by the abbreviation Ant., written in green.) One person recites the first word or two of the antiphon and then all join in to recite the rest.

If following the rubrics, all should sit at the beginning of the first psalm until the Reading.

As with the Hymn, when praying the psalm or canticle, the green dot (✦) marks off alternating strophes. The first person or group should pray the first strophe, and the second should follow, continuing to alternate, changing at every green dot (✦).

4 **End each psalm or canticle** by reciting the "Glory to the Father". All should bow their heads (or stand and bow) while the Blessed Trinity is named.

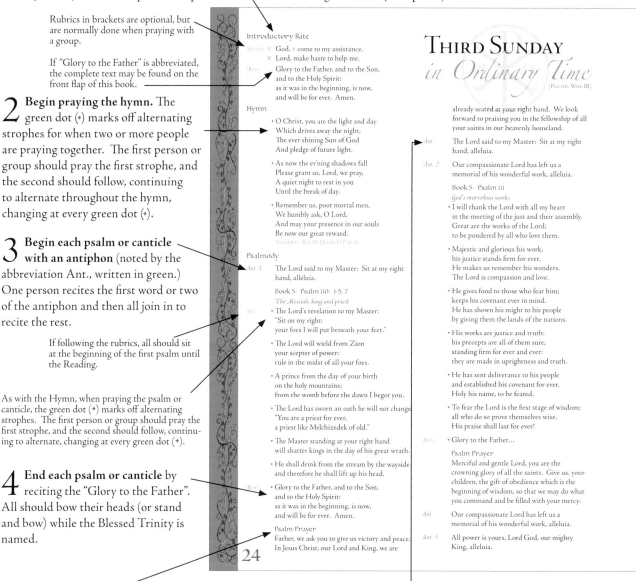

Introductory Rite

[Stand] ℣. God, ✠ come to my assistance.
℟. Lord, make haste to help me.
[Bow] Glory to the Father, and to the Son,
and to the Holy Spirit:
as it was in the beginning, is now,
and will be for ever. Amen.

Hymn

✦ O Christ, you are the light and day
Which drives away the night,
The ever shining Sun of God
And pledge of future light.

✦ As now the ev'ning shadows fall
Please grant us, Lord, we pray,
A quiet night to rest in you
Until the break of day.

✦ Remember us, poor mortal men,
We humbly ask, O Lord,
And may your presence in our souls
Be now our great reward.
Translation: Rev. M. Quinn, O.P. et al.

Psalmody

Ant. 1 The Lord said to my Master: Sit at my right hand, alleluia.

Book 5: Psalm 110: 1-5, 7
The Messiah, king and priest

[Sit] ✦ The Lord's revelation to my Master:
"Sit on my right:
your foes I will put beneath your feet."

✦ The Lord will wield from Zion
your scepter of power:
rule in the midst of all your foes.

✦ A prince from the day of your birth
on the holy mountains;
from the womb before the dawn I begot you.

✦ The Lord has sworn an oath he will not change
"You are a priest for ever,
a priest like Melchizedek of old."

✦ The Master standing at your right hand
will shatter kings in the day of his great wrath.

✦ He shall drink from the stream by the wayside
and therefore he shall lift up his head.

[Bow] ✦ Glory to the Father, and to the Son,
and to the Holy Spirit:
as it was in the beginning, is now,
and will be for ever. Amen.

Psalm Prayer
Father, we ask you to give us victory and peace.
In Jesus Christ, our Lord and King, we are

24

already seated at your right hand. We look forward to praising you in the fellowship of all your saints in our heavenly homeland.

Ant. The Lord said to my Master: Sit at my right hand, alleluia.

Ant. 2 Our compassionate Lord has left us a memorial of his wonderful work, alleluia.

Book 5: Psalm 111
God's marvelous works

✦ I will thank the Lord with all my heart
in the meeting of the just and their assembly.
Great are the works of the Lord;
to be pondered by all who love them.

✦ Majestic and glorious his work,
his justice stands firm for ever.
He makes us remember his wonders.
The Lord is compassion and love.

✦ He gives food to those who fear him;
keeps his covenant ever in mind.
He has shown his might to his people
by giving them the lands of the nations.

✦ His works are justice and truth:
his precepts are all of them sure,
standing firm for ever and ever:
they are made in uprightness and truth.

✦ He has sent deliverance to his people
and established his covenant for ever.
Holy his name, to be feared.

✦ To fear the Lord is the first stage of wisdom;
all who do so prove themselves wise.
His praise shall last for ever!

[Bow] ✦ Glory to the Father…

Psalm Prayer
Merciful and gentle Lord, you are the crowning glory of all the saints. Give us, your children, the gift of obedience which is the beginning of wisdom, so that we may do what you command and be filled with your mercy.

Ant. Our compassionate Lord has left us a memorial of his wonderful work, alleluia.

Ant. 3 All power is yours, Lord God, our mighty King, alleluia.

5 **A Psalm Prayer** may follow the psalm. This prayer is always optional. If you choose to recite it, all present should recite it together.

6 After the psalm or canticle is completed, all repeat the antiphon together.

7 **Repeat steps 3-6** for the next psalm, and then for the canticle.

8 Whoever is leading the prayer stands for the Reading.

The complete Magnificat prayer can be found on the back flap of this book.

After the Magnificat is recited, its antiphon is repeated. Although the antiphons for the psalms and other canticles are printed a second time, the antiphon for the Magnificat is not printed again. So you need to go back and recite the antiphon as it appears just before the Magnificat.

Canticle based on Revelation 19: 1-7
The wedding of the Lamb

• Alleluia.
Salvation, glory, and power to our God:
(℟ Alleluia.)
his judgments are honest and true.
℟ Alleluia, alleluia.

• Alleluia.
Sing praise to our God, all you his servants,
(℟ Alleluia.)
all who worship him reverently, great and small.
℟ Alleluia, alleluia.

• Alleluia.
The Lord our all-powerful God is King;
(℟ Alleluia.)
let us rejoice, sing praise, and give him glory.
℟ Alleluia, alleluia.

• Alleluia.
The wedding feast of the Lamb has begun,
(℟ Alleluia.)
and his bride is prepared to welcome him.
℟ Alleluia, alleluia.

[Bow] • Glory to the Father…

Ant. All power is yours, Lord God, our mighty King, alleluia.

Reading: 1 Peter 1: 3-7

Praised be the God and Father /of our Lord Jesus Christ, /he who in his great mercy /gave us new birth; /a birth unto hope which draws its life /from the resurrection of Jesus Christ from the dead; /a birth to an imperishable inheritance, /incapable of fading or defilement, /which is kept in heaven for you /who are guarded with God's power through faith; /a birth to a salvation which stands ready /to be revealed in the last days.
There is cause for rejoicing here. You may for a time have to suffer the distress of many trials; but this is so that your faith, which is more precious than the passing splendor of fire-tried gold, may by its genuineness lead to praise, glory, and honor when Jesus Christ appears.

Responsory

℣ The whole creation proclaims the greatness of your glory.
℟ The whole creation proclaims the greatness of your glory.
℣ Eternal ages praise
℟ the greatness of your glory.

[Bow] ℣ Glory to the Father, and to the Son, and to the Holy Spirit.
℟ The whole creation proclaims the greatness of your glory.

Canticle Of Mary

Ant. The Spirit of the Lord rests upon me; he has sent me to preach the good news to the poor.
Magnificat: Luke 1: 46-55
My soul ✠ proclaims the… [See Prayer On Back Flap. Then Repeat The Antiphon Above.]

Intercessions

Introductory Formula
The world was created by the Word of God, re-created by his redemption, and it is continually renewed by his love. Rejoicing in him we call out:
℟ Renew the wonders of your love, Lord.

Petitions
℣ We give thanks to God whose power is revealed in nature,
℟ and whose providence is revealed in history.
℣ Through your Son, the herald of reconciliation, the victor of the cross,
℟ free us from empty fear and hopelessness.
℣ May all those who love and pursue justice,
℟ work together without deceit to build a world of true peace.
℣ Be with the oppressed, free the captives, console the sorrowing, feed the hungry, strengthen the weak,
℟ in all people reveal the victory of your cross.
℣ After your Son's death and burial you raised him up again in glory,
℟ grant that the faithful departed may live with him.

The Lord's Prayer
Our Father… [See Prayer On Back Flap.]

Prayer

All-powerful and ever-living God, direct your love that is within us, that our efforts in the name of your Son may bring mankind to unity and peace. We ask this through our Lord Jesus Christ, your Son, who lives and reigns with you and the Holy Spirit, one God, for ever and ever. Amen.

Closing Rite Or Dismissal
[See Closing Rite on Back Flap.]

25

---

11 **Recite the Intercessions.** If there are two or more present, one person recites the Introductory Formula. The others recite the response (indicated by the symbol ℟). Then they alternate between the versicles and responsories. In some places the first response (in italics) is repeated after each response in the Petitions.

12 **Recite The Lord's Prayer**, with one person beginning it and all others joining in. (The complete Lord's Prayer can be found on the back flap of this book.)

13 **The Prayer** is recited either by one person or all together. All respond with "Amen", as indicated by the red.'

14 **The Closing Rite** may be done in two ways. The first is done when a priest or deacon leads a group in Evening Prayer. The second is done when a layman leads the prayer or when it is recited alone. (The complete Closing Rite can be found on the back flap of this book.)

15 **Sunday Evening Prayer** is completed after the Closing Rite.

---

9 **Recite the Response To The Word of God.** If there are two or more present, the versicles (indicated by the symbol ℣) are recited by the person who read the Reading. All others respond by reciting the responses (indicated by the symbol ℟).

10 **The Canticle of Mary** follows the same procedure as the psalms and other canticles. It begins with an antiphon, then the canticle is recited, either alternating between strophes or in unison. After the "Glory to the Father" the antiphon is repeated again.

Evening Prayerbook
Sunday Vespers
Liturgy of the Hours

Introductory Rite

[Stand] V. God, ✠ come to my assistance.
R. Lord, make haste to help me.

[Bow] Glory to the Father, and to the Son,
and to the Holy Spirit:
as it was in the beginning, is now,
and will be for ever. Amen.

Hymn

✦ Creator of the stars of night,
Your people's everlasting light,
Jesus, Redeemer, save us all,
And hear your servants when they call.

✦ Now, grieving that the ancient curse
Should doom to death a universe,
You heal all men who need your grace
To save and heal a ruined race.

✦ At whose great name, majestic now,
All knees must bend, all hearts must bow;
All things in heaven and on earth adore,
And own thee King for evermore.

[Bow] ✦ To God the Father, God the Son,
And God the Spirit, Three in One,
Praise, honor, might, and glory be
From age to age eternally.
Translator: J.M. Neale and others, alt.

Psalmody

Ant. 1   Rejoice, daughter of Zion; shout for joy,
daughter of Jerusalem, alleluia.

Book 5: Psalm 110: 1-5, 7
The Messiah, king and priest

[Sit] ✦ The Lord's revelation to my Master:
"Sit on my right:
your foes I will put beneath your feet."

✦ The Lord will wield from Zion
your scepter of power:
rule in the midst of all your foes.

✦ A prince from the day of your birth
on the holy mountains;
from the womb before the dawn I begot you.

✦ The Lord has sworn an oath he will not change.
"You are a priest for ever,
a priest like Melchizedek of old."

✦ The Master standing at your right hand
will shatter kings in the day of his great wrath.

✦ He shall drink from the stream by the wayside
and therefore he shall lift up his head.

[Bow] ✦ Glory to the Father…

FIRST SUNDAY
Of Advent
[Psalter, Week I]

Psalm Prayer
Father, we ask you to give us victory and peace.
In Jesus Christ, our Lord and King, we are
already seated at your right hand. We look
forward to praising you in the fellowship of all
your saints in our heavenly homeland.

Ant.   Rejoice, daughter of Zion; shout for joy,
daughter of Jerusalem, alleluia.

Ant. 2   Christ our King will come to us:
the Lamb of God foretold by John.

Book 2: Psalm 114
The Israelites are delivered from the bondage of Egypt

✦ When Israel came forth from Egypt,
Jacob's sons from an alien people,
Judah became the Lord's temple,
Israel became his kingdom.

✦ The sea fled at the sight:
the Jordan turned back on its course,
the mountains leapt like rams
and the hills like yearling sheep.

✦ Why was it, sea, that you fled,
that you turned back, Jordan, on your course?
Mountains, that you leapt like rams,
hills, like yearling sheep?

✦ Tremble, O earth, before the Lord,
in the presence of the God of Jacob,
who turns the rock into a pool
and flint into a spring of water.

[Bow] ✦ Glory to the Father…

Psalm Prayer
Almighty God, ever-living mystery of unity and
trinity, you gave life to the new Israel by birth
from water and the Spirit, and made it a chosen
race, a royal priesthood, a people set apart as
your eternal possession. May all those you have
called to walk in the splendor of the new light
render you fitting service and adoration.

Ant.   Christ our King will come to us:
the Lamb of God foretold by John.

Ant. 3   I am coming soon, says the Lord; I will give
to everyone the reward his deeds deserve.

Canticle Based On Revelation 19: 1-7

The wedding of the Lamb

+ Alleluia.
Salvation, glory, and power to our God:
(℟ Alleluia.)
his judgments are honest and true.
℟ Alleluia (alleluia).

+ Alleluia.
Sing praise to our God, all you his servants,
(℟ Alleluia.)
all who worship him reverently, great and small.
℟ Alleluia (alleluia).

+ Alleluia.
The Lord our all-powerful God is King;
(℟ Alleluia.)
let us rejoice, sing praise, and give him glory.
℟ Alleluia (alleluia).

+ Alleluia.
The wedding feast of the Lamb has begun,
(℟ Alleluia.)
and his bride is prepared to welcome him.
℟ Alleluia (alleluia).

[Bow] + Glory to the Father…

Ant. I am coming soon, says the Lord; I will give
to everyone the reward his deeds deserve.

Reading: Philippians 4: 4-7

Rejoice in the Lord always! I say it again.
Rejoice! Everyone should see how unselfish
you are. The Lord is near. Dismiss all anxiety
from your minds. Present your needs to God
in every form of prayer and in petitions full
of gratitude. Then God's own peace, which is
beyond all understanding, will stand guard over
your hearts and minds, in Christ Jesus.

Responsory

℣ Lord, show us your mercy and love.
℟ Lord, show us your mercy and love.
℣ And grant us your salvation,
℟ your mercy and love.
[Bow] ℣ Glory to the Father, and to the Son,
and to the Holy Spirit.
℟ Lord, show us your mercy and love.

Canticle Of Mary

Ant. Do not be afraid, Mary, you have found favor
[Stand] with God; you will conceive and give birth to a
Son, alleluia.

Magnificat: Luke 1:46-55
My soul + proclaims…

[See Prayer On Back Flap, Then Repeat The Antiphon Above.]

Intercessions

Introductory Formula
To Jesus Christ, our Redeemer, the way, the
truth, and the life, let us make our humble
prayer:
℟ Come and stay with us, Lord.

Petitions
℣ Son of the Most High, your coming
was announced to the Virgin Mary by
Gabriel,
℟ come and rule over your people for ever.
℣ Holy One of God, in your presence
John the Baptist leapt in Elizabeth's womb,
℟ bring the joy of salvation to all the earth.
℣ Jesus the Savior, the angel revealed your name
to Joseph the just man,
℟ come and save your people from their sins.
℣ Light of the world, for whom Simeon
and all the just waited,
℟ come and comfort us.
℣ O Rising Sun that never sets, Zechariah
foretold that you would visit us from above,
℟ come and shine on those who dwell in
darkness and the shadow of death.

The Lord's Prayer
Our Father… [See Prayer On Back Flap]

Prayer

All-powerful God,
increase our strength of will for doing good
that Christ may find an eager welcome
at his coming
and call us to his side in the kingdom
of heaven,
where he lives and reigns with you
and the Holy Spirit,
one God, for ever and ever. Amen.

Closing Rite Or Dismissal

[When Priest Or Deacon Presides]
℣ The Lord be with you.
℟ And also with you.
[Bow] May almighty God bless you, + the Father,
and the Son, and the Holy Spirit.
℟ Amen.
℣ Go in peace.
℟ Thanks be to God.

[When Priest Or Deacon Do Not Preside, And In Individual Recitation]
+ May the Lord bless us, protect us from all evil
and bring us to everlasting life.
℟ Amen.

Introductory Rite

[See Introductory Rite on Front Flap]

Hymn

♦ Creator of the stars of night,
Your people's everlasting light,
Jesus, Redeemer, save us all,
And hear your servants when they call.

♦ Now, grieving that the ancient curse
Should doom to death a universe,
You heal all men who need your grace
To save and heal a ruined race.

♦ At whose great name, majestic now,
All knees must bend, all hearts must bow;
All things in heaven and on earth adore,
And own thee King for evermore.

[Bow] ♦ To God the Father, God the Son,
And God the Spirit, Three in One,
Praise, honor, might, and glory be
From age to age eternally.

Translator: J.M. Neale and others, alt.

Psalmody

Ant. 1   The Lord will come on the clouds of heaven
with great power and might, alleluia.

Book 5: Psalm 110: 1-5, 7
The Messiah, king and priest

[Sit] ♦ The Lord's revelation to my Master:
"Sit on my right:
your foes I will put beneath your feet."

♦ The Lord will wield from Zion
your scepter of power:
rule in the midst of all your foes.

♦ A prince from the day of your birth
on the holy mountains;
from the womb before the dawn I begot you.

♦ The Lord has sworn an oath he will not change.
"You are a priest for ever,
a priest like Melchizedek of old."

♦ The Master standing at your right hand
will shatter kings in the day of his great wrath.

♦ He shall drink from the stream by the wayside
and therefore he shall lift up his head.

[Bow] ♦ Glory to the Father, and to the Son,
and to the Holy Spirit:
as it was in the beginning, is now,
and will be for ever. Amen.

Psalm Prayer
Almighty God, bring the kingdom of Christ,
your anointed one, to its fullness. May the

SECOND SUNDAY
Of Advent

perfect offering of your Son, eternal priest of
the new Jerusalem, be offered in every place to
your name, and make all nations a holy people
for you.

Ant.   The Lord will come on the clouds of heaven
with great power and might, alleluia.

Ant. 2   The Lord will come; he is true to his word. If
he seems to delay, keep watch for him, for he
will surely come, alleluia.

Book 5: Psalm 115
Praise of the true God

♦ Not to us, Lord, not to us,
but to your name give the glory
for the sake of your love and your truth,
lest the heathen say: "Where is their God?"

♦ But our God is in the heavens;
he does whatever he wills.
Their idols are silver and gold,
the work of human hands.

♦ They have mouths but they cannot speak;
they have eyes but they cannot see;
they have ears but they cannot hear;
they have nostrils but they cannot smell.

♦ With their hands they cannot feel;
with their feet they cannot walk.
No sound comes from their throats.
Their makers will come to be like them
and so will all who trust in them.

♦ Sons of Israel, trust in the Lord;
he is their help and their shield.
Sons of Aaron, trust in the Lord;
he is their help and their shield.

♦ You who fear him, trust in the Lord;
he is their help and their shield.
He remembers us, and he will bless us;
he will bless the sons of Israel.
He will bless the sons of Aaron.

♦ The Lord will bless those who fear him,
the little no less than the great:
to you may the Lord grant increase,
to you and all your children.

♦ May you be blessed by the Lord,
the maker of heaven and earth.

The heavens belong to the Lord
but the earth he has given to men.

✦ The dead shall not praise the Lord,
nor those who go down into the silence.
But we who live bless the Lord
now and for ever. Amen.

[Bow]   ✦ Glory to the Father…

Psalm Prayer

Father, creator…[See psalm prayer on front flap]

Ant.   The Lord will come; he is true to his word. If
he seems to delay, keep watch for him, for he
will surely come, alleluia.

Ant. 3   The Lord our king and lawgiver will come to
save us.

Canticle Based On Revelation 19: 1-7
The wedding of the Lamb

✦ Alleluia.
Salvation, glory, and power to our God:
(℟ Alleluia.)
his judgments are honest and true.
℟ Alleluia (alleluia).

✦ Alleluia.
Sing praise to our God, all you his servants,
(℟ Alleluia.)
all who worship him reverently, great and small.
℟ Alleluia (alleluia).

✦ Alleluia.
The Lord our all-powerful God is King;
(℟ Alleluia.)
let us rejoice, sing praise, and give him glory.
℟ Alleluia (alleluia).

✦ Alleluia.
The wedding feast of the Lamb has begun,
(℟ Alleluia.)
and his bride is prepared to welcome him.
℟ Alleluia (alleluia).

[Bow]   ✦ Glory to the Father…

Ant.   The Lord our king and lawgiver will come to
save us.

Reading: Philippians 4: 4-7

Rejoice in the Lord always! I say it again.
Rejoice! Everyone should see how unselfish
you are. The Lord is near. Dismiss all anxiety
from your minds. Present your needs to God
in every form of prayer and in petitions full
of gratitude. Then God's own peace, which
is beyond all understanding, will stand guard
over your hearts and minds, in Christ Jesus.

Responsory

℣   Lord, show us your mercy and love.
℟   Lord, show us your mercy and love.
℣   And grant us your salvation,
℟   your mercy and love.
[Bow]   ℣   Glory to the Father, and to the Son,
and to the Holy Spirit.
℟   Lord, show us your mercy and love.

Canticle Of Mary

Ant.
[Stand]   Blessed are you, O Virgin Mary, for your
great faith; all that the Lord promised you will
come to pass through you, alleluia.

Magnificat: Luke 1: 46-55
My soul ✠ proclaims the… [See Prayer On Back
Flap. Then Repeat The Antiphon Above.]

Intercessions

Introductory Formula
To Christ the Lord, who was born of the
Virgin Mary, let us pray with joyful hearts:
℟   Come, Lord Jesus!

Petitions
℣   Lord Jesus, in the mystery of your incarnation,
you revealed your glory to the world,
℟   give us new life by your coming.
℣   You have taken our weakness upon yourself,
℟   grant us your mercy.
℣   You redeemed the world from sin by your first
coming in humility,
℟   free us from all guilt when you come again
in glory.
℣   You live and rule over all,
℟   in your goodness bring us to our eternal
inheritance.
℣   You sit at the right hand of the Father,
℟   gladden the souls of the dead with your light.

The Lord's Prayer
Our Father… [See prayer on back flap]

Prayer

God of power and mercy,
open our hearts in welcome.
Remove the things that hinder us from
receiving Christ with joy,
so that we may share his wisdom
and become one with him
when he comes in glory,
for he lives and reigns with you
and the Holy Spirit,
one God, for ever and ever. Amen

Closing Rite Or Dismissal [See Back Flap.]

Introductory Rite

[Stand] V. God, ✝ come to my assistance.

R. Lord, make haste to help me.

[Bow] Glory to the Father…

Hymn

✦ Creator of the stars of night,
Your people's everlasting light,
Jesus, Redeemer, save us all,
And hear your servants when they call.

✦ Now, grieving that the ancient curse
Should doom to death a universe,
You heal all men who need your grace
To save and heal a ruined race.

✦ At whose great name, majestic now,
All knees must bend, all hearts must bow;
All things in heaven and on earth adore,
And own thee King for evermore.

[Bow] ✦ To God the Father, God the Son,
And God the Spirit, Three in One,
Praise, honor, might, and glory be
From age to age eternally.

Translator: J.M. Neale and others, alt.

Psalmody

Ant. 1   Our Lord will come to claim his glorious
throne in the assembly of the princes.

Book 5: Psalm 110: 1-5, 7
The Messiah, king and priest

[Sit] ✦ The Lord's revelation to my Master:
"Sit on my right:
your foes I will put beneath your feet."

✦ The Lord will wield from Zion
your scepter of power:
rule in the midst of all your foes.

✦ A prince from the day of your birth
on the holy mountains;
from the womb before the dawn I begot you.

✦ The Lord has sworn an oath he will not change.
"You are a priest for ever,
a priest like Melchizedek of old."

✦ The Master standing at your right hand
will shatter kings in the day of his great wrath.

✦ He shall drink from the stream by the wayside
and therefore he shall lift up his head.

[Bow] ✦ Glory to the Father…

Psalm Prayer
Father, we ask you to give us victory and peace.
In Jesus Christ, our Lord and King, we are

THIRD SUNDAY
Of Advent
[Psalter, Week III]

already seated at your right hand. We look
forward to praising you in the fellowship of all
your saints in our heavenly homeland.

Ant.   Our Lord will come to claim his glorious throne
in the assembly of the princes.

Ant. 2   Let the mountains break out with joy and the
hills with answering gladness, for the world's
true light, the Lord, comes with power and
might.

Book 5: Psalm 111
God's marvelous works

✦ I will thank the Lord with all my heart
in the meeting of the just and their assembly.
Great are the works of the Lord;
to be pondered by all who love them.

✦ Majestic and glorious his work,
his justice stands firm for ever.
He makes us remember his wonders.
The Lord is compassion and love.

✦ He gives food to those who fear him;
keeps his covenant ever in mind.
He has shown his might to his people
by giving them the lands of the nations.

✦ His works are justice and truth:
his precepts are all of them sure,
standing firm for ever and ever:
they are made in uprightness and truth.

✦ He has sent deliverance to his people
and established his covenant for ever.
Holy his name, to be feared.

✦ To fear the Lord is the first stage of wisdom;
all who do so prove themselves wise.
His praise shall last for ever!

[Bow] ✦ Glory to the Father…

Psalm Prayer
Merciful and gentle Lord, you are the crowning
glory of all the saints. Give us, your children,
the gift of obedience which is the beginning of
wisdom, so that we may do what you command
and be filled with your mercy.

Ant.   Let the mountains break out with joy and the

6

hills with answering gladness, for the world's true light, the Lord, comes with power and might.

Ant. 3 Let us live in holiness and love as we patiently await our blessed hope, the coming of our Savior.

Canticle based on Revelation 19: 1-7
The wedding of the Lamb

✦ Alleluia.
Salvation, glory, and power to our God:
(℟ Alleluia.)
his judgments are honest and true.
℟ Alleluia (alleluia).

✦ Alleluia.
Sing praise to our God, all you his servants,
(℟ Alleluia.)
all who worship him reverently, great and small.
℟ Alleluia (alleluia).

✦ Alleluia.
The Lord our all-powerful God is King;
(℟ Alleluia.)
let us rejoice, sing praise, and give him glory.
℟ Alleluia (alleluia).

✦ Alleluia.
The wedding feast of the Lamb has begun,
(℟ Alleluia.)
and his bride is prepared to welcome him.
℟ Alleluia (alleluia).

[BOW] ✦ Glory to the Father…

Ant. Let us live in holiness and love as we patiently await our blessed hope, the coming of our Savior.

Reading: Philippians 4: 4-7

Rejoice in the Lord always! I say it again. Rejoice! Everyone should see how unselfish you are. The Lord is near. Dismiss all anxiety from your minds. Present your needs to God in every form of prayer and in petitions full of gratitude. Then God's own peace, which is beyond all understanding, will stand guard over your hearts and minds, in Christ Jesus.

Responsory

℣ Lord, show us your mercy and love.
℟ Lord, show us your mercy and love.
℣ And grant us your salvation,
℟ your mercy and love.
[BOW] ℣ Glory to the Father, and to the Son, and to the Holy Spirit.
℟ Lord, show us your mercy and love.

Canticle Of Mary

Ant.
[STAND] Are you the One whose coming was foretold, or should we look for another? Tell John what you see: the blind have their sight restored, the dead are raised to life, the poor have the good news preached to them, alleluia.

Magnificat: Luke 1: 46-55
My soul ✠ proclaims the… [SEE PRAYER ON BACK FLAP. THEN REPEAT THE ANTIPHON ABOVE.]

Intercessions

Introductory Formula
To Jesus Christ, our Redeemer, the way, the truth, and the life, let us make our humble prayer:
℟ Come and stay with us, Lord.

Petitions
℣ Son of the Most High, your coming was announced to the Virgin Mary by Gabriel,
℟ come and rule over your people for ever.
℣ Holy One of God, in your presence John the Baptist leapt in Elizabeth's womb,
℟ bring the joy of salvation to all the earth.
℣ Jesus the Savior, the angel revealed your name to Joseph the just man,
℟ come and save your people from their sins.
℣ Light of the world, for whom Simeon and all the just waited,
℟ come and comfort us.
℣ O Rising Sun that never sets, Zechariah foretold that you would visit us from above,
℟ come and shine on those who dwell in darkness and the shadow of death.

The Lord's Prayer
Our Father… [SEE PRAYER ON BACK FLAP]

Prayer

Lord God,
may we, your people,
who look forward to the birthday of Christ
experience the joy of salvation
and celebrate that feast with love
  and thanksgiving.
We ask this through our Lord Jesus Christ,
  your Son,
who lives and reigns with you
  and the Holy Spirit,
one God, for ever and ever. Amen.

Closing Rite Or Dismissal

[SEE CLOSING RITE ON BACK FLAP]

Introductory Rite

[Stand] ℣. God, ✠ come to my assistance.
℟. Lord, make haste to help me.

[Bow] Glory to the Father, and to the Son,
and to the Holy Spirit:
as it was in the beginning, is now,
and will be for ever. Amen.

Hymn

✦ Behold, a rose of Judah
From tender branch has sprung,
From Jesse's lineage coming,
As men of old have sung.
It came a flower bright
Amid the cold of winter,
When half spent was the night.

✦ Isaiah has foretold it
In words of promise sure,
And Mary's arms enfold it,
A virgin meek and pure.
Through God's eternal will
She bore to men a savior
At midnight calm and still.

Translator: Composite

Psalmody

Ant. 1 See how glorious he is, coming forth as Savior
of all peoples!

Book 5: Psalm 110: 1-5, 7
The Messiah, king and priest

[Sit] ✦ The Lord's revelation to my Master:
"Sit on my right:
your foes I will put beneath your feet."

✦ The Lord will wield from Zion
your scepter of power:
rule in the midst of all your foes.

✦ A prince from the day of your birth
on the holy mountains;
from the womb before the dawn I begot you.

✦ The Lord has sworn an oath he will not change.
"You are a priest for ever,
a priest like Melchizedek of old."

✦ The Master standing at your right hand
will shatter kings in the day of his great wrath.

✦ He shall drink from the stream by the wayside
and therefore he shall lift up his head.

[Bow] ✦ Glory to the Father…

Psalm Prayer
Father, we ask you to give us victory and peace.
In Jesus Christ, our Lord and King, we are
already seated at your right hand. We look

FOURTH SUNDAY
Of Advent
[Psalter, Week IV]

forward to praising you in the fellowship of all
your saints in our heavenly homeland.

Ant. See how glorious he is, coming forth as Savior
of all peoples!

Ant. 2 Crooked paths will be straightened, and rough
ways made smooth. Come, O Lord, do not
delay, alleluia.

Book 5: Psalm 112
The happiness of the just man

✦ Happy the man who fears the Lord,
who takes delight in all his commands.
His sons will be powerful on earth;
the children of the upright are blessed.

✦ Riches and wealth are in his house;
his justice stands firm for ever.
He is a light in the darkness for the upright:
he is generous, merciful and just.

✦ The good man takes pity and lends,
he conducts his affairs with honor.
The just man will never waver:
he will be remembered for ever.

✦ He has no fear of evil news;
with a firm heart he trusts in the Lord.
With a steadfast heart he will not fear;
he will see the downfall of his foes.

✦ Open-handed, he gives to the poor;
his justice stands firm for ever.
His head will be raised in glory.

✦ The wicked man sees and is angry,
grinds his teeth and fades away;
the desire of the wicked leads to doom.

[Bow] ✦ Glory to the Father…

Psalm Prayer
Lord God, you are the eternal light which
illumines the hearts of good people. Help us
to love you, to rejoice in your glory, and so to
live in this world as to avoid harsh judgment in
the next. May we come to see the light of your
countenance.

Ant. Crooked paths will be straightened, and rough
ways made smooth. Come, O Lord, do not
delay, alleluia.

Ant. 3   Ever wider will his kingdom spread, eternally at peace, alleluia.

Canticle based on Revelation 19: 1-7
The wedding of the Lamb

+ Alleluia.
Salvation, glory, and power to our God:
(℟ Alleluia.)
his judgments are honest and true.
℟ Alleluia (alleluia).

+ Alleluia.
Sing praise to our God, all you his servants,
(℟ Alleluia.)
all who worship him reverently, great and small.
℟ Alleluia (alleluia).

+ Alleluia.
The Lord our all-powerful God is King;
(℟ Alleluia.)
let us rejoice, sing praise, and give him glory.
℟ Alleluia (alleluia).

+ Alleluia.
The wedding feast of the Lamb has begun,
(℟ Alleluia.)
and his bride is prepared to welcome him.
℟ Alleluia (alleluia).

[Bow]   + Glory to the Father…

Ant.   Ever wider will his kingdom spread, eternally at peace, alleluia.

Reading: Philippians 4: 4-7

Rejoice in the Lord always! I say it again. Rejoice! Everyone should see how unselfish you are. The Lord is near. Dismiss all anxiety from your minds. Present your needs to God in every form of prayer and in petitions full of gratitude. Then God's own peace, which is beyond all understanding, will stand guard over your hearts and minds, in Christ Jesus.

Responsory

℣. Lord, show us your mercy and love.
℟. Lord, show us your mercy and love.
℣. And grant us your salvation,
℟. your mercy and love.
[Bow]   ℣. Glory to the Father, and to the Son, and to the Holy Spirit.
℟. Lord, show us your mercy and love.

Canticle Of Mary

Ant.   O Wisdom, O holy Word of God, you govern
[Stand]   all creation with your strong yet tender care. Come and show your people the way to salvation.

Magnificat: Luke 1: 46-55
My soul ✠ proclaims the… [See Prayer On Back Flap. Then Repeat The Antiphon Above.]

Intercessions

Introductory Formula
To Christ the Lord, who was born of the Virgin Mary, let us pray with joyful hearts:
℟ Come, Lord Jesus!

Petitions
℣. Lord Jesus, in the mystery of your incarnation, you revealed your glory to the world,
℟ give us new life by your coming.
℣. You have taken our weakness upon yourself,
℟ grant us your mercy.
℣. You redeemed the world from sin by your first coming in humility,
℟ free us from all guilt when you come again in glory.
℣. You live and rule over all,
℟ in your goodness bring us to our eternal inheritance.
℣. You sit at the right hand of the Father,
℟ gladden the souls of the dead with your light.

The Lord's Prayer
Our Father… [See prayer on back flap]

Prayer

Lord,
fill our hearts with your love,
and as you revealed to us by an angel
the coming of your Son as man,
so lead us through his suffering and death
to the glory of his resurrection,
for he lives and reigns with you
    and the Holy Spirit,
one God, for ever and ever. Amen.

Closing Rite Or Dismissal

[When Priest Or Deacon Presides]
℣. The Lord be with you.
℟. And also with you.
[Bow]   May almighty God bless you, + the Father, and the Son, and the Holy Spirit.
℟. Amen.
℣. Go in peace.
℟. Thanks be to God.

[When Priest Or Deacon Do Not Preside, And In Individual Recitation]
+ May the Lord bless us, protect us from all evil and bring us to everlasting life.
℟. Amen.

9

Introductory Rite

[See Introductory Rite on Front Flap]

Hymn

✦ What child is this, who, laid to rest,
On Mary's lap is sleeping?
Whom angels greet with anthems sweet,
While shepherds watch are keeping?
This, this is Christ the King,
Whom shepherds guard and angels sing;
Haste, haste to bring him laud,
The Babe, the Son of Mary.

✦ Why lies he in such mean estate,
Where ox and ass are feeding?
Good Christian, fear, for sinners here
The silent Word is pleading.
Nails, spear, shall pierce him through,
The cross be borne for me, for you:
Hail, hail, the Word made flesh,
The Babe, the Son of Mary!

✦ So bring him incense, gold and myrrh,
Come peasant, king, to own Him;
The King of kings salvation brings,
Let loving hearts enthrone him.
Raise, raise the song on high,
The Virgin sings her lullaby:
Joy, joy, for Christ is born,
The Babe, the Son of Mary!

Text: William Chatterton Dix, 1837-1898

Psalmody

Ant. 1   You have been endowed from your birth with princely gifts; in eternal splendor, before the dawn of light on earth, I have begotten you.

Book 5: Psalm 110: 1-5, 7
The Messiah, king and priest

[Sit]   ✦ The Lord's revelation to my Master:
"Sit on my right:
your foes I will put beneath your feet."

✦ The Lord will wield from Zion
your scepter of power:
rule in the midst of all your foes.

✦ A prince from the day of your birth
on the holy mountains;
from the womb before the dawn I begot you.

✦ The Lord has sworn an oath he will not change.
"You are a priest for ever,
a priest like Melchizedek of old."

✦ The Master standing at your right hand
will shatter kings in the day of his great wrath.

CHRISTMAS
Birth of Christ

✦ He shall drink from the stream by the wayside
and therefore he shall lift up his head.

[Bow]   ✦ Glory to the Father…

Ant.   You have been endowed from your birth with princely gifts; in eternal splendor, before the dawn of light on earth, I have begotten you.

Ant. 2   With the Lord is unfailing love;
great is his power to save.

Book 5: Psalm 130
A cry from the depths

✦ Out of the depths I cry to you, O Lord,
Lord, hear my voice!
O let your ears be attentive
to the voice of my pleading.

✦ If you, O Lord, should mark our guilt,
Lord, who would survive?
But with you is found forgiveness:
for this we revere you.

✦ My soul is waiting for the Lord.
I count on his word.
My soul is longing for the Lord
more than watchman for daybreak.
Let the watchman count on daybreak
and Israel on the Lord.

✦ Because with the Lord there is mercy
and fullness of redemption,
Israel indeed he will redeem
from all its iniquity.

[Bow]   ✦ Glory to the Father…

Ant.   With the Lord is unfailing love;
great is his power to save.

Ant. 3   In the beginning, before time began, the Word was God; today he is born, the Savior of the world.

Canticle: Colossians 1: 12-20

✦ Let us give thanks to the Father
for having made you worthy
to share the lot of the saints
in light.

✦ He rescued us
from the power of darkness
and brought us

into the kingdom of his beloved Son.
Through him we have redemption,
the forgiveness of our sins.

✦ He is the image of the invisible God,
the first-born of all creatures.
In him everything in heaven and on earth was
     created,
things visible and invisible.

✦ All were created through him;
all were created for him.
He is before all else that is.
In him everything continues in being.

✦ It is he who is head of the body, the church!
he who is the beginning,
the first-born of the dead,
so that primacy may be his in everything.

✦ It pleased God to make absolute fullness
     reside in him
and, by means of him, to reconcile everything
     in his person,
both on earth and in the heavens,
making peace through the blood of his cross.

[Bow] ✦ Glory to the Father…

Ant.   In the beginning, before time began, the Word
was God; today he is born, the Savior of the
world.

Reading: 1 John 1: 1-3

This is what we proclaim to you: /what was
from the beginning, /what we have heard,
/what we have seen with our eyes, /what
we have looked upon /and our hands have
touched—/we speak of the word of life.
/(This life became visible; /we have seen and
bear witness to it, /and we proclaim to you
the eternal life /that was present to the Father
/and became visible to us.) /What we have
seen and heard /we proclaim in turn to you
/so that you may share life with us. /This
fellowship of ours is with the Father /and with
his Son, Jesus Christ.

Responsory

℣. The Word was made man, alleluia, alleluia.
℟. The Word was made man, alleluia, alleluia.
℣. He lived among us,
℟. alleluia, alleluia.
[Bow] ℣. Glory to the Father, and to the Son,
and to the Holy Spirit.
℟. The Word was made man, alleluia, alleluia.

Canticle Of Mary

Ant.   Christ the Lord is born today; today, the
[Stand] Savior has appeared. Earth echoes songs of
angel choirs, archangels' joyful praise. Today
on earth his friends exult: Glory to God in
the highest, alleluia.

Magnificat: Luke 1: 46-55
My soul ✦ proclaims the… [See Prayer On Back
Flap. Then Repeat The Antiphon Above.]

Intercessions

Introductory Formula
At the birth of Jesus, angels proclaimed peace
to the world. We worship him now with joy,
and we pray with hearts full of faith:
℟. May your birth bring peace to all.

Petitions
℣. Lord, fill your holy people with whatever good
they need,
℟. let the mystery of your birth be the source of
our peace.
℣. You came as chief shepherd and guardian of
our lives,
℟. let the Pope and bishops be faithful channels
of your many gifts of grace.
℣. King from all eternity, you desired to be born
within time and to experience the day-to-day
life of men and women,
℟. share your gift of unending life with us, weak
people, doomed to death.
℣. Awaited from the beginning of the world, you
came only in the fullness of time,
℟. now reveal your presence to those who are still
expecting you.
℣. You became man and gave new life to our
human condition in the grip of death,
℟. now give the fullness of life to all who
have died.

The Lord's Prayer
Our Father… [See prayer on back flap]

Prayer

Lord God,
we praise you for creating man,
and still more for restoring him in Christ.
Your Son shared our weakness:
may we share his glory,
for he lives and reigns with you
   and the Holy Spirit,
one God, for ever and ever. Amen.

Closing Rite Or Dismissal

[See Closing Rite on Back Flap]

Introductory Rite

[Stand] V. God, ✠ come to my assistance.

R. Lord, make haste to help me.

[Bow] Glory to the Father...

Hymn

✦ Sing of Mary, pure and lowly,
Virgin mother undefiled,
Sing of God's own Son most holy
Who became her little child.
Fairest child of fairest mother,
God the Lord, who came to earth,
Word made flesh, our very brother,
Takes our nature by his birth.

✦ Sing of Jesus, son of Mary,
In the home at Nazareth.
Toil and labor cannot weary
Love enduring unto death.
Constant was the love he gave her,
Though he went forth from her side,
Forth to preach and heal and suffer,
Till on Calvary he died.

[Bow] ✦ Glory be to God the Father,
Glory be to God the Son:
Glory be to God the Spirit,
Glory to the Three in One.
From the heart of blessed Mary,
From all saints the song ascends,
And the Church the strain re-echoes
Unto earth's remotest ends.

Text: Anonymous, 1914

Psalmody

Ant. 1   After three days, Jesus was found in the
temple, seated in the midst of the doctors,
listening to them and asking them questions.

Book 5: Psalm 122
Holy city Jerusalem

[Sit] ✦ I rejoiced when I heard them say:
"Let us go to God's house."
And now our feet are standing
within your gates, O Jerusalem.

✦ Jerusalem is built as a city
strongly compact.
It is there that the tribes go up,
the tribes of the Lord.

✦ For Israel's law it is,
there to praise the Lord's name.
There were set the thrones of judgment
of the house of David.

✦ For the peace of Jerusalem pray:
"Peace be to your homes!

HOLY FAMILY
in the Christmas Octave

May peace reign in your walls,
in your palaces, peace!"

✦ For love of my brethren and friends
I say: "Peace upon you!"
For love of the house of the Lord
I will ask for your good.

[Bow] ✦ Glory to the Father, and to the Son,
and to the Holy Spirit:
as it was in the beginning, is now,
and will be for ever. Amen.

Ant.   After three days, Jesus was found in the temple,
seated in the midst of the doctors, listening to
them and asking them questions.

Ant. 2   Jesus returned with Mary and Joseph to
Nazareth; there he lived and was obedient to
them.

Book 5: Psalm 127
Apart from God our labors are worthless

✦ If the Lord does not build the house,
in vain do its builders labor;
if the Lord does not watch over the city,
in vain does the watchman keep vigil.

✦ In vain is your earlier rising,
your going later to rest,
you who toil for the bread you eat:
when he pours gifts on his beloved
while they slumber.

✦ Truly sons are a gift from the Lord,
a blessing, the fruit of the womb.
Indeed the sons of youth
are like arrows in the hand of a warrior.

✦ O the happiness of the man
who has filled his quiver with these arrows!
He will have no cause for shame
when he disputes with his foes in the gateways.

[Bow] ✦ Glory to the Father...

Ant.   Jesus returned with Mary and Joseph to
Nazareth; there he lived and was obedient to
them.

Ant. 3   Jesus grew in wisdom with the years and was
pleasing to God and men.

Canticle: Ephesians 1: 3-10

✦ Praised be the God and Father
of our Lord Jesus Christ,
who bestowed on us in Christ
every spiritual blessing in the heavens.

✦ God chose us in him
before the world began,
to be holy
and blameless in his sight.

✦ He predestined us
to be his adopted sons through Jesus Christ,
such was his will and pleasure,
that all might praise the glorious favor
he has bestowed on us in his beloved.

✦ In him and through his blood,
we have been redeemed,
and our sins forgiven,
so immeasurably generous
is God's favor to us.

✦ God has given us the wisdom
to understand fully the mystery,
the plan he was pleased
to decree in Christ.

✦ A plan to be carried out
in Christ, in the fullness of time,
to bring all things into one in him,
in the heavens and on the earth.

[Bow]   ✦ Glory to the Father…

Ant.   Jesus grew in wisdom with the years and was
pleasing to God and men.

Reading: Philippians 2: 6-7

Though he was in the form of God, Christ
Jesus did not deem equality with God
something to be grasped at. Rather, he
emptied himself and took the form of a slave,
being born in the likeness of men. He was
known to be of human estate.

Responsory

℣. He had to become like his brothers in every
way to show the fullness of his mercy.

℟. He had to become like his brothers in every
way to show the fullness of his mercy.

℣. He was seen on earth and lived among men
and women,

℟. to show the fullness of his mercy.

[Bow] ℣. Glory to the Father, and to the Son,
and to the Holy Spirit.

℟. He had to become like his brothers in every
way to show the fullness of his mercy.

Canticle Of Mary

Ant.
[Stand]   Son, why have you done this to us? Think
what anguish your father and I have endured
looking for you. But why did you look for
me? Did you not know that I had to be in my
Father's house?

Magnificat: Luke 1: 46-55
My soul ✠ proclaims the… [See Prayer On Back
Flap. Then Repeat The Antiphon Above.]

Intercessions

Introductory Formula
Let us adore the Son of the living God who
humbled himself to become a son of a human
family, and let us proclaim:
℟. Lord, you are the model and Savior of all.

Petitions
℣. Christ, by the mystery of your subjection to
Mary and Joseph,
℟. teach all people reverence and obedience to
lawful authority.
℣. You loved your parents and were loved
by them,
℟. establish our families in mutual love
and peace.
℣. You were eager to be about your
Father's business,
℟. may he be honored in every home.
℣. Christ, after three days your anxious parents
found you in your Father's house,
℟. teach all to seek first the kingdom of God.
℣. Christ, you have made Mary and Joseph
sharers in heavenly glory,
℟. admit the dead into the family of the blessed.

The Lord's Prayer
Our Father… [See prayer on back flap]

Prayer

Father,
help us to live as the holy family,
united in respect and love.
Bring us to the joy and peace
of your eternal home.
Grant this through our Lord Jesus Christ,
your Son,
who lives and reigns with you
and the Holy Spirit,
one God, for ever and ever. Amen.

Closing Rite Or Dismissal

[See Closing Rite on Back Flap]

Introductory Rite

[STAND] V. God, + come to my assistance.

R. Lord, make haste to help me.

[BOW] Glory to the Father, and to the Son,
and to the Holy Spirit:
as it was in the beginning, is now,
and will be for ever. Amen.

Hymn

+ Virgin born, we bow before you;
Blessed was the womb that bore you;
Mary, Mother meek and mild,
Blessed was she in her Child.
Blessed was the maid that fed you;
Blessed was the hand that led you;
Blessed was the parent's eye
That watched your slumbering infancy.

+ Blessed she by all creation,
Who brought forth the world's salvation;
And blessed they forever blest,
Who love you most and serve you best.
Virgin born, we bow before you:
Blessed was the womb that bore you;
Mary, Mother meek and mild,
Blessed was she in her Child.

Text: R. Heber, 1783-1826, alt.

Psalmody

Ant. 1   O marvelous exchange! Man's Creator has
become man, born of a virgin. We have been
made sharers in the divinity of Christ who
humbled himself to share in our humanity.

Book 5: Psalm 122
Holy city Jerusalem

[SIT] + I rejoiced when I heard them say:
"Let us go to God's house."
And now our feet are standing
within your gates, O Jerusalem.

+ Jerusalem is built as a city
strongly compact.
It is there that the tribes go up,
the tribes of the Lord.

+ For Israel's law it is,
there to praise the Lord's name.
There were set the thrones of judgment
of the house of David.

+ For the peace of Jerusalem pray:
"Peace be to your homes!
May peace reign in your walls,
in your palaces, peace!"

+ For love of my brethren and friends
I say: "Peace upon you!"

For love of the house of the Lord
I will ask for your good.

[BOW] + Glory to the Father, and to the Son,
and to the Holy Spirit:
as it was in the beginning, is now,
and will be for ever. Amen.

Ant.   O marvelous exchange! Man's Creator has
become man, born of a virgin. We have been
made sharers in the divinity of Christ who
humbled himself to share in our humanity.

Ant. 2   By your miraculous birth from the virgin you
have fulfilled the Scriptures: like a gentle rain
falling upon the earth you have come down to
save your people. O God, we praise you.

Book 5: Psalm 127
Apart from God our labors are worthless

+ If the Lord does not build the house,
in vain do its builders labor;
if the Lord does not watch over the city,
in vain does the watchman keep vigil.

+ In vain is your earlier rising,
your going later to rest,
you who toil for the bread you eat,
when he pours gifts on his beloved
while they slumber.

+ Truly sons are a gift from the Lord,
a blessing, the fruit of the womb.
Indeed the sons of youth
are like arrows in the hand of a warrior.

+ O the happiness of the man
who has filled his quiver with these arrows!
He will have no cause for shame
when he disputes with his foes in the gateways.

[BOW] + Glory to the Father…

Ant.   By your miraculous birth from the virgin you
have fulfilled the Scriptures: like a gentle rain
falling upon the earth you have come down to
save your people. O God, we praise you.

Ant. 3   Your blessed and fruitful virginity is like the
bush, flaming yet unburned, which Moses saw
on Sinai. Pray for us, Mother of God.

14

Canticle: Ephesians 1: 3-10

✦ Praised be the God and Father
of our Lord Jesus Christ,
who bestowed on us in Christ
every spiritual blessing in the heavens.

✦ God chose us in him
before the world began,
to be holy
and blameless in his sight.

✦ He predestined us
to be his adopted sons through Jesus Christ,
such was his will and pleasure,
that all might praise the glorious favor
he has bestowed on us in his beloved.

✦ In him and through his blood,
we have been redeemed,
and our sins forgiven,
so immeasurably generous
is God's favor to us.

✦ God has given us the wisdom
to understand fully the mystery,
the plan he was pleased
to decree in Christ.

✦ A plan to be carried out
in Christ, in the fullness of time,
to bring all things into one in him,
in the heavens and on the earth.

[Bow] ✦ Glory to the Father…

Ant. Your blessed and fruitful virginity is like the bush, flaming yet unburned, which Moses saw on Sinai. Pray for us, Mother of God.

Reading: Galatians 4: 3-7

While we were not yet of age we were like slaves subordinated to the elements of the world; but when the designated time had come, God sent forth his Son born of a woman, born under the law, to deliver from the law those who were subjected to it, so that we might receive our status as adopted sons. The proof that you are sons is the fact that God has sent forth into our hearts the spirit of his Son which cries out "Abba!" ("Father!") You are no longer a slave but a son! And the fact that you are a son makes you an heir, by God's design.

Responsory

℣. The Word was made man, alleluia, alleluia.
℟. The Word was made man, alleluia, alleluia.

℣. He lived among us,
℟. alleluia, alleluia.
[Bow] ℣. Glory to the Father, and to the Son, and to the Holy Spirit.
℟. The Word was made man, alleluia, alleluia.

Canticle Of Mary

Ant. Blessed is the womb which bore you, O
[Stand] Christ, and the breast that nursed you, Lord and Savior of the world, alleluia.

Magnificat: Luke 1: 46-55
My soul ✟ proclaims the… [See Prayer On Back Flap. Then Repeat The Antiphon Above.]

Intercessions

Introductory Formula
To Christ, Emmanuel, whom the Virgin conceived and brought forth, let us give praise and pray to him:
℟. Son of the Virgin Mary, hear us.

Petitions
℣. You gave Mary the joy of motherhood,
℟. give all parents true joy in their children.
℣. King of peace, your kingdom is one of justice and peace,
℟. help us to seek the paths of peace.
℣. You came to make the human race the holy people of God,
℟. bring all nations to acknowledge the unifying bond of your love.
℣. By your birth you strengthened family ties,
℟. help families to come to a greater love for one another.
℣. You desired to be born into the days of time,
℟. grant that our departed brothers and sisters may be born into the day of eternity.

The Lord's Prayer
Our Father… [See prayer on back flap]

Prayer

God our Father,
may we always profit by the prayers
of the Virgin Mother Mary,
for you bring us life and salvation
through Jesus Christ her Son
who lives and reigns with you
and the Holy Spirit,
one God, for ever and ever. Amen.

Closing Rite Or Dismissal

[See Closing Rite on Back Flap]

Introductory Rite

[See Introductory Rite on Front Flap]

Hymn

◆ Virgin born, we bow before you;
Blessed was the womb that bore you;
Mary, Mother meek and mild,
Blessed was she in her Child.
Blessed was the maid that fed you;
Blessed was the hand that led you;
Blessed was the parent's eye
That watched your slumbering infancy.

◆ Blessed she by all creation,
Who brought forth the world's salvation;
And blessed they forever blest,
Who love you most and serve you best.
Virgin born, we bow before you:
Blessed was the womb that bore you;
Mary, Mother meek and mild,
Blessed was she in her Child.

Text: R. Heber, 1783-1826, alt.

Psalmody

Ant. 1   This pledge of new redemption and promise
of eternal joy, prepared through ages past, has
dawned for us today.

Book 5: Psalm 110: 1-5, 7
The Messiah, king and priest

[Sit]   ◆ The Lord's revelation to my Master:
"Sit on my right:
your foes I will put beneath your feet."

◆ The Lord will wield from Zion
your scepter of power:
rule in the midst of all your foes.

◆ A prince from the day of your birth
on the holy mountains;
from the womb before the dawn I begot you.

◆ The Lord has sworn an oath he will not change.
"You are a priest for ever,
a priest like Melchizedek of old."

◆ The Master standing at your right hand
will shatter kings in the day of his great wrath.

◆ He shall drink from the stream by the wayside
and therefore he shall lift up his head.

[Bow]   ◆ Glory to the Father…

Psalm Prayer
Almighty God,…[See psalm prayer on front flap]

Ant.   This pledge of new redemption and promise
of eternal joy, prepared through ages past, has
dawned for us today.

Ant. 2   The Lord has made manifest his steadfast love
for us.

SECOND SUNDAY
after Christmas

Book 5: Psalm 115
Praise of the true God

◆ Not to us, Lord, not to us,
but to your name give the glory
for the sake of your love and your truth,
lest the heathen say: "Where is their God?"

◆ But our God is in the heavens;
he does whatever he wills.
Their idols are silver and gold,
the work of human hands.

◆ They have mouths but they cannot speak;
they have eyes but they cannot see;
they have ears but they cannot hear;
they have nostrils but they cannot smell.

◆ With their hands they cannot feel;
with their feet they cannot walk.
No sound comes from their throats.
Their makers will come to be like them
and so will all who trust in them.

◆ Sons of Israel, trust in the Lord;
he is their help and their shield.
Sons of Aaron, trust in the Lord;
he is their help and their shield.

◆ You who fear him, trust in the Lord;
he is their help and their shield.
He remembers us, and he will bless us;
he will bless the sons of Israel.
He will bless the sons of Aaron.

◆ The Lord will bless those who fear him,
the little no less than the great:
to you may the Lord grant increase,
to you and all your children.

◆ May you be blessed by the Lord,
the maker of heaven and earth.
The heavens belong to the Lord
but the earth he has given to men.

◆ The dead shall not praise the Lord,
nor those who go down into the silence.
But we who live bless the Lord
now and for ever. Amen.

[Bow]   ◆ Glory to the Father…

Psalm Prayer
Father, creator…[See psalm prayer on front flap]

Ant. The Lord has made manifest his steadfast love for us.

Ant. 3 The Lord, the King of kings, is born for us; the day of the world's salvation has come; the promise of our redemption is fulfilled, alleluia.

Canticle based on Revelation 19: 1-7
The wedding of the Lamb

♦ Alleluia.
Salvation, glory, and power to our God:
(℟ Alleluia.)
his judgments are honest and true.
℟ Alleluia (alleluia).

♦ Alleluia.
Sing praise to our God, all you his servants,
(℟ Alleluia.)
all who worship him reverently, great and small.
℟ Alleluia (alleluia).

♦ Alleluia.
The Lord our all-powerful God is King;
(℟ Alleluia.)
let us rejoice, sing praise, and give him glory.
℟ Alleluia (alleluia).

♦ Alleluia.
The wedding feast of the Lamb has begun,
(℟ Alleluia.)
and his bride is prepared to welcome him.
℟ Alleluia (alleluia).

[Bow] ♦ Glory to the Father…

Ant. The Lord, the King of kings, is born for us; the day of the world's salvation has come; the promise of our redemption is fulfilled, alleluia.

Reading: 1 John 1: 1-3

This is what we proclaim to you: /what was from the beginning, /what we have heard, /what we have seen with our eyes, /what we have looked upon /and our hands have touched—/we speak of the word of life. /(This life became visible; /we have seen and bear witness to it, /and we proclaim to you the eternal life /that was present to the Father /and became visible to us.) /What we have seen and heard /we proclaim in turn to you /so that you may share life with us. /This fellowship of ours is with the Father /and with his Son, Jesus Christ.

Responsory

℣. The Word was made man, alleluia, alleluia.
℟. The Word was made man, alleluia, alleluia.
℣. He lived among us,
℟. alleluia, alleluia.

[Bow] ℣. Glory to the Father, and to the Son, and to the Holy Spirit.
℟. The Word was made man, alleluia, alleluia.

Canticle Of Mary

Ant. Blessed is the womb that bore the Son of the
[Stand] Eternal Father, and blessed are the breasts that nursed Christ the Lord.

Magnificat: Luke 1: 46-55
My soul ✠ proclaims the… [See Prayer On Back.]

Intercessions

Introductory Formula
At the birth of Jesus, angels proclaimed peace to the world. We worship him now with joy, and we pray with hearts full of faith:
℟ May your birth bring peace to all.

Petitions
℣. Lord, fill your holy people with whatever good they need,
℟. let the mystery of your birth be the source of our peace.
℣. You came as chief shepherd and guardian of our lives,
℟. let the Pope and bishops be faithful channels of your many gifts of grace.
℣. King from all eternity, you desired to be born within time and to experience the day-to-day life of men and women,
℟. share your gift of unending life with us, weak people, doomed to death.
℣. Awaited from the beginning of the world, you came only in the fullness of time,
℟. now reveal your presence to those who are still expecting you.
℣. You became man and gave new life to our human condition in the grip of death,
℟. now give the fullness of life to all who have died.

The Lord's Prayer
Our Father… [See prayer on back flap]

Prayer

God of power and life,
glory of all who believe in you,
fill the world with your splendor
and show the nations the light of your truth.
We ask this through our Lord Jesus Christ,
your Son,
who lives and reigns with you
and the Holy Spirit,
one God, for ever and ever. Amen.

Closing Rite Or Dismissal [See Back Flap.]

Introductory Rite

[Stand] V. God, ✠ come to my assistance.

R. Lord, make haste to help me.

[Bow] Glory to the Father, and to the Son,
and to the Holy Spirit:
as it was in the beginning, is now,
and will be for ever. Amen.

Hymn

As with gladness men of old,
Did the guiding star behold,
As with joy they hailed its light,
Leading onwards, beaming bright,
So, most gracious God, may we
Evermore be led to thee.

As with joyful steps they sped
To that lowly manger-bed,
There to bend the knee before
Him whom heaven and earth adore,
So may we with willing feet
Ever seek thy mercy-seat.

As they offered gifts most rare
At that manger rude and bare,
So may we with holy joy,
Pure, and free from sin's alloy,
All our costliest treasures bring,
Christ, to thee our heavenly king.

Holy Jesus, every day
Keep us in the narrow way;
And, when earthly things are past,
Bring our ransomed souls at last
Where they need no star to guide,
Where no clouds thy glory hide.

In the heavenly country bright
Need they no created light;
Thou its light, its joy, its crown,
Thou its sun which goes not down:
There for ever may we sing
Alleluias to our king.

Text: W. Chatteron Dix, 1837-1898

Psalmody

Ant. 1 He comes in splendor, the King who is our peace;
he is supreme over all the kings of the earth.

Book 5: Psalm 110: 1-5, 7
The Messiah, king and priest

[Sit] The Lord's revelation to my Master:
"Sit on my right:
your foes I will put beneath your feet."

The Lord will wield from Zion
your scepter of power:
rule in the midst of all your foes.

THE EPIPHANY
of the Lord

A prince from the day of your birth
on the holy mountains;
from the womb before the dawn I begot you.

The Lord has sworn an oath he will not change.
"You are a priest for ever,
a priest like Melchizedek of old."

The Master standing at your right hand
will shatter kings in the day of his great wrath.

He shall drink from the stream by the wayside
and therefore he shall lift up his head.

[Bow] Glory to the Father, and to the Son,
and to the Holy Spirit:
as it was in the beginning, is now,
and will be for ever. Amen.

Ant. He comes in splendor, the King who is our
peace; he is supreme over all the kings of the
earth.

Ant. 2 A light has shone through the darkness for the
upright of heart; the Lord is gracious, merciful
and just.

Book 5: Psalm 112
The happiness of the just man

Happy the man who fears the Lord,
who takes delight in all his commands.
His sons will be powerful on earth;
the children of the upright are blessed.

Riches and wealth are in his house;
his justice stands firm for ever.
He is a light in the darkness for the upright:
he is generous, merciful and just.

The good man takes pity and lends,
he conducts his affairs with honor.
The just man will never waver:
he will be remembered for ever.

He has no fear of evil news;
with a firm heart he trusts in the Lord.
With a steadfast heart he will not fear;
he will see the downfall of his foes.

Open-handed, he gives to the poor;
his justice stands firm for ever.
His head will be raised in glory.

♦ The wicked man sees and is angry,
grinds his teeth and fades away;
the desire of the wicked leads to doom.

[Bow] ♦ Glory to the Father, and to the Son,
and to the Holy Spirit:
as it was in the beginning, is now,
and will be for ever. Amen.

Ant. A light has shone through the darkness for the
upright of heart; the Lord is gracious, merciful
and just.

Ant. 3 All the people, whom you have made, will
come and worship before you, Lord.

Canticle: Revelation 15: 3-4
♦ Mighty and wonderful are your works,
Lord God Almighty!
Righteous and true are your ways,
O King of the nations!

♦ Who would dare refuse you honor,
or the glory due your name, O Lord?

♦ Since you alone are holy,
all nations shall come
and worship in your presence.
Your mighty deeds are clearly seen.

[Bow] ♦ Glory to the Father…

Ant. All the people, whom you have made, will
come and worship before you, Lord.

Reading: Titus 3: 4-7

When the kindness and love of God our
Savior appeared, he saved us; not because
of any righteous deeds we had done, but
because of his mercy. He saved us through the
baptism of new birth and renewal by the Holy
Spirit. This Spirit he lavished on us through
Jesus Christ our Savior, that we might be
justified by his grace and become heirs, in
hope, of eternal life.

Responsory

℣. All peoples will be blessed in him, men and
women of every race.
℟. All peoples will be blessed in him, men and
women of every race.
℣. All nations will acclaim his glory.
℟. Men and women of every race.
[Bow] ℣. Glory to the Father, and to the Son,
and to the Holy Spirit.
℟. All peoples will be blessed in him, men and
women of every race.

Canticle Of Mary

Ant.
[Stand]
Three mysteries mark this holy day: today the
star leads the Magi to the infant Christ; today
water is changed into wine for the wedding
feast; today Christ wills to be baptized by
John in the river Jordan to bring us salvation.

Magnificat: Luke 1: 46-55
My soul ✠ proclaims the… [See Prayer On Back
Flap. Then Repeat The Antiphon Above.]

Intercessions

Introductory Formula
On this day our Savior was adored by the
Magi. Let us also worship him with joy as we
pray to him:
℟. Save the poor, O Lord.

Petitions
℣. King of the nations, you called the Magi to
adore you as the first representatives of
the nations,
℟. give us a willing spirit of adoration and service.
℣. King of glory, you judge your people
with justice,
℟. grant mankind an abundant measure of peace.
℣. King of ages, you endure from age to age,
℟. send your word as fresh spring rain falling on
our hearts.
℣. King of justice, you desire to free the poor
who have no advocate,
℟. be compassionate to the suffering and
the afflicted.
℣. Lord, your name is blessed for all ages,
℟. show the wonders of your saving power to our
deceased brothers and sisters.

The Lord's Prayer
Our Father… [See prayer on back flap]

Prayer

Father,
you revealed your Son to the nations
by the guidance of a star.
Lead us to your glory in heaven
by the light of faith.
We ask this through our Lord Jesus Christ,
your Son,
who lives and reigns with you
and the Holy Spirit,
one God, for ever and ever. Amen.

Closing Rite Or Dismissal

[See Closing Rite on Back Flap]

19

Introductory Rite

[STAND] V. God, ✢ come to my assistance.

R. Lord, make haste to help me.

[BOW] Glory to the Father, and to the Son,
and to the Holy Spirit:
as it was in the beginning, is now,
and will be for ever. Amen.

Hymn

Sing praise to our Creator,
O sons of Adam's race;
God's children by adoption,
Baptized into his grace.

REFRAIN: *Praise the holy Trinity,*
Undivided Unity;
Holy God, Mighty God,
God Immortal, be adored.

To Jesus Christ give glory,
God's coeternal Son;
As members of his Body
We live in him as one.

REFRAIN *Praise the holy Trinity...*

Now praise the Holy Spirit
Poured forth upon the earth;
Who sanctifies and guides us,
Confirmed in our rebirth.

REFRAIN *Praise the holy Trinity...*
Text: Omer Westendorf, 1961

Psalmody

Ant. 1 The Father's voice resounded from the heavens:
This is my Son in whom I delight, listen to
what he says to you.

Book 5: Psalm 110: 1-5, 7
The Messiah, king and priest

[SIT] The Lord's revelation to my Master:
"Sit on my right:
your foes I will put beneath your feet."

The Lord will wield from Zion
your scepter of power:
rule in the midst of all your foes.

A prince from the day of your birth
on the holy mountains;
from the womb before the dawn I begot you.

The Lord has sworn an oath he will not change.
"You are a priest for ever,
a priest like Melchizedek of old."

The Master standing at your right hand
will shatter kings in the day of his great wrath.

THE BAPTISM
of the Lord

He shall drink from the stream by the wayside
and therefore he shall lift up his head.

[BOW] Glory to the Father, and to the Son,
and to the Holy Spirit:
as it was in the beginning, is now,
and will be for ever. Amen.

Ant. The Father's voice resounded from the
heavens: This is my Son in whom I delight,
listen to what he says to you.

Ant. 2 In the Jordan river our Savior crushed the
serpent's head and wrested us free from
his grasp.

Book 5: Psalm 112
The happiness of the just man

Happy the man who fears the Lord,
who takes delight in all his commands.
His sons will be powerful on earth;
the children of the upright are blessed.

Riches and wealth are in his house;
his justice stands firm for ever.
He is a light in the darkness for the upright:
he is generous, merciful and just.

The good man takes pity and lends,
he conducts his affairs with honor.
The just man will never waver:
he will be remembered for ever.

He has no fear of evil news;
with a firm heart he trusts in the Lord.
With a steadfast heart he will not fear;
he will see the downfall of his foes.

Open-handed, he gives to the poor;
his justice stands firm for ever.
His head will be raised in glory.

The wicked man sees and is angry,
grinds his teeth and fades away;
the desire of the wicked leads to doom.

[BOW] Glory to the Father, and to the Son,
and to the Holy Spirit:
as it was in the beginning, is now,
and will be for ever. Amen.

Ant. In the Jordan river our Savior crushed the serpent's head and wrested us free from his grasp.

Ant. 3 A wondrous mystery is declared to us today: the Creator of the universe has washed away our sins in the waters of the Jordan.

Canticle: Revelation 15: 3-4

✦ Mighty and wonderful are your works,
Lord God Almighty!
Righteous and true are your ways,
O King of the nations!

✦ Who would dare refuse you honor,
or the glory due your name, O Lord?

✦ Since you alone are holy,
all nations shall come
and worship in your presence.
Your mighty deeds are clearly seen.

[Bow] ✦ Glory to the Father…

Ant. A wondrous mystery is declared to us today: the Creator of the universe has washed away our sins in the waters of the Jordan.

Reading: Acts 10: 37-39

I take it you know what has been reported all over Judea about Jesus of Nazareth, beginning in Galilee with the baptism John preached; of the way God anointed him with the Holy Spirit and power. He went about doing good works and healing all who were in the grip of the devil, and God was with him. We are witnesses to all that he did in the land of the Jews and in Jerusalem.

Responsory

℣. Christ comes to us. He comes in water and in blood.

℟. Christ comes to us. He comes in water and in blood.

℣. Jesus Christ our Lord.

℟. Comes in water and in blood.

[Bow] ℣. Glory to the Father, and to the Son, and to the Holy Spirit.

℟. Christ comes to us. He comes in water and in blood.

Canticle Of Mary

Ant.
[Stand] Christ Jesus loved us, poured out his blood to wash away our sins, and made us a kingdom and priests for God our Father. To him be glory and honor for ever.

Magnificat: Luke 1: 46-55
My soul ✠ proclaims the… [See Prayer On Back Flap. Then Repeat The Antiphon Above.]

Intercessions

Introductory Formula
Our Redeemer desired to be baptized in the Jordan by John; let us make our petition to him:

℟. Lord, send forth your Spirit upon us.

Petitions
℣. Christ, Servant of God, the Father acknowledged you as his own Son with whom he was pleased,

℟. send forth your Spirit upon us.

℣. Christ, Chosen One of God, you did not break the crushed reed or extinguish the wavering flame,

℟. have mercy on all who are seeking you in good faith.

℣. Christ, Son of God, the Father called you to be a light to the nations in the new covenant,

℟. open the eyes of the blind by the waters of baptism.

℣. Christ, Savior of mankind, the Father anointed you with the Holy Spirit for the ministry of salvation,

℟. lead all to see you and to believe in you, that they may have eternal life.

℣. Christ, our hope, you lead those in darkness to the light of salvation,

℟. receive our departed brothers and sisters into your kingdom.

The Lord's Prayer
Our Father… [See prayer on back flap]

Prayer

Almighty, eternal God,
when the Spirit descended upon Jesus
at his baptism in the Jordan,
you revealed him as your own beloved Son.
Keep us, your children born of water
   and the Spirit,
faithful to our calling.
We ask this through our Lord Jesus Christ,
   your Son,
who lives and reigns with you
   and the Holy Spirit,
one God, for ever and ever. Amen.

Closing Rite Or Dismissal

[See Closing Rite on Back Flap]

Introductory Rite

[See Introductory Rite on Front Flap]

Hymn

♦ Love divine, all loves excelling,
Joy of heaven to earth come down,
And impart to us, here dwelling,
Grace and mercy all around.
Jesus, source of all compassion,
Pure, unbounded love you share;
Grant us many choicest blessings,
Keep us in your loving care.

♦ Come, O source of inspiration,
Pure and spotless let us be:
Let us see your true salvation,
Perfect in accord with thee.
Praising Father for all glory
With the Spirit and the Son;
Everlasting thanks we give thee,
Undivided, love, in one.

Text: C. Wesley, 1707-1788, adapted by C.T. Andrews 1968

Psalmody

Ant. 1 Christ our Lord is a priest for ever, like
Melchizedek of old, alleluia.

Book 5: Psalm 110: 1-5, 7
The Messiah, king and priest

[Sit] ♦ The Lord's revelation to my Master:
"Sit on my right:
your foes I will put beneath your feet."

♦ The Lord will wield from Zion
your scepter of power:
rule in the midst of all your foes.

♦ A prince from the day of your birth
on the holy mountains;
from the womb before the dawn I begot you.

♦ The Lord has sworn an oath he will not change.
"You are a priest for ever,
a priest like Melchizedek of old."

♦ The Master standing at your right hand
will shatter kings in the day of his great wrath.

♦ He shall drink from the stream by the wayside
and therefore he shall lift up his head.

[Bow] ♦ Glory to the Father, and to the Son,
and to the Holy Spirit:
as it was in the beginning, is now,
and will be for ever. Amen.

Psalm Prayer
Almighty God, bring the kingdom of Christ,
your anointed one, to its fullness. May the
perfect offering of your Son, eternal priest of

SECOND SUNDAY
in Ordinary Time

the new Jerusalem, be offered in every place to
your name, and make all nations a holy people
for you.

Ant. Christ our Lord is a priest for ever, like
Melchizedek of old, alleluia.

Ant. 2 God dwells in highest heaven; he has power to
do all he wills, alleluia.

Book 5: Psalm 115
Praise of the true God

♦ Not to us, Lord, not to us,
but to your name give the glory
for the sake of your love and your truth,
lest the heathen say: "Where is their God?"

♦ But our God is in the heavens;
he does whatever he wills.
Their idols are silver and gold,
the work of human hands.

♦ They have mouths but they cannot speak;
they have eyes but they cannot see;
they have ears but they cannot hear;
they have nostrils but they cannot smell.

♦ With their hands they cannot feel;
with their feet they cannot walk.
No sound comes from their throats.
Their makers will come to be like them
and so will all who trust in them.

♦ Sons of Israel, trust in the Lord;
he is their help and their shield.
Sons of Aaron, trust in the Lord;
he is their help and their shield.

♦ You who fear him, trust in the Lord;
he is their help and their shield.
He remembers us, and he will bless us;
he will bless the sons of Israel.
He will bless the sons of Aaron.

♦ The Lord will bless those who fear him,
the little no less than the great:
to you may the Lord grant increase,
to you and all your children.

♦ May you be blessed by the Lord,
the maker of heaven and earth.
The heavens belong to the Lord
but the earth he has given to men.

✛ The dead shall not praise the Lord,
   nor those who go down into the silence.
   But we who live bless the Lord
   now and for ever. Amen.

[Bow] ✛ Glory to the Father…

Psalm Prayer
Father, creator… [See psalm prayer on front flap]

Ant. God dwells in highest heaven; he has power to
        do all he wills, alleluia.

Ant. 3 Praise God, all you who serve him, both great
          and small, alleluia.

Canticle based on Revelation 19: 1-7
The wedding of the Lamb
✛ Alleluia.
   Salvation, glory, and power to our God:
   (℟ Alleluia.)
   his judgments are honest and true.
℟ Alleluia (alleluia).

✛ Alleluia.
   Sing praise to our God, all you his servants,
   (℟ Alleluia.)
   all who worship him reverently, great and small.
℟ Alleluia (alleluia).

✛ Alleluia.
   The Lord our all-powerful God is King;
   (℟ Alleluia.)
   let us rejoice, sing praise, and give him glory.
℟ Alleluia (alleluia).

✛ Alleluia.
   The wedding feast of the Lamb has begun,
   (℟ Alleluia.)
   and his bride is prepared to welcome him.
℟ Alleluia (alleluia).

[Bow] ✛ Glory to the Father…

Ant. Praise God, all you who serve him, both great
        and small, alleluia.

Reading: 2 Thessalonians 2: 13-14

We are bound to thank God for you always,
beloved brothers in the Lord, because you are
the first fruits of those whom God has chosen
for salvation, in holiness of spirit and fidelity
to truth. He called you through our preaching
of the good news so that you might achieve the
glory of our Lord Jesus Christ.

Responsory

℣ Our Lord is great, mighty is his power.
℟ Our Lord is great, mighty is his power.
℣ His wisdom is beyond compare,
℟ mighty is his power.

[Bow] ℣ Glory to the Father, and to the Son,
            and to the Holy Spirit.
       ℟ Our Lord is great, mighty is his power.

Canticle Of Mary

Ant. There was a wedding in Cana of Galilee, and
[Stand] Jesus was there with Mary his mother.

Magnificat: Luke 1: 46-55
My soul ✛ proclaims the… [See Prayer On Back
Flap. Then Repeat The Antiphon Above.]

Intercessions

Introductory Formula
All praise and honor to Christ! He lives for
ever to intercede for us, and he is able to save
those who approach the Father in his name.
Sustained by our faith, let us call upon him:
℟ Remember your people, Lord.

Petitions
℣ As the day draws to a close, Sun of Justice, we
   invoke your name upon the whole human race,
℟ so that all men may enjoy your never
   failing light.
℣ Preserve the covenant which you have ratified
   in your blood,
℟ cleanse and sanctify your Church.
℣ Remember your assembly, Lord,
℟ your dwelling place.
℣ Guide travelers along the path of peace
   and prosperity,
℟ so that they may reach their destinations in
   safety and joy.
℣ Receive the souls of the dead, Lord,
℟ grant them your favor and the gift of
   eternal glory.

The Lord's Prayer
Our Father… [See prayer on back flap]

Prayer

Father of heaven and earth,
hear our prayers,
and show us the way to peace in the world.
Grant this through our Lord Jesus Christ,
   your Son,
who lives and reigns with you
   and the Holy Spirit,
one God, for ever and ever. Amen.

Closing Rite Or Dismissal

[See Closing Rite on Back Flap]

Introductory Rite

[Stand] V. God, + come to my assistance.
R. Lord, make haste to help me.

[Bow] Glory to the Father, and to the Son,
and to the Holy Spirit:
as it was in the beginning, is now,
and will be for ever. Amen.

Hymn

* O Christ, you are the light and day
Which drives away the night,
The ever shining Sun of God
And pledge of future light.

* As now the ev'ning shadows fall
Please grant us, Lord, we pray,
A quiet night to rest in you
Until the break of day.

* Remember us, poor mortal men,
We humbly ask, O Lord,
And may your presence in our souls
Be now our great reward.
Translator: Rev. M. Quinn, O.P. et al.

Psalmody

Ant. 1 The Lord said to my Master: Sit at my right
hand, alleluia.

Book 5: Psalm 110: 1-5, 7
The Messiah, king and priest

[Sit] * The Lord's revelation to my Master:
"Sit on my right:
your foes I will put beneath your feet."

* The Lord will wield from Zion
your scepter of power:
rule in the midst of all your foes.

* A prince from the day of your birth
on the holy mountains;
from the womb before the dawn I begot you.

* The Lord has sworn an oath he will not change.
"You are a priest for ever,
a priest like Melchizedek of old."

* The Master standing at your right hand
will shatter kings in the day of his great wrath.

* He shall drink from the stream by the wayside
and therefore he shall lift up his head.

[Bow] * Glory to the Father, and to the Son,
and to the Holy Spirit:
as it was in the beginning, is now,
and will be for ever. Amen.

Psalm Prayer
Father, we ask you to give us victory and peace.
In Jesus Christ, our Lord and King, we are

already seated at your right hand. We look
forward to praising you in the fellowship of all
your saints in our heavenly homeland.

Ant. The Lord said to my Master: Sit at my right
hand, alleluia.

Ant. 2 Our compassionate Lord has left us a
memorial of his wonderful work, alleluia.

Book 5: Psalm III
God's marvelous works

* I will thank the Lord with all my heart
in the meeting of the just and their assembly.
Great are the works of the Lord;
to be pondered by all who love them.

* Majestic and glorious his work,
his justice stands firm for ever.
He makes us remember his wonders.
The Lord is compassion and love.

* He gives food to those who fear him;
keeps his covenant ever in mind.
He has shown his might to his people
by giving them the lands of the nations.

* His works are justice and truth:
his precepts are all of them sure,
standing firm for ever and ever:
they are made in uprightness and truth.

* He has sent deliverance to his people
and established his covenant for ever.
Holy his name, to be feared.

* To fear the Lord is the first stage of wisdom;
all who do so prove themselves wise.
His praise shall last for ever!

[Bow] * Glory to the Father...

Psalm Prayer
Merciful and gentle Lord, you are the
crowning glory of all the saints. Give us, your
children, the gift of obedience which is the
beginning of wisdom, so that we may do what
you command and be filled with your mercy.

Ant. Our compassionate Lord has left us a
memorial of his wonderful work, alleluia.

Ant. 3 All power is yours, Lord God, our mighty
King, alleluia.

THIRD SUNDAY
in Ordinary Time
[Psalter, Week III]

Canticle based on Revelation 19: 1-7
The wedding of the Lamb

+ Alleluia.
Salvation, glory, and power to our God:
(℟ Alleluia.)
his judgments are honest and true.
℟ Alleluia (alleluia).

+ Alleluia.
Sing praise to our God, all you his servants,
(℟ Alleluia.)
all who worship him reverently, great and small.
℟ Alleluia (alleluia).

+ Alleluia.
The Lord our all-powerful God is King;
(℟ Alleluia.)
let us rejoice, sing praise, and give him glory.
℟ Alleluia (alleluia).

+ Alleluia.
The wedding feast of the Lamb has begun,
(℟ Alleluia.)
and his bride is prepared to welcome him.
℟ Alleluia (alleluia).

[Bow] + Glory to the Father…

Ant. All power is yours, Lord God, our mighty King, alleluia.

Reading: 1 Peter 1: 3-7

Praised be the God and Father /of our Lord Jesus Christ, /he who in his great mercy /gave us new birth; /a birth unto hope which draws its life /from the resurrection of Jesus Christ from the dead; /a birth to an imperishable inheritance, /incapable of fading or defilement, /which is kept in heaven for you /who are guarded with God's power through faith; /a birth to a salvation which stands ready /to be revealed in the last days.

There is cause for rejoicing here. You may for a time have to suffer the distress of many trials; but this is so that your faith, which is more precious than the passing splendor of fire-tried gold, may by its genuineness lead to praise, glory, and honor when Jesus Christ appears.

Responsory

℣ The whole creation proclaims the greatness of your glory.
℟ The whole creation proclaims the greatness of your glory.
℣ Eternal ages praise
℟ the greatness of your glory.

[Bow] ℣ Glory to the Father, and to the Son, and to the Holy Spirit.
℟ The whole creation proclaims the greatness of your glory.

Canticle Of Mary

Ant.
[Stand] The Spirit of the Lord rests upon me; he has sent me to preach the good news to the poor.

Magnificat: Luke 1: 46-55
My soul ✠ proclaims the… [See Prayer On Back Flap. Then Repeat The Antiphon Above.]

Intercessions

Introductory Formula
The world was created by the Word of God, re-created by his redemption, and it is continually renewed by his love. Rejoicing in him we call out:
℟ Renew the wonders of your love, Lord.

Petitions
℣ We give thanks to God whose power is revealed in nature,
℟ and whose providence is revealed in history.
℣ Through your Son, the herald of reconciliation, the victor of the cross,
℟ free us from empty fear and hopelessness.
℣ May all those who love and pursue justice,
℟ work together without deceit to build a world of true peace.
℣ Be with the oppressed, free the captives, console the sorrowing, feed the hungry, strengthen the weak,
℟ in all people reveal the victory of your cross.
℣ After your Son's death and burial you raised him up again in glory,
℟ grant that the faithful departed may live with him.

The Lord's Prayer
Our Father… [See prayer on back flap]

Prayer

All-powerful and ever-living God,
direct your love that is within us,
that our efforts in the name of your Son
may bring mankind to unity and peace.
We ask this through our Lord Jesus Christ,
  your Son,
who lives and reigns with you
  and the Holy Spirit,
one God, for ever and ever. Amen.

Closing Rite Or Dismissal

[See Closing Rite on Back Flap]

25

Introductory Rite

[STAND] V. God, + come to my assistance.

R. Lord, make haste to help me.

[BOW] Glory to the Father, and to the Son,
and to the Holy Spirit:
as it was in the beginning, is now,
and will be for ever. Amen.

Hymn

✦ Love divine, all loves excelling,
Joy of heaven to earth come down,
And impart to us, here dwelling,
Grace and mercy all around.
Jesus, source of all compassion,
Pure, unbounded love you share;
Grant us many choicest blessings,
Keep us in your loving care.

✦ Come, O source of inspiration,
Pure and spotless let us be:
Let us see your true salvation,
Perfect in accord with thee.
Praising Father for all glory
With the Spirit and the Son;
Everlasting thanks we give thee,
Undivided, love, in one.

Text: C. Wesley, 1707-1788, adapted by C.T. Andrews 1968

Psalmody

Ant. 1 In eternal splendor, before the dawn of light on
earth, I have begotten you, alleluia.

Book 5: Psalm 110: 1-5, 7
The Messiah, king and priest

[SIT] ✦ The Lord's revelation to my Master:
"Sit on my right:
your foes I will put beneath your feet."

✦ The Lord will wield from Zion
your scepter of power:
rule in the midst of all your foes.

✦ A prince from the day of your birth
on the holy mountains;
from the womb before the dawn I begot you.

✦ The Lord has sworn an oath he will not change.
"You are a priest for ever,
a priest like Melchizedek of old."

✦ The Master standing at your right hand
will shatter kings in the day of his great wrath.

✦ He shall drink from the stream by the wayside
and therefore he shall lift up his head.

[BOW] ✦ Glory to the Father…

Psalm Prayer
Father, we ask you to give us victory and peace.

FOURTH SUNDAY
in Ordinary Time
[PSALTER, WEEK IV]

In Jesus Christ, our Lord and King, we are
already seated at your right hand. We look
forward to praising you in the fellowship of all
your saints in our heavenly homeland.

Ant. In eternal splendor, before the dawn of light
on earth, I have begotten you, alleluia.

Ant. 2 Blessed are they who hunger and thirst for
holiness; they will be satisfied.

Book 5: Psalm 112
The happiness of the just man

✦ Happy the man who fears the Lord,
who takes delight in all his commands.
His sons will be powerful on earth;
the children of the upright are blessed.

✦ Riches and wealth are in his house;
his justice stands firm for ever.
He is a light in the darkness for the upright:
he is generous, merciful and just.

✦ The good man takes pity and lends,
he conducts his affairs with honor.
The just man will never waver:
he will be remembered for ever.

✦ He has no fear of evil news;
with a firm heart he trusts in the Lord.
With a steadfast heart he will not fear;
he will see the downfall of his foes.

✦ Open-handed, he gives to the poor;
his justice stands firm for ever.
His head will be raised in glory.

✦ The wicked man sees and is angry,
grinds his teeth and fades away;
the desire of the wicked leads to doom.

[BOW] ✦ Glory to the Father…

Psalm Prayer
Lord God, you are the eternal light which
illumines the hearts of good people. Help us
to love you, to rejoice in your glory, and so to
live in this world as to avoid harsh judgment in
the next. May we come to see the light of your
countenance.

Ant. Blessed are they who hunger and thirst for
holiness; they will be satisfied.

Ant. 3 Praise God, all you who serve him, both great and small, alleluia.

Canticle based on Revelation 19: 1-7
The wedding of the Lamb

✦ Alleluia.
Salvation, glory, and power to our God:
(℟ Alleluia.)
his judgments are honest and true.
℟ Alleluia (alleluia).

✦ Alleluia.
Sing praise to our God, all you his servants,
(℟ Alleluia.)
all who worship him reverently, great and small.
℟ Alleluia (alleluia).

✦ Alleluia.
The Lord our all-powerful God is King;
(℟ Alleluia.)
let us rejoice, sing praise, and give him glory.
℟ Alleluia (alleluia).

✦ Alleluia.
The wedding feast of the Lamb has begun,
(℟ Alleluia.)
and his bride is prepared to welcome him.
℟ Alleluia (alleluia).

[Bow] ✦ Glory to the Father…

Ant. Praise God, all you who serve him, both great and small, alleluia.

Reading: Hebrews 12: 22-24

You have drawn near to Mount Zion and the city of the living God, the heavenly Jerusalem, to myriads of angels in festal gathering, to the assembly of the first-born enrolled in heaven, to God the judge of all, to the spirits of just men made perfect, to Jesus, the mediator of a new covenant, and to the sprinkled blood which speaks more eloquently than that of Abel.

Responsory

℣. Our Lord is great, mighty is his power.
℟. Our Lord is great, mighty is his power.
℣. His wisdom is beyond compare,
℟. mighty is his power.
[Bow] ℣. Glory to the Father, and to the Son, and to the Holy Spirit.
℟. Our Lord is great, mighty is his power.

Canticle Of Mary

Ant. They all marveled at the words that came
[Stand] forth from the mouth of God.

Magnificat: Luke 1: 46-55
My soul ✠ proclaims the… [See Prayer On Back Flap. Then Repeat The Antiphon Above.]

Intercessions

Introductory Formula
Rejoicing in the Lord, from whom all good things come, let us pray:
℟ Lord, hear our prayer.

Petitions
℣ Father and Lord of all, you sent your Son into the world, that your name might be glorified in every place,
℟ strengthen the witness of your Church among the nations.
℣ Make us obedient to the teachings of your apostles,
℟ and bound to the truth of our faith.
℣ As you love the innocent,
℟ render justice to those who are wronged.
℣ Free those in bondage and give sight to the blind,
℟ raise up the fallen and protect the stranger.
℣ Fulfill your promise to those who already sleep in your peace,
℟ through your Son grant them a blessed resurrection.

The Lord's Prayer
Our Father… [See prayer on back flap]

Prayer

Lord our God,
help us to love you with all our hearts
and to love all men as you love them.
Grant this through our Lord Jesus Christ,
  your Son,
who lives and reigns with you
  and the Holy Spirit,
one God, for ever and ever. Amen.

Closing Rite Or Dismissal

[When Priest Or Deacon Presides]
℣. The Lord be with you.
℟ And also with you.
[Bow] May almighty God bless you, ✠ the Father, and the Son, and the Holy Spirit.
℟. Amen.
℣. Go in peace.
℟. Thanks be to God.

[When Priest Or Deacon Do Not Preside, And In Individual Recitation]
✠ May the Lord bless us, protect us from all evil and bring us to everlasting life.
Amen.

27

Introductory Rite

[Stand] V. God, + come to my assistance.
         R. Lord, make haste to help me.

[Bow]   Glory to the Father, and to the Son,
         and to the Holy Spirit:
         as it was in the beginning, is now,
         and will be for ever. Amen.

Hymn

    ✦ When Mary brought her treasure
      Unto the holy place,
      No eye of man could measure
      The joy upon her face.
      He was but six weeks old,
      Her plaything and her pleasure,
      Her silver and her gold.

    ✦ Then Simeon, on him gazing
      With wonder and with love,
      His aged voice up-raising
      Gave thanks to God above:
      "Now welcome sweet release!
      For I, my Savior praising,
      May die at last in peace."

    ✦ As by the sun in splendor
      The flags of night are furled,
      So darkness shall surrender
      To Christ who lights the world,
      To Christ the star of day,
      Who once was small and tender,
      A candle's gentle ray.

      Text: Jan Struther 1901-1953

Psalmody

Ant. 1   The Holy Spirit had revealed to Simeon that he
         would not see death until he had seen the Lord.

         Book 5: Psalm 110: 1-5, 7
         The Messiah, king and priest

[Sit]   ✦ The Lord's revelation to my Master:
          "Sit on my right:
          your foes I will put beneath your feet."

        ✦ The Lord will wield from Zion
          your scepter of power:
          rule in the midst of all your foes.

        ✦ A prince from the day of your birth
          on the holy mountains;
          from the womb before the dawn I begot you.

        ✦ The Lord has sworn an oath he will not change.
          "You are a priest for ever,
          a priest like Melchizedek of old."

        ✦ The Master standing at your right hand
          will shatter kings in the day of his great wrath.

Presentation
of the Lord

    ✦ He shall drink from the stream by the wayside
      and therefore he shall lift up his head.

[Bow]   ✦ Glory to the Father…

Ant.   The Holy Spirit had revealed to Simeon that
        he would not see death until he had seen the
        Lord.

Ant. 2 As the law prescribed, they offered to the Lord
        a pair of turtle doves or two young pigeons.

        Book 5: Psalm 130
        A cry from the depths

    ✦ Out of the depths I cry to you, O Lord,
      Lord, hear my voice!
      O let your ears be attentive
      to the voice of my pleading.

    ✦ If you, O Lord, should mark our guilt,
      Lord, who would survive?
      But with you is found forgiveness:
      for this we revere you.

    ✦ My soul is waiting for the Lord.
      I count on his word.
      My soul is longing for the Lord
      more than watchman for daybreak.
      Let the watchman count on daybreak
      and Israel on the Lord.

    ✦ Because with the Lord there is mercy
      and fullness of redemption,
      Israel indeed he will redeem
      from all its iniquity.

[Bow]   ✦ Glory to the Father…

Ant.   As the law prescribed, they offered to the Lord
        a pair of turtle doves or two young pigeons.

Ant. 3 My own eyes have seen the salvation which
        you have prepared in the sight of every people.

        Canticle: Colossians 1: 12-20

    ✦ Let us give thanks to the Father
      for having made you worthy
      to share the lot of the saints
      in light.

    ✦ He rescued us
      from the power of darkness

28

and brought us
into the kingdom of his beloved Son.
Through him we have redemption,
the forgiveness of our sins.

✦ He is the image of the invisible God,
the first-born of all creatures.
In him everything in heaven and on
   earth was created,
things visible and invisible.

✦ All were created through him;
all were created for him.
He is before all else that is.
In him everything continues in being.

✦ It is he who is head of the body, the church!
he who is the beginning,
the first-born of the dead,
so that primacy may be his in everything.

✦ It pleased God to make absolute fullness
   reside in him
and, by means of him, to reconcile everything
   in his person,
both on earth and in the heavens,
making peace through the blood of his cross.

[Bow]   ✦ Glory to the Father...

Ant.   My own eyes have seen the salvation which
you have prepared in the sight of every people.

Reading: Hebrews 4: 15-16

We do not have a high priest who is unable
to sympathize with our weakness, but one
who was tempted in every way that we are, yet
never sinned. So let us confidently approach
the throne of grace to receive mercy and favor
and to find help in time of need.

Responsory

℣. The Lord has made known his saving power.
℟. The Lord has made known his saving power.
℣. Which he has prepared in the sight
of every people.
℟. His saving power.
[Bow] ℣. Glory to the Father, and to the Son,
and to the Holy Spirit.
℟. The Lord has made known his saving power.

Canticle Of Mary

Ant.   Today the Blessed Virgin Mary presented
[Stand]   the Child Jesus in the temple; and Simeon,
inspired by the Holy Spirit, took him in his
arms, and gave thanks to God.

Magnificat: Luke 1: 46-55
My soul ✠ proclaims the... [See Prayer On Back Flap. Then Repeat The Antiphon Above.]

Intercessions

Introductory Formula
Today our Savior was presented in the temple.
Let us adore him as we say:
℟ Lord, may our eyes see your saving power.

Petitions
℣ Christ Jesus, you are the light that enlightens
all nations,
℟ shine upon those who do not know you, that
they may come to believe in you, the one,
true God.
℣ You are the redeemer and the glory of your
people Israel,
℟ may your Church proclaim your salvation to
the ends of the earth.
℣ Jesus, desire of the nations, Simeon, the just
man, rejoiced at your coming,
℟ lead all men to recognize that you still come
to them.
℣ Lord, when you were presented in the temple,
Simeon foretold that a sword of sorrow would
pierce your mother's heart,
℟ strengthen us to accept the sufferings we
endure for the sake of your name.
℣ Christ Jesus, joy of all the saints, Simeon
longed to see you before he died, and his
prayer was answered,
℟ hear our plea for all the dead who still yearn to
see you face to face.

The Lord's Prayer
Our Father... [See prayer on back flap]

Prayer

All-powerful Father,
Christ your Son became man for us
and was presented in the temple.
May he free our hearts from sin
and bring us into your presence.
We ask this through our Lord Jesus Christ,
   your Son,
who lives and reigns with you
   and the Holy Spirit,
one God, for ever and ever. Amen.

Closing Rite Or Dismissal

[See Closing Rite on Back Flap]

Introductory Rite

[STAND] V. God, ✠ come to my assistance.

R. Lord, make haste to help me.

[BOW] Glory to the Father, and to the Son,
and to the Holy Spirit:
as it was in the beginning, is now,
and will be for ever. Amen.

Hymn

✦ O Christ, you are the light and day
Which drives away the night,
The ever shining Sun of God
And pledge of future light.

✦ As now the ev'ning shadows fall
Please grant us, Lord, we pray,
A quiet night to rest in you
Until the break of day.

✦ Remember us, poor mortal men,
We humbly ask, O Lord,
And may your presence in our souls
Be now our great reward.

Translator: Rev. M. Quinn, O.P. et al.

Psalmody

Ant. 1 The Lord will stretch forth his mighty scepter
from Zion, and he will reign for ever, alleluia.

Book 5: Psalm 110: 1-5, 7
The Messiah, king and priest

[SIT] ✦ The Lord's revelation to my Master:
"Sit on my right:
your foes I will put beneath your feet."

✦ The Lord will wield from Zion
your scepter of power:
rule in the midst of all your foes.

✦ A prince from the day of your birth
on the holy mountains;
from the womb before the dawn I begot you.

✦ The Lord has sworn an oath he will not change.
"You are a priest for ever,
a priest like Melchizedek of old."

✦ The Master standing at your right hand
will shatter kings in the day of his great wrath.

✦ He shall drink from the stream by the wayside
and therefore he shall lift up his head.

[BOW] ✦ Glory to the Father…

Psalm Prayer
Father, we ask you to give us victory and peace.
In Jesus Christ, our Lord and King, we are
already seated at your right hand. We look
forward to praising you in the fellowship of all
your saints in our heavenly homeland.

30

FIFTH SUNDAY
in Ordinary Time
[PSALTER, WEEK I]

Ant. The Lord will stretch forth his mighty scepter
from Zion, and he will reign for ever, alleluia.

Ant. 2 The earth is shaken to its depths before the
glory of your face.

Book 2: Psalm 114
*The Israelites are delivered from the bondage of
Egypt*

✦ When Israel came forth from Egypt,
Jacob's sons from an alien people,
Judah became the Lord's temple,
Israel became his kingdom.

✦ The sea fled at the sight:
the Jordan turned back on its course,
the mountains leapt like rams
and the hills like yearling sheep.

✦ Why was it, sea, that you fled,
that you turned back, Jordan, on your course?
Mountains, that you leapt like rams,
hills, like yearling sheep?

✦ Tremble, O earth, before the Lord,
in the presence of the God of Jacob,
who turns the rock into a pool
and flint into a spring of water.

[BOW] ✦ Glory to the Father…

Psalm Prayer
Almighty God, ever-living mystery of unity
and trinity, you gave life to the new Israel by
birth from water and the Spirit, and made
it a chosen race, a royal priesthood, a people
set apart as your eternal possession. May all
those you have called to walk in the splendor
of the new light render you fitting service and
adoration.

Ant. The earth is shaken to its depths before the
glory of your face.

Ant. 3 All power is yours, Lord God, our mighty
King, alleluia.

Canticle based on Revelation 19: 1-7
The wedding of the Lamb

✦ Alleluia.
Salvation, glory, and power to our God:
(R. Alleluia.)
his judgments are honest and true.

R. Alleluia (alleluia).

+ Alleluia.
Sing praise to our God, all you his servants,
(℟ Alleluia.)
all who worship him reverently, great and small.
℟ Alleluia (alleluia).

+ Alleluia.
The Lord our all-powerful God is King;
(℟ Alleluia.)
let us rejoice, sing praise, and give him glory.
℟ Alleluia (alleluia).

+ Alleluia.
The wedding feast of the Lamb has begun,
(℟ Alleluia.)
and his bride is prepared to welcome him.
℟ Alleluia (alleluia).

[Bow] + Glory to the Father…

Ant. All power is yours, Lord God, our mighty King, alleluia.

Reading: 2 Corinthians 1: 3-7

Praised be God, the Father of our Lord Jesus Christ, the Father of mercies and the God of all consolation! He comforts us in all our afflictions and thus enables us to comfort those who are in trouble, with the same consolation we have received from him. As we have shared much in the suffering of Christ, so through Christ do we share abundantly in his consolation. If we are afflicted it is for your encouragement and salvation, and when we are consoled it is for your consolation, so that you may endure patiently the same sufferings we endure. Our hope for you is firm because we know that just as you share in the sufferings, so you will share in the consolation.

Responsory

℣ The whole creation proclaims the greatness of your glory.
℟ The whole creation proclaims the greatness of your glory.
℣ Eternal ages praise
℟ the greatness of your glory.
[Bow] ℣ Glory to the Father, and to the Son, and to the Holy Spirit.
℟ The whole creation proclaims the greatness of your glory.

Canticle Of Mary

Ant. Master, we have worked all night and have
[Stand] caught nothing; but if you say so, I will lower the nets again.

Magnificat: Luke 1: 46-55
My soul ✠ proclaims the… [See Prayer On Back Flap. Then Repeat The Antiphon Above.]

Intercessions

Introductory Formula
Christ the Lord is our head; we are his members. In joy let us call out to him:
℟ Lord, may your kingdom come.

Petitions
℣ Christ our Savior, make your Church a more vivid symbol of the unity of all mankind,
℟ make it more effectively the sacrament of salvation for all peoples.
℣ Through your presence, guide the college of bishops in union with the Pope,
℟ give them the gifts of unity, love and peace.
℣ Bind all Christians more closely to yourself, their divine Head,
℟ lead them to proclaim your kingdom by the witness of their lives.
℣ Grant peace to the world,
℟ let every land flourish in justice and security.
℣ Grant to the dead the glory of resurrection,
℟ and give us a share in their happiness.

The Lord's Prayer
Our Father… [See prayer on back flap]

Prayer

Father,
watch over your family
and keep us safe in your care,
for all our hope is in you.
Grant this through our Lord Jesus Christ,
  your Son,
who lives and reigns with you
  and the Holy Spirit,
one God, for ever and ever. Amen.

Closing Rite Or Dismissal

[When Priest Or Deacon Presides]
℣ The Lord be with you.
℟ And also with you.
[Bow] May almighty God bless you, + the Father, and the Son, and the Holy Spirit.
℟ Amen.
℣ Go in peace.
℟ Thanks be to God.

[When Priest Or Deacon Do Not Preside, And In Individual Recitation]
+ May the Lord bless us, protect us from all evil and bring us to everlasting life.
℟ Amen.

Introductory Rite

[See Introductory Rite on Front Flap]

Hymn

◆ Love divine, all loves excelling,
Joy of heaven to earth come down,
And impart to us, here dwelling,
Grace and mercy all around.
Jesus, source of all compassion,
Pure, unbounded love you share;
Grant us many choicest blessings,
Keep us in your loving care.

◆ Come, O source of inspiration,
Pure and spotless let us be:
Let us see your true salvation,
Perfect in accord with thee.
Praising Father for all glory
With the Spirit and the Son;
Everlasting thanks we give thee,
Undivided, love, in one.

Text: C. Wesley, 1707-1788, adapted by C.T. Andrews 1968

Psalmody

Ant. 1   Christ our Lord is a priest for ever, like
Melchizedek of old, alleluia.

Book 5: Psalm 110: 1-5, 7
The Messiah, king and priest

[Sit]   ◆ The Lord's revelation to my Master:
"Sit on my right:
your foes I will put beneath your feet."

◆ The Lord will wield from Zion
your scepter of power:
rule in the midst of all your foes.

◆ A prince from the day of your birth
on the holy mountains;
from the womb before the dawn I begot you.

◆ The Lord has sworn an oath he will not change.
"You are a priest for ever,
a priest like Melchizedek of old."

◆ The Master standing at your right hand
will shatter kings in the day of his great wrath.

◆ He shall drink from the stream by the wayside
and therefore he shall lift up his head.

[Bow]   ◆ Glory to the Father…

Psalm Prayer
Almighty God, bring the kingdom of Christ,
your anointed one, to its fullness. May the
perfect offering of your Son, eternal priest of
the new Jerusalem, be offered in every place to
your name, and make all nations a holy people
for you.

SIXTH SUNDAY
in Ordinary Time
[Psalter, Week II]

Ant.   Christ our Lord is a priest for ever, like
Melchizedek of old, alleluia.

Ant. 2   God dwells in highest heaven;
he has power to do all he wills, alleluia.

Book 5: Psalm 115
'Praise' of the 'true' God

◆ Not to us, Lord, not to us,
but to your name give the glory
for the sake of your love and your truth,
lest the heathen say: "Where is their God?"

◆ But our God is in the heavens;
he does whatever he wills.
Their idols are silver and gold,
the work of human hands.

◆ They have mouths but they cannot speak;
they have eyes but they cannot see;
they have ears but they cannot hear;
they have nostrils but they cannot smell.

◆ With their hands they cannot feel;
with their feet they cannot walk.
No sound comes from their throats.
Their makers will come to be like them
and so will all who trust in them.

◆ Sons of Israel, trust in the Lord;
he is their help and their shield.
Sons of Aaron, trust in the Lord;
he is their help and their shield.

◆ You who fear him, trust in the Lord;
he is their help and their shield.
He remembers us, and he will bless us;
he will bless the sons of Israel.
He will bless the sons of Aaron.

◆ The Lord will bless those who fear him,
the little no less than the great:
to you may the Lord grant increase,
to you and all your children.

◆ May you be blessed by the Lord,
the maker of heaven and earth.
The heavens belong to the Lord
but the earth he has given to men.

◆ The dead shall not praise the Lord,
nor those who go down into the silence.
But we who live bless the Lord
now and for ever. Amen.

[Bow] ✦ Glory to the Father...

Psalm Prayer

Father, creator and ruler of heaven and earth, you made man in your likeness to subdue the earth and master it, and to recognize the work of your hands in created beauty. Grant that your children, thus surrounded on all sides by signs of your presence, may live continually in Christ, praising you through him and with him.

Ant. God dwells in highest heaven;
he has power to do all he wills, alleluia.

Ant. 3 Praise God, all you who serve him, both great and small, alleluia.

Canticle based on Revelation 19: 1-7
The wedding of the Lamb

✦ Alleluia.
Salvation, glory, and power to our God:
(℟ Alleluia.)
his judgments are honest and true.
℟ Alleluia (alleluia).

✦ Alleluia.
Sing praise to our God, all you his servants,
(℟ Alleluia.)
all who worship him reverently, great and small.
℟ Alleluia (alleluia).

✦ Alleluia.
The Lord our all-powerful God is King;
(℟ Alleluia.)
let us rejoice, sing praise, and give him glory.
℟ Alleluia (alleluia).

✦ Alleluia.
The wedding feast of the Lamb has begun,
(℟ Alleluia.)
and his bride is prepared to welcome him.
℟ Alleluia (alleluia).

[Bow] ✦ Glory to the Father...

Ant. Praise God, all you who serve him, both great and small, alleluia.

Reading: 2 Thessalonians 2: 13-14

We are bound to thank God for you always, beloved brothers in the Lord, because you are the first fruits of those whom God has chosen for salvation, in holiness of spirit and fidelity to truth. He called you through our preaching of the good news so that you might achieve the glory of our Lord Jesus Christ.

Responsory

℣ Our Lord is great, mighty is his power.
℟ Our Lord is great, mighty is his power.

℣ His wisdom is beyond compare,
℟ mighty is his power.
[Bow] ℣ Glory to the Father, and to the Son, and to the Holy Spirit.
℟ Our Lord is great, mighty is his power.

Canticle Of Mary

Ant. Blessed are you who are poor, for the kingdom
[Stand] of God is yours. And blessed are you who hunger now; you shall be satisfied.

Magnificat: Luke 1: 46-55
My soul ✠ proclaims the... [See Prayer On Back Flap. Then Repeat The Antiphon Above.]

Intercessions

Introductory Formula
All praise and honor to Christ! He lives for ever to intercede for us, and he is able to save those who approach the Father in his name. Sustained by our faith, let us call upon him:
℟ Remember your people, Lord.

Petitions
℣ As the day draws to a close, Sun of Justice, we invoke your name upon the whole human race,
℟ so that all men may enjoy your never failing light.
℣ Preserve the covenant which you have ratified in your blood,
℟ cleanse and sanctify your Church.
℣ Remember your assembly, Lord,
℟ your dwelling place.
℣ Guide travelers along the path of peace and prosperity,
℟ so that they may reach their destinations in safety and joy.
℣ Receive the souls of the dead, Lord,
℟ grant them your favor and the gift of eternal glory.

The Lord's Prayer
Our Father... [See prayer on back flap]

Prayer

God our Father,
you have promised to remain for ever
with those who do what is just and right.
Help us to live in your presence.
We ask this through our Lord Jesus Christ,
  your Son,
who lives and reigns with you
  and the Holy Spirit,
one God, for ever and ever. Amen.

Closing Rite Or Dismissal

[See Closing Rite on Back Flap]

33

Introductory Rite

[STAND] V. God, + come to my assistance.
R. Lord, make haste to help me.

[BOW] Glory to the Father, and to the Son,
and to the Holy Spirit:
as it was in the beginning, is now,
and will be for ever. Amen.

Hymn

✦ O Christ, you are the light and day
Which drives away the night,
The ever shining Sun of God
And pledge of future light.

✦ As now the ev'ning shadows fall
Please grant us, Lord, we pray,
A quiet night to rest in you
Until the break of day.

✦ Remember us, poor mortal men,
We humbly ask, O Lord,
And may your presence in our souls
Be now our great reward.

Translator: Rev. M. Quinn, O.P. et al.

Psalmody

Ant. 1   The Lord said to my Master:
Sit at my right hand, alleluia.

Book 5: Psalm 110: 1-5, 7
The Messiah, king and priest

[SIT] ✦ The Lord's revelation to my Master:
"Sit on my right:
your foes I will put beneath your feet."

✦ The Lord will wield from Zion
your scepter of power:
rule in the midst of all your foes.

✦ A prince from the day of your birth
on the holy mountains;
from the womb before the dawn I begot you.

✦ The Lord has sworn an oath he will not change.
"You are a priest for ever,
a priest like Melchizedek of old."

✦ The Master standing at your right hand
will shatter kings in the day of his great wrath.

✦ He shall drink from the stream by the wayside
and therefore he shall lift up his head.

[BOW] ✦ Glory to the Father, and to the Son,
and to the Holy Spirit:
as it was in the beginning, is now,
and will be for ever. Amen.

Psalm Prayer
Father, we ask you to give us victory and peace.
In Jesus Christ, our Lord and King, we are

already seated at your right hand. We look
forward to praising you in the fellowship of all
your saints in our heavenly homeland.

Ant.   The Lord said to my Master:
Sit at my right hand, alleluia.

Ant. 2   Our compassionate Lord has left us a
memorial of his wonderful work, alleluia.

Book 5: Psalm 111
God's marvelous works

✦ I will thank the Lord with all my heart
in the meeting of the just and their assembly.
Great are the works of the Lord;
to be pondered by all who love them.

✦ Majestic and glorious his work,
his justice stands firm for ever.
He makes us remember his wonders.
The Lord is compassion and love.

✦ He gives food to those who fear him;
keeps his covenant ever in mind.
He has shown his might to his people
by giving them the lands of the nations.

✦ His works are justice and truth:
his precepts are all of them sure,
standing firm for ever and ever:
they are made in uprightness and truth.

✦ He has sent deliverance to his people
and established his covenant for ever.
Holy his name, to be feared.

✦ To fear the Lord is the first stage of wisdom;
all who do so prove themselves wise.
His praise shall last for ever!

[BOW] ✦ Glory to the Father...

Psalm Prayer
Merciful and gentle Lord, you are the
crowning glory of all the saints. Give us, your
children, the gift of obedience which is the
beginning of wisdom, so that we may do what
you command and be filled with your mercy.

Ant.   Our compassionate Lord has left us a
memorial of his wonderful work, alleluia.

Ant. 3   All power is yours, Lord God, our mighty
King, alleluia.

Canticle based on Revelation 19: 1-7
The wedding of the Lamb

✠ Alleluia.
Salvation, glory, and power to our God:
(℟ Alleluia.)
his judgments are honest and true.
℟ Alleluia (alleluia).

✠ Alleluia.
Sing praise to our God, all you his servants,
(℟ Alleluia.)
all who worship him reverently, great and small.
℟ Alleluia (alleluia).

✠ Alleluia.
The Lord our all-powerful God is King;
(℟ Alleluia.)
let us rejoice, sing praise, and give him glory.
℟ Alleluia (alleluia).

✠ Alleluia.
The wedding feast of the Lamb has begun,
(℟ Alleluia.)
and his bride is prepared to welcome him.
℟ Alleluia (alleluia).

[Bow] ✠ Glory to the Father...

Ant. All power is yours, Lord God, our mighty King, alleluia.

Reading: 1 Peter 1: 3-7

Praised be the God and Father /of our Lord Jesus Christ, /he who in his great mercy /gave us new birth; /a birth unto hope which draws its life /from the resurrection of Jesus Christ from the dead; /a birth to an imperishable inheritance, /incapable of fading or defilement, /which is kept in heaven for you /who are guarded with God's power through faith; /a birth to a salvation which stands ready /to be revealed in the last days.

There is cause for rejoicing here. You may for a time have to suffer the distress of many trials; but this is so that your faith, which is more precious than the passing splendor of fire-tried gold, may by its genuineness lead to praise, glory, and honor when Jesus Christ appears.

Responsory

℣ The whole creation proclaims the greatness of your glory.
℟ The whole creation proclaims the greatness of your glory.
℣ Eternal ages praise
℟ the greatness of your glory.

[Bow] ℣ Glory to the Father, and to the Son, and to the Holy Spirit.
℟ The whole creation proclaims the greatness of your glory.

Canticle Of Mary

Ant.
[Stand] Do not judge others, and you will not be judged, for as you have judged them, so God will judge you.

Magnificat: Luke 1: 46-55
My soul ✠ proclaims the... [See Prayer On Back Flap. Then Repeat The Antiphon Above.]

Intercessions

Introductory Formula
The world was created by the Word of God, re-created by his redemption, and it is continually renewed by his love. Rejoicing in him we call out:
℟ Renew the wonders of your love, Lord.

Petitions
℣ We give thanks to God whose power is revealed in nature,
℟ and whose providence is revealed in history.
℣ Through your Son, the herald of reconciliation, the victor of the cross,
℟ free us from empty fear and hopelessness.
℣ May all those who love and pursue justice,
℟ work together without deceit to build a world of true peace.
℣ Be with the oppressed, free the captives, console the sorrowing, feed the hungry, strengthen the weak,
℟ in all people reveal the victory of your cross.
℣ After your Son's death and burial you raised him up again in glory,
℟ grant that the faithful departed may live with him.

The Lord's Prayer
Our Father... [See prayer on back flap]

Prayer

Father,
keep before us the wisdom and love
you have revealed in your Son.
Help us to be like him
in word and deed,
for he lives and reigns with you
and the Holy Spirit,
one God, for ever and ever. Amen.

Closing Rite Or Dismissal
[See Closing Rite on Back Flap]

Introductory Rite

[Stand] V. God, ✠ come to my assistance.

R. Lord, make haste to help me.

[Bow] Glory to the Father, and to the Son,
and to the Holy Spirit:
as it was in the beginning, is now,
and will be for ever. Amen.

Hymn

+ Love divine, all loves excelling,
Joy of heaven to earth come down,
And impart to us, here dwelling,
Grace and mercy all around.
Jesus, source of all compassion,
Pure, unbounded love you share;
Grant us many choicest blessings,
Keep us in your loving care.

+ Come, O source of inspiration,
Pure and spotless let us be:
Let us see your true salvation,
Perfect in accord with thee.
Praising Father for all glory
With the Spirit and the Son;
Everlasting thanks we give thee,
Undivided, love, in one.

Text: C. Wesley, 1707-1788, adapted by C.T. Andrews 1968

Psalmody

Ant. 1 In eternal splendor, before the dawn of light on earth, I have begotten you, alleluia.

Book 5: Psalm 110: 1-5, 7
The Messiah, king and priest

[Sit] + The Lord's revelation to my Master:
"Sit on my right:
your foes I will put beneath your feet."

+ The Lord will wield from Zion
your scepter of power:
rule in the midst of all your foes.

+ A prince from the day of your birth
on the holy mountains;
from the womb before the dawn I begot you.

+ The Lord has sworn an oath he will not change.
"You are a priest for ever,
a priest like Melchizedek of old."

+ The Master standing at your right hand
will shatter kings in the day of his great wrath.

+ He shall drink from the stream by the wayside
and therefore he shall lift up his head.

[Bow] + Glory to the Father...

Psalm Prayer
Father, we ask you to give us victory and peace.

In Jesus Christ, our Lord and King, we are already seated at your right hand. We look forward to praising you in the fellowship of all your saints in our heavenly homeland.

Ant. In eternal splendor, before the dawn of light on earth, I have begotten you, alleluia.

Ant. 2 Blessed are they who hunger and thirst for holiness; they will be satisfied.

Book 5: Psalm 112
The happiness of the just man

+ Happy the man who fears the Lord,
who takes delight in all his commands.
His sons will be powerful on earth;
the children of the upright are blessed.

+ Riches and wealth are in his house;
his justice stands firm for ever.
He is a light in the darkness for the upright:
he is generous, merciful and just.

+ The good man takes pity and lends,
he conducts his affairs with honor.
The just man will never waver:
he will be remembered for ever.

+ He has no fear of evil news;
with a firm heart he trusts in the Lord.
With a steadfast heart he will not fear;
he will see the downfall of his foes.

+ Open-handed, he gives to the poor;
his justice stands firm for ever.
His head will be raised in glory.

+ The wicked man sees and is angry,
grinds his teeth and fades away;
the desire of the wicked leads to doom.

[Bow] + Glory to the Father...

Psalm Prayer
Lord God, you are the eternal light which illumines the hearts of good people. Help us to love you, to rejoice in your glory, and so to live in this world as to avoid harsh judgment in the next. May we come to see the light of your countenance.

Ant. Blessed are they who hunger and thirst for holiness; they will be satisfied.

EIGHTH SUNDAY
in Ordinary Time
[Psalter, Week IV]

Ant. 3   Praise God, all you who serve him, both great
and small, alleluia.

Canticle based on Revelation 19: 1-7
The wedding of the Lamb

✦ Alleluia.
Salvation, glory, and power to our God:
(℟ Alleluia.)
his judgments are honest and true.
℟ Alleluia (alleluia).

✦ Alleluia.
Sing praise to our God, all you his servants,
(℟ Alleluia.)
all who worship him reverently, great and small.
℟ Alleluia (alleluia).

✦ Alleluia.
The Lord our all-powerful God is King;
(℟ Alleluia.)
let us rejoice, sing praise, and give him glory.
℟ Alleluia (alleluia).

✦ Alleluia.
The wedding feast of the Lamb has begun,
(℟ Alleluia.)
and his bride is prepared to welcome him.
℟ Alleluia (alleluia).

[Bow]   ✦ Glory to the Father…

Ant.   Praise God, all you who serve him, both great
and small, alleluia.

Reading: Hebrews 12: 22-24

You have drawn near to Mount Zion and the
city of the living God, the heavenly Jerusalem,
to myriads of angels in festal gathering, to the
assembly of the first-born enrolled in heaven, to
God the judge of all, to the spirits of just men
made perfect, to Jesus, the mediator of a new
covenant, and to the sprinkled blood which
speaks more eloquently than that of Abel.

Responsory

℣ Our Lord is great, mighty is his power.
℟ Our Lord is great, mighty is his power.
℣ His wisdom is beyond compare,
℟ mighty is his power.
[Bow]   ℣ Glory to the Father, and to the Son,
and to the Holy Spirit.
℟ Our Lord is great, mighty is his power.

Canticle Of Mary

Ant.   A good tree cannot bear bad fruit, nor a bad
[Stand]   tree good fruit.

Magnificat: Luke 1: 46-55
My soul ✠ proclaims the… [See Prayer On Back
Flap. Then Repeat The Antiphon Above.]

Intercessions

Introductory Formula
Rejoicing in the Lord, from whom all good
things come, let us pray:
℟ Lord, hear our prayer.

Petitions
℣ Father and Lord of all, you sent your Son into
the world, that your name might be glorified
in every place,
℟ strengthen the witness of your Church among
the nations.
℣ Make us obedient to the teachings of
your apostles,
℟ and bound to the truth of our faith.
℣ As you love the innocent,
℟ render justice to those who are wronged.
℣ Free those in bondage and give sight to
the blind,
℟ raise up the fallen and protect the stranger.
℣ Fulfill your promise to those who already
sleep in your peace,
℟ through your Son grant them a blessed
resurrection.

The Lord's Prayer
Our Father… [See prayer on back flap]

Prayer

Lord,
guide the course of world events
and give your Church the joy and peace
of serving you in freedom.
We ask this through our Lord Jesus Christ,
your Son,
who lives and reigns with you
and the Holy Spirit,
one God, for ever and ever. Amen.

Closing Rite Or Dismissal

[When Priest Or Deacon Presides]
℣ The Lord be with you.
℟ And also with you.
[Bow]   May almighty God bless you, + the Father,
and the Son, and the Holy Spirit.
℟ Amen.
℣ Go in peace.
℟ Thanks be to God.
[When Priest Or Deacon Do Not Preside, And In Individual Recitation]
+ May the Lord bless us, protect us from all evil
and bring us to everlasting life.
℟ Amen.

Introductory Rite

V. God, ✠ come to my assistance.

R. Lord, make haste to help me.

Glory to the Father, and to the Son,
and to the Holy Spirit:
as it was in the beginning, is now,
and will be for ever. Amen.

Hymn

✦ O Christ, you are the light and day
Which drives away the night,
The ever shining Sun of God
And pledge of future light.

✦ As now the ev'ning shadows fall
Please grant us, Lord, we pray,
A quiet night to rest in you
Until the break of day.

✦ Remember us, poor mortal men,
We humbly ask, O Lord,
And may your presence in our souls
Be now our great reward.

Translator: Rev. M. Quinn, O.P. et al.

Psalmody

Ant. 1 The Lord will stretch forth his mighty scepter
from Zion, and he will reign for ever, alleluia.

Book 5: Psalm 110: 1-5, 7
The Messiah, king and priest

✦ The Lord's revelation to my Master:
"Sit on my right:
your foes I will put beneath your feet."

✦ The Lord will wield from Zion
your scepter of power:
rule in the midst of all your foes.

✦ A prince from the day of your birth
on the holy mountains;
from the womb before the dawn I begot you.

✦ The Lord has sworn an oath he will not change.
"You are a priest for ever,
a priest like Melchizedek of old."

✦ The Master standing at your right hand
will shatter kings in the day of his great wrath.

✦ He shall drink from the stream by the wayside
and therefore he shall lift up his head.

✦ Glory to the Father…

Psalm Prayer
Father, we ask you to give us victory and peace.
In Jesus Christ, our Lord and King, we are
already seated at your right hand. We look
forward to praising you in the fellowship of all
your saints in our heavenly homeland.

NINTH SUNDAY
in Ordinary Time

Ant. The Lord will stretch forth his mighty scepter
from Zion, and he will reign for ever, alleluia.

Ant. 2 The earth is shaken to its depths before the
glory of your face.

Book 2: Psalm 114
The Israelites are delivered from the bondage of Egypt

✦ When Israel came forth from Egypt,
Jacob's sons from an alien people,
Judah became the Lord's temple,
Israel became his kingdom.

✦ The sea fled at the sight:
the Jordan turned back on its course,
the mountains leapt like rams
and the hills like yearling sheep.

✦ Why was it, sea, that you fled,
that you turned back, Jordan, on your course?
Mountains, that you leapt like rams,
hills, like yearling sheep?

✦ Tremble, O earth, before the Lord,
in the presence of the God of Jacob,
who turns the rock into a pool
and flint into a spring of water.

✦ Glory to the Father…

Psalm Prayer
Almighty God, ever-living mystery of unity and
trinity, you gave life to the new Israel by birth
from water and the Spirit, and made it a chosen
race, a royal priesthood, a people set apart as
your eternal possession. May all those you have
called to walk in the splendor of the new light
render you fitting service and adoration.

Ant. The earth is shaken to its depths before the
glory of your face.

Ant. 3 All power is yours, Lord God, our mighty
King, alleluia.

Canticle based on Revelation 19: 1-7
The wedding of the Lamb

✦ Alleluia.
Salvation, glory, and power to our God:
(R. Alleluia.)
his judgments are honest and true.

R. Alleluia (alleluia).

✦ Alleluia.
Sing praise to our God, all you his servants,
(℟ Alleluia.)
all who worship him reverently, great and small.
℟ Alleluia (alleluia).

✦ Alleluia.
The Lord our all-powerful God is King;
(℟ Alleluia.)
let us rejoice, sing praise, and give him glory.
℟ Alleluia (alleluia).

✦ Alleluia.
The wedding feast of the Lamb has begun,
(℟ Alleluia.)
and his bride is prepared to welcome him.
℟ Alleluia (alleluia).

[Bow] ✦ Glory to the Father…

Ant. All power is yours, Lord God, our mighty King, alleluia.

Reading: 2 Corinthians 1: 3-7

Praised be God, the Father of our Lord Jesus Christ, the Father of mercies and the God of all consolation! He comforts us in all our afflictions and thus enables us to comfort those who are in trouble, with the same consolation we have received from him. As we have shared much in the suffering of Christ, so through Christ do we share abundantly in his consolation. If we are afflicted it is for your encouragement and salvation, and when we are consoled it is for your consolation, so that you may endure patiently the same sufferings we endure. Our hope for you is firm because we know that just as you share in the sufferings, so you will share in the consolation.

Responsory

℣ The whole creation proclaims the greatness of your glory.
℟ The whole creation proclaims the greatness of your glory.
℣ Eternal ages praise
℟ the greatness of your glory.
[Bow] ℣ Glory to the Father, and to the Son, and to the Holy Spirit.
℟ The whole creation proclaims the greatness of your glory.

Canticle Of Mary

Ant. Lord, I am not worthy to have you enter my
[Stand] house; just say the word and my servant will be healed.

Magnificat: Luke 1: 46-55
My soul ✠ proclaims the… [See Prayer On Back Flap. Then Repeat The Antiphon Above.]

Intercessions

Introductory Formula
Christ the Lord is our head; we are his members. In joy let us call out to him:
℟ Lord, may your kingdom come.

Petitions
℣ Christ our Savior, make your Church a more vivid symbol of the unity of all mankind,
℟ make it more effectively the sacrament of salvation for all peoples.
℣ Through your presence, guide the college of bishops in union with the Pope,
℟ give them the gifts of unity, love and peace.
℣ Bind all Christians more closely to yourself, their divine Head,
℟ lead them to proclaim your kingdom by the witness of their lives.
℣ Grant peace to the world,
℟ let every land flourish in justice and security.
℣ Grant to the dead the glory of resurrection,
℟ and give us a share in their happiness.

The Lord's Prayer
Our Father… [See prayer on back flap]

Prayer

Father,
your love never fails.
Hear our call.
Keep us from danger
and provide for all our needs.
Grant this through our Lord Jesus Christ,
your Son,
who lives and reigns with you
and the Holy Spirit,
one God, for ever and ever. Amen.

Closing Rite Or Dismissal

[When Priest Or Deacon Presides]
℣ The Lord be with you.
℟ And also with you.
[Bow] May almighty God bless you, + the Father, and the Son, and the Holy Spirit.
℟ Amen.
℣ Go in peace.
℟ Thanks be to God.

[When Priest Or Deacon Do Not Preside, And In Individual Recitation]
+ May the Lord bless us, protect us from all evil and bring us to everlasting life.
℟ Amen.

Introductory Rite

[STAND] V. God, + come to my assistance.
R. Lord, make haste to help me.

[BOW] Glory to the Father, and to the Son,
and to the Holy Spirit:
as it was in the beginning, is now,
and will be for ever. Amen.

Hymn

+ This is our accepted time,
This is our salvation;
Prayer and fasting are our hope,
Penance, our vocation.
God of pardon and of love,
Mercy past all measure,
You alone can grant us peace,
You, our holy treasure.

+ Lord, look down upon your sons,
Look upon their yearning;
Man is dust, and unto dust
He shall be returning.
Lift him up, O Lord of life,
Flesh has gained him sadness,
Hear his plea, bestow on him
Everlasting gladness.

Text: Michael Gannon, alt., 1955

Psalmody

Ant. 1 Worship your Lord and God; serve him alone.

Book 5: Psalm 110: 1-5, 7
The Messiah, king and priest

[SIT] + The Lord's revelation to my Master:
"Sit on my right:
your foes I will put beneath your feet."

+ The Lord will wield from Zion
your scepter of power:
rule in the midst of all your foes.

+ A prince from the day of your birth
on the holy mountains;
from the womb before the dawn I begot you.

+ The Lord has sworn an oath he will not change.
"You are a priest for ever,
a priest like Melchizedek of old."

+ The Master standing at your right hand
will shatter kings in the day of his great wrath.

+ He shall drink from the stream by the wayside
and therefore he shall lift up his head.

[BOW] + Glory to the Father, and to the Son,
and to the Holy Spirit:
as it was in the beginning, is now,
and will be for ever. Amen.

FIRST SUNDAY
in Lent
[PSALTER, WEEK I]

Psalm Prayer
Father, we ask you to give us victory and peace.
In Jesus Christ, our Lord and King, we are
already seated at your right hand. We look
forward to praising you in the fellowship of all
your saints in our heavenly homeland.

Ant. Worship your Lord and God; serve him alone.

Ant. 2 This is the time when you can win God's favor,
the day when you can be saved.

Book 2: Psalm 114
The Israelites are delivered from the bondage of Egypt

+ When Israel came forth from Egypt,
Jacob's sons from an alien people,
Judah became the Lord's temple,
Israel became his kingdom.

+ The sea fled at the sight:
the Jordan turned back on its course,
the mountains leapt like rams
and the hills like yearling sheep.

+ Why was it, sea, that you fled,
that you turned back, Jordan, on your course?
Mountains, that you leapt like rams,
hills, like yearling sheep?

+ Tremble, O earth, before the Lord,
in the presence of the God of Jacob,
who turns the rock into a pool
and flint into a spring of water.

[BOW] + Glory to the Father…

Psalm Prayer
Almighty God, ever-living mystery of unity and
trinity, you gave life to the new Israel by birth
from water and the Spirit, and made it a chosen
race, a royal priesthood, a people set apart as
your eternal possession. May all those you have
called to walk in the splendor of the new light
render you fitting service and adoration.

Ant. This is the time when you can win God's favor,
the day when you can be saved.

Ant. 3 Now we must go up to Jerusalem where all
that has been written about the Son of Man
will be fulfilled.

Canticle: 1 Peter 2: 21-24

The willing acceptance of his passion by Christ, the servant of God

✦ Christ suffered for you,
and left you an example
to have you follow in his footsteps.

✦ He did no wrong;
no deceit was found in his mouth.
when he was insulted,
he returned no insult.

✦ When he was made to suffer,
he did not counter with threats.
instead he delivered himself up
to the One who judges justly.

✦ In his own body
he brought your sins to the cross,
so that all of us, dead to sin,
could live in accord with God's will.

✦ By his wounds you were healed.

[Bow] ✦ Glory to the Father…

Ant. Now we must go up to Jerusalem where all
that has been written about the Son of Man
will be fulfilled.

Reading: 1 Corinthians 9: 24-27

While all the runners in the stadium take
part in the race, the award goes to one man.
In that case, run so as to win! Athletes deny
themselves all sorts of things. They do this to
win a crown of leaves that withers, but we a
crown that is imperishable. I do not run like a
man who loses sight of the finish line. I do not
fight as if I were shadowboxing. What I do is
discipline my own body and master it, for fear
that after having preached to others I myself
should be rejected.

Responsory

℣. Listen to us, O Lord, and have mercy, for we
have sinned against you.

℟. Listen to us, O Lord, and have mercy, for we
have sinned against you.

℣. Christ Jesus, hear our humble petitions,

℟. for we have sinned against you.

[Bow] ℣. Glory to the Father, and to the Son,
and to the Holy Spirit.

℟. Listen to us, O Lord, and have mercy, for we
have sinned against you.

Canticle Of Mary

Ant.
[Stand]
Watch over us, eternal Savior; do not let the
cunning tempter seize us. We place all our
trust in your unfailing help.

Magnificat: Luke 1: 46-55
My soul ✠ proclaims the… [See Prayer On Back
Flap. Then Repeat The Antiphon Above.]

Intercessions

Introductory Formula
All praise to God the Father who brought his
chosen people to rebirth from imperishable
seed through his eternal Word. Let us ask
him as his children:

℟. Lord, be gracious to your people.

Petitions
℣. God of mercy, hear the prayers we offer for all
your people,
may they hunger for your word more than for
bodily food.

℣. Give us a sincere and active love for our own
nation and for all mankind,

℟. may we work always to build a world of peace
and goodness.

℣. Look with love on all to be reborn in baptism,

℟. that they may be living stones in your temple
of the Spirit.

℣. You moved Nineveh to repentance by the
preaching of Jonah,

℟. in your mercy touch the hearts of sinners by
the preaching of your word.

℣. May the dying go in hope to meet Christ
their judge,

℟. may they rejoice for ever in the vision of
your glory.

The Lord's Prayer
Our Father… [See prayer on back flap]

Prayer

Father,
through our observance of Lent,
help us to understand the meaning
of your Son's death and resurrection,
and teach us to reflect it in our lives.
Grant this through our Lord Jesus Christ,
your Son,
who lives and reigns with you
and the Holy Spirit,
one God, for ever and ever. Amen.

Closing Rite Or Dismissal
[See Closing Rite on Back Flap]

41

Introductory Rite

[STAND] ℣. God, ✠ come to my assistance.

℟. Lord, make haste to help me.

[BOW]   Glory to the Father…

Hymn

✦ When I survey the wondrous cross
On which the Prince of glory died,
My richest gain I count but loss,
And pour contempt on all my pride.

✦ Forbid it, Lord, that I should boast,
Save in the death of Christ my God;
The vain delights that charm me most:
I sacrifice them to his blood.

✦ See from his head, his hands, his feet
What grief and love flow mingling down;
Did e'er such Love and sorrow meet,
Or thorns compose so rich a crown?

✦ Were all the realm of nature mine,
That were a present far too small;
Love so amazing, so divine,
Demands my soul, my life, my all.

Text: Isaac Watts, 1674-1748, slightly adapted

Psalmody

Ant. 1   In holy splendor the Lord will send forth your
mighty scepter from Zion.

Book 5: Psalm 110: 1-5, 7
The Messiah, king and priest

[SIT] ✦ The Lord's revelation to my Master:
"Sit on my right:
your foes I will put beneath your feet."

✦ The Lord will wield from Zion
your scepter of power:
rule in the midst of all your foes.

✦ A prince from the day of your birth
on the holy mountains;
from the womb before the dawn I begot you.

✦ The Lord has sworn an oath he will not change.
"You are a priest for ever,
a priest like Melchizedek of old."

✦ The Master standing at your right hand
will shatter kings in the day of his great wrath.

✦ He shall drink from the stream by the wayside
and therefore he shall lift up his head.

[BOW]   ✦ Glory to the Father…

Psalm Prayer
Almighty God,… [SEE PSALM PRAYER ON FRONT FLAP]

Ant.   In holy splendor the Lord will send forth your
mighty scepter from Zion.

SECOND SUNDAY
in Lent
[PSALTER, WEEK II]

Ant. 2   We worship the one true God who made
heaven and earth.

Book 5: Psalm 115
Praise of the true God

✦ Not to us, Lord, not to us,
but to your name give the glory
for the sake of your love and your truth,
lest the heathen say: "Where is their God?"

✦ But our God is in the heavens;
he does whatever he wills.
Their idols are silver and gold,
the work of human hands.

✦ They have mouths but they cannot speak;
they have eyes but they cannot see;
they have ears but they cannot hear;
they have nostrils but they cannot smell.

✦ With their hands they cannot feel;
with their feet they cannot walk.
No sound comes from their throats.
Their makers will come to be like them
and so will all who trust in them.

✦ Sons of Israel, trust in the Lord;
he is their help and their shield.
Sons of Aaron, trust in the Lord;
he is their help and their shield.

✦ You who fear him, trust in the Lord;
he is their help and their shield.
He remembers us, and he will bless us;
he will bless the sons of Israel.
He will bless the sons of Aaron.

✦ The Lord will bless those who fear him,
the little no less than the great:
to you may the Lord grant increase,
to you and all your children.

✦ May you be blessed by the Lord,
the maker of heaven and earth.
The heavens belong to the Lord
but the earth he has given to men.

✦ The dead shall not praise the Lord,
nor those who go down into the silence.
But we who live bless the Lord
now and for ever. Amen.

42

[Bow] ✦ Glory to the Father…

Psalm Prayer
Father, creator…[See psalm prayer on front flap]

Ant. We worship the one true God who made heaven and earth.

Ant. 3 God did not spare his own Son but gave him up for us all.

Canticle: 1 Peter 2: 21-24
The willing acceptance of his passion by Christ, the servant of God

✦ Christ suffered for you,
and left you an example
to have you follow in his footsteps.

✦ He did no wrong;
no deceit was found in his mouth.
when he was insulted,
he returned no insult.

✦ When he was made to suffer,
he did not counter with threats.
instead he delivered himself up
to the One who judges justly.

✦ In his own body
he brought your sins to the cross,
so that all of us, dead to sin,
could live in accord with God's will.

✦ By his wounds you were healed.

[Bow] ✦ Glory to the Father…

Ant. God did not spare his own Son but gave him up for us all.

Reading: 1 Corinthians 9: 24-27

While all the runners in the stadium take part in the race, the award goes to one man. In that case, run so as to win! Athletes deny themselves all sorts of things. They do this to win a crown of leaves that withers, but we a crown that is imperishable. I do not run like a man who loses sight of the finish line. I do not fight as if I were shadowboxing. What I do is discipline my own body and master it, for fear that after having preached to others I myself should be rejected.

Responsory

℣. Listen to us, O Lord, and have mercy, for we have sinned against you.
℟. Listen to us, O Lord, and have mercy, for we have sinned against you.
℣. Christ Jesus, hear our humble petitions,
℟. for we have sinned against you.

[Bow] ℣. Glory to the Father, and to the Son,
and to the Holy Spirit.
℟. Listen to us, O Lord, and have mercy, for we have sinned against you.

Canticle Of Mary

Ant.
[Stand] Tell no one about the vision you have seen until the Son of Man has risen from the dead.

Magnificat: Luke 1: 46-55
My soul ✠ proclaims the… [See Prayer On Back Flap. Then Repeat The Antiphon Above.]

Intercessions

Introductory Formula
Let us give thanks continually to Christ, our teacher and our head, who came to serve and to do good to all. In humility and confidence let us ask him:
℟. Come, Lord, to visit your family.

Petitions
℣. Lord, be present to the bishops and priests of your Church, who share your role as head and shepherd,
℟. may they lead your people to the Father under your guidance.
℣. May your angel be with all who travel,
℟. to keep them safe in soul and body.
℣. Teach us to serve the needs of others,
℟. and to be like you, who came to serve, not to be served.
℣. Grant that in the human family, brother may always help brother,
℟. so that, with your assistance, it may be a city compact and strong.
℣. Have mercy on all the dead,
℟. bring them to the vision of your glory.

The Lord's Prayer
Our Father… [See prayer on back flap]

Prayer

God our Father,
help us to hear your Son.
Enlighten us with your word,
that we may find the way to your glory.
We ask this through our Lord Jesus Christ,
your Son,
who lives and reigns with you
and the Holy Spirit,
one God, for ever and ever. Amen.

Closing Rite Or Dismissal

[See Closing Rite on Back Flap]

Introductory Rite

[STAND] V. God, ✠ come to my assistance.

R. Lord, make haste to help me.

[BOW] Glory to the Father, and to the Son,
and to the Holy Spirit:
as it was in the beginning, is now,
and will be for ever. Amen.

Hymn

✦ This is our accepted time,
This is our salvation;
Prayer and fasting are our hope,
Penance, our vocation.
God of pardon and of love,
Mercy past all measure,
You alone can grant us peace,
You, our holy treasure.

✦ Lord, look down upon your sons,
Look upon their yearning;
Man is dust, and unto dust
He shall be returning.
Lift him up, O Lord of life,
Flesh has gained him sadness,
Hear his plea, bestow on him
Everlasting gladness.

Text: Michael Gannon, alt., 1955

Psalmody

Ant. 1   Lord, all-powerful King, free us for the sake of
your name. Give us time to turn from our sins.

Book 5: Psalm 110: 1-5, 7
The Messiah, king and priest

[SIT] ✦ The Lord's revelation to my Master:
"Sit on my right:
your foes I will put beneath your feet."

✦ The Lord will wield from Zion
your scepter of power:
rule in the midst of all your foes.

✦ A prince from the day of your birth
on the holy mountains;
from the womb before the dawn I begot you.

✦ The Lord has sworn an oath he will not change.
"You are a priest for ever,
a priest like Melchizedek of old."

✦ The Master standing at your right hand
will shatter kings in the day of his great wrath.

✦ He shall drink from the stream by the wayside
and therefore he shall lift up his head.

[BOW] ✦ Glory to the Father…

THIRD SUNDAY
in Lent
[PSALTER, WEEK III]

Psalm Prayer
Father, we ask you to give us victory and
peace. In Jesus Christ, our Lord and King, we
are already seated at your right hand. We look
forward to praising you in the fellowship of all
your saints in our heavenly homeland.

Ant.   Lord, all-powerful King, free us for the sake
of your name. Give us time to turn from our
sins.

Ant. 2   We have been redeemed by the precious blood
of Christ, the lamb without blemish.

Book 5: Psalm 111
God's marvelous works

✦ I will thank the Lord with all my heart
in the meeting of the just and their assembly.
Great are the works of the Lord;
to be pondered by all who love them.

✦ Majestic and glorious his work,
his justice stands firm for ever.
He makes us remember his wonders.
The Lord is compassion and love.

✦ He gives food to those who fear him;
keeps his covenant ever in mind.
He has shown his might to his people
by giving them the lands of the nations.

✦ His works are justice and truth:
his precepts are all of them sure,
standing firm for ever and ever:
they are made in uprightness and truth.

✦ He has sent deliverance to his people
and established his covenant for ever.
Holy his name, to be feared.

✦ To fear the Lord is the first stage of wisdom;
all who do so prove themselves wise.
His praise shall last for ever!

[BOW] ✦ Glory to the Father…

Psalm Prayer
Merciful and gentle Lord, you are the
crowning glory of all the saints. Give us, your
children, the gift of obedience which is the
beginning of wisdom, so that we may do what
you command and be filled with your mercy.

Ant. We have been redeemed by the precious blood of Christ, the lamb without blemish.

Ant. 3 Ours were the sufferings he bore; ours the torments he endured.

Canticle: 1 Peter 2: 21-24

The willing acceptance of his passion by Christ, the servant of God

✦ Christ suffered for you,
and left you an example
to have you follow in his footsteps.

✦ He did no wrong;
no deceit was found in his mouth.
when he was insulted,
he returned no insult.

✦ When he was made to suffer,
he did not counter with threats.
instead he delivered himself up
to the One who judges justly.

✦ In his own body
he brought your sins to the cross,
so that all of us, dead to sin,
could live in accord with God's will.

✦ By his wounds you were healed.

[Bow] ✦ Glory to the Father…

Ant. Ours were the sufferings he bore; ours the torments he endured.

Reading: 1 Corinthians 9: 24-27

While all the runners in the stadium take part in the race, the award goes to one man. In that case, run so as to win! Athletes deny themselves all sorts of things. They do this to win a crown of leaves that withers, but we a crown that is imperishable. I do not run like a man who loses sight of the finish line. I do not fight as if I were shadowboxing. What I do is discipline my own body and master it, for fear that after having preached to others I myself should be rejected.

Responsory

℣. Listen to us, O Lord, and have mercy, for we have sinned against you.

℟. Listen to us, O Lord, and have mercy, for we have sinned against you.

℣. Christ Jesus, hear our humble petitions,

℟. for we have sinned against you.

[Bow] ℣. Glory to the Father, and to the Son, and to the Holy Spirit.

℟. Listen to us, O Lord, and have mercy, for we have sinned against you.

Canticle Of Mary

Ant.
[Stand] Whoever drinks the water that I shall give will never be thirsty again, says the Lord.

Magnificat: Luke 1: 46-55

My soul ✠ proclaims the… [See Prayer On Back Flap. Then Repeat The Antiphon Above.]

Intercessions

Introductory Formula

All praise to God the Father who brought his chosen people to rebirth from imperishable seed through his eternal Word. Let us ask him as his children:

℟. Lord, be gracious to your people.

Petitions

℣. God of mercy, hear the prayers we offer for all your people,

℟. may they hunger for your word more than for bodily food.

℣. Give us a sincere and active love for our own nation and for all mankind,

℟. may we work always to build a world of peace and goodness.

℣. Look with love on all to be reborn in baptism,

℟. that they may be living stones in your temple of the Spirit.

℣. You moved Nineveh to repentance by the preaching of Jonah,

℟. in your mercy touch the hearts of sinners by the preaching of your word.

℣. May the dying go in hope to meet Christ their judge,

℟. may they rejoice for ever in the vision of your glory.

The Lord's Prayer

Our Father… [See prayer on back flap]

Prayer

Father,
You have taught us to overcome our sins
by prayer, fasting and works of mercy.
When we are discouraged by our weakness,
give us confidence in your love.
We ask this through our Lord Jesus Christ,
your Son,
who lives and reigns with you
and the Holy Spirit,
one God, for ever and ever. Amen.

Closing Rite Or Dismissal

[See Closing Rite on Back Flap]

Introductory Rite

[Stand] V. God, ✠ come to my assistance.
R. Lord, make haste to help me.

[Bow] Glory to the Father, and to the Son,
and to the Holy Spirit:
as it was in the beginning, is now,
and will be for ever. Amen.

Hymn

◆ Lord, who throughout these forty days
For us did fast and pray,
Teach us with you to mourn our sins,
And close by you to stay.

◆ As you with Satan did contend
And did the vict'ry win,
O give us strength in you to fight,
In you to conquer sin.

◆ As you did hunger and did thirst,
So teach us, gracious Lord,
To die to self and so to live
By your most holy word.

◆ Abide with us, that through this life
Of suff'ring and of pain,
An Easter of unending joy
We may at last attain.

Text: Claudia Hernaman, 1838-1898, alt.

Psalmody

Ant. 1   God has appointed Christ to be the judge of the living and the dead.

Book 5: Psalm 110: 1-5, 7
The Messiah, king and priest

[Sit] ◆ The Lord's revelation to my Master:
"Sit on my right:
your foes I will put beneath your feet."

◆ The Lord will wield from Zion
your scepter of power:
rule in the midst of all your foes.

◆ A prince from the day of your birth
on the holy mountains;
from the womb before the dawn I begot you.

◆ The Lord has sworn an oath he will not change.
"You are a priest for ever,
a priest like Melchizedek of old."

◆ The Master standing at your right hand
will shatter kings in the day of his great wrath.

◆ He shall drink from the stream by the wayside
and therefore he shall lift up his head.

[Bow] ◆ Glory to the Father…

FOURTH SUNDAY
in Lent
[Psalter, Week IV]

Psalm Prayer
Father, we ask you to give us victory and peace. In Jesus Christ, our Lord and King, we are already seated at your right hand. We look forward to praising you in the fellowship of all your saints in our heavenly homeland.

Ant.   God has appointed Christ to be the judge of the living and the dead.

Ant. 2   Happy the man who shows mercy for the Lord's sake; he will stand firm for ever.

Book 5: Psalm 112
The happiness of the just man

◆ Happy the man who fears the Lord,
who takes delight in all his commands.
His sons will be powerful on earth;
the children of the upright are blessed.

◆ Riches and wealth are in his house;
his justice stands firm for ever.
He is a light in the darkness for the upright:
he is generous, merciful and just.

◆ The good man takes pity and lends,
he conducts his affairs with honor.
The just man will never waver:
he will be remembered for ever.

◆ He has no fear of evil news;
with a firm heart he trusts in the Lord.
With a steadfast heart he will not fear;
he will see the downfall of his foes.

◆ Open-handed, he gives to the poor;
his justice stands firm for ever.
His head will be raised in glory.

◆ The wicked man sees and is angry,
grinds his teeth and fades away;
the desire of the wicked leads to doom.

[Bow] ◆ Glory to the Father…

Psalm Prayer
Lord God, you are the eternal light which illumines the hearts of good people. Help us to love you, to rejoice in your glory, and so to live in this world as to avoid harsh judgment in the next. May we come to see the light of your countenance.

Ant.   Happy the man who shows mercy for the Lord's sake; he will stand firm for ever.

Ant. 3 Those things, which God foretold through his prophets concerning the sufferings that Christ would endure, have been fulfilled.

Canticle: 1 Peter 2: 21-24

The willing acceptance of his passion by Christ, the servant of God

✦ Christ suffered for you,
and left you an example
to have you follow in his footsteps.

✦ He did no wrong;
no deceit was found in his mouth.
when he was insulted,
he returned no insult.

✦ When he was made to suffer,
he did not counter with threats.
instead he delivered himself up
to the One who judges justly.

✦ In his own body
he brought your sins to the cross,
so that all of us, dead to sin,
could live in accord with God's will.

✦ By his wounds you were healed.

[Bow] ✦ Glory to the Father...

Ant. Those things, which God foretold through his prophets concerning the sufferings that Christ would endure, have been fulfilled.

Reading: 1 Corinthians 9: 24-27

While all the runners in the stadium take part in the race, the award goes to one man. In that case, run so as to win! Athletes deny themselves all sorts of things. They do this to win a crown of leaves that withers, but we a crown that is imperishable. I do not run like a man who loses sight of the finish line. I do not fight as if I were shadowboxing. What I do is discipline my own body and master it, for fear that after having preached to others I myself should be rejected.

Responsory

℣. Listen to us, O Lord, and have mercy, for we have sinned against you.

℟. Listen to us, O Lord, and have mercy, for we have sinned against you.

℣. Christ Jesus, hear our humble petitions,

℟. for we have sinned against you.

[Bow] ℣. Glory to the Father, and to the Son, and to the Holy Spirit.

℟. Listen to us, O Lord, and have mercy, for we have sinned against you.

Canticle Of Mary

Ant.
[Stand] My son, you have been with me all the time and everything I have is yours. But we had to feast and rejoice, because your brother was dead and has come to life again; he was lost to us and now has been found.

Magnificat: Luke 1: 46-55

My soul ✠ proclaims the... [See Prayer On Back Flap. Then Repeat The Antiphon Above.]

Intercessions

Introductory Formula
Let us give thanks continually to Christ, our teacher and our head, who came to serve and to do good to all. In humility and confidence let us ask him:

℟. Come, Lord, to visit your family.

Petitions
℣. Lord, be present to the bishops and priests of your Church, who share your role as head and shepherd,

℟. may they lead your people to the Father under your guidance.

℣. May your angel be with all who travel,

℟. to keep them safe in soul and body.

℣. Teach us to serve the needs of others,

℟. and to be like you, who came to serve, not to be served.

℣. Grant that in the human family, brother may always help brother,

℟. so that, with your assistance, it may be a city compact and strong.

℣. Have mercy on all the departed,

℟. bring them to the vision of your glory.

The Lord's Prayer
Our Father... [See prayer on back flap]

Prayer

Father of peace,
we are joyful in your Word,
your Son Jesus Christ,
who reconciles us to you.
Let us hasten toward Easter
with the eagerness of faith and love.
We ask this through our Lord Jesus Christ,
  your Son,
who lives and reigns with you
  and the Holy Spirit,
one God, for ever and ever. Amen.

Closing Rite Or Dismissal

[See Closing Rite on Back Flap]

Introductory Rite

[See Introductory Rite on Front Flap]

Hymn

Refrain: ✦ *Draw near, O Lord, our God, graciously hear us,*
Guilty of sinning before you.

✦ O King exalted, Savior of all nations,
See how our grieving lifts our eyes to heaven;
Hear us, Redeemer, as we beg forgiveness.

Refrain ✦ *Draw near, O Lord...*

✦ Might of the Father, Keystone of God's temple,
Way of salvation, Gate to heaven's glory;
Sin has enslaved us; free your sons from
bondage.

Refrain ✦ *Draw near, O Lord...*

✦ We pray you, O God, throned in strength and
splendor,
Hear from your kingdom this, our song of
sorrow:
Show us your mercy, pardon our offenses.

Refrain ✦ *Draw near, O Lord...*

✦ Humbly confessing countless sins committed,
Our hearts are broken, laying bare their secrets;
Cleanse us, Redeemer, boundless in
compassion.

Refrain ✦ *Draw near, O Lord...*

✦ Innocent captive, unresisting victim,
Liars denounced you, sentenced for the guilty;
Once you redeemed us: now renew us, Jesus.

Refrain ✦ *Draw near, O Lord...*
Translator: Melvin Farrell, S.S., 1961

Psalmody

Ant. 1   As the serpent was lifted up in the desert, so
the Son of Man must be lifted up.

Book 5: Psalm 110: 1-5, 7
The Messiah, king and priest

[Sit] ✦ The Lord's revelation to my Master:
"Sit on my right:
your foes I will put beneath your feet."

✦ The Lord will wield from Zion
your scepter of power:
rule in the midst of all your foes.

✦ A prince from the day of your birth
on the holy mountains;
from the womb before the dawn I begot you.

✦ The Lord has sworn an oath he will not change.
"You are a priest for ever,
a priest like Melchizedek of old."

Fifth Sunday *in Lent*

✦ The Master standing at your right hand
will shatter kings in the day of his great wrath.

✦ He shall drink from the stream by the wayside
and therefore he shall lift up his head.

[Bow] ✦ Glory to the Father...

Psalm Prayer
Father, we ask you to give us victory and peace.
In Jesus Christ, our Lord and King, we are
already seated at your right hand. We look
forward to praising you in the fellowship of all
your saints in our heavenly homeland.

Ant.   As the serpent was lifted up in the desert, so
the Son of Man must be lifted up.

Ant. 2   The Lord of hosts protects us and sets us free;
he guides and saves his people.

Book 2: Psalm 114
The Israelites are delivered from the bondage of Egypt

✦ When Israel came forth from Egypt,
Jacob's sons from an alien people,
Judah became the Lord's temple,
Israel became his kingdom.

✦ The sea fled at the sight:
the Jordan turned back on its course,
the mountains leapt like rams
and the hills like yearling sheep.

✦ Why was it, sea, that you fled,
that you turned back, Jordan, on your course?
Mountains, that you leapt like rams,
hills, like yearling sheep?

✦ Tremble, O earth, before the Lord,
in the presence of the God of Jacob,
who turns the rock into a pool
and flint into a spring of water.

[Bow] ✦ Glory to the Father...

Psalm Prayer
Almighty God, ever-living mystery of unity
and trinity, you gave life to the new Israel by
birth from water and the Spirit, and made
it a chosen race, a royal priesthood, a people
set apart as your eternal possession. May all
those you have called to walk in the splendor

of the new light render you fitting service and adoration.

Ant. The Lord of hosts protects us and sets us free; he guides and saves his people.

Ant. 3 He was pierced for our offenses and burdened with our sins. By his wounds we are healed.

Canticle: 1 Peter 2: 21-24
The willing acceptance of his passion by Christ, the servant of God

✛ Christ suffered for you,
and left you an example
to have you follow in his footsteps.

✛ He did no wrong;
no deceit was found in his mouth.
when he was insulted,
he returned no insult.

✛ When he was made to suffer,
he did not counter with threats.
instead he delivered himself up
to the One who judges justly.

✛ In his own body
he brought your sins to the cross,
so that all of us, dead to sin,
could live in accord with God's will.

✛ By his wounds you were healed.

[Bow] ✛ Glory to the Father…

Ant. He was pierced for our offenses and burdened with our sins. By his wounds we are healed.

Reading: Acts 13: 26-30

My brothers, it was to us that this message of salvation was sent forth. The inhabitants of Jerusalem and their rulers failed to recognize him, and in condemning him they fulfilled the words of the prophets which we read sabbath after sabbath. Even though they found no charge against him which deserved death, they begged Pilate to have him executed. Once they had brought about all that had been written of him, they took him down from the tree and laid him in a tomb. Yet God raised him from the dead.

Responsory

℣ Listen to us, O Lord, and have mercy, for we have sinned against you.
℟ Listen to us, O Lord, and have mercy, for we have sinned against you.
℣ Christ Jesus, hear our humble petitions,
℟ for we have sinned against you.

[Bow] ℣ Glory to the Father, and to the Son, and to the Holy Spirit.
℟ Listen to us, O Lord, and have mercy, for we have sinned against you.

Canticle Of Mary

Ant. When I am lifted up from the earth, I will
[Stand] draw all people to myself.

Magnificat: Luke 1: 46-55
My soul ✛ proclaims the… [See Prayer On Back Flap. Then Repeat The Antiphon Above.]

Intercessions

Introductory Formula
All praise to God the Father who brought his chosen people to rebirth from imperishable seed through his eternal Word. Let us ask him as his children:
℟ Lord, be gracious to your people.

Petitions
℣ God of mercy, hear the prayers we offer for all your people,
℟ may they hunger for your word more than for bodily food.
℣ Give us a sincere and active love for our own nation and for all mankind,
℟ and goodness.
℣ Look with love on all to be reborn in baptism,
℟ that they may be living stones in your temple of the Spirit.
℣ You moved Nineveh to repentance by the preaching of Jonah,
℟ in your mercy touch the hearts of sinners by the preaching of your word.
℣ May the dying go in hope to meet Christ their judge,
℟ may they rejoice for ever in the vision of your glory.

The Lord's Prayer
Our Father… [See prayer on back flap]

Prayer

Father,
help us to be like Christ your Son,
who loved the world and died for our Salvation.
Inspire us by his love,
guide us by his example,
who lives and reigns with you
and the Holy Spirit,
one God, for ever and ever. Amen.

Closing Rite Or Dismissal

[See Closing Rite on Back Flap]

Introductory Rite

[See Introductory Rite on Front Flap]

Hymn

✦ O Sacred Head, surrounded
By crown of piercing thorn.
O Bleeding Head, so wounded,
Reviled and put to scorn.
Our sins have marred the glory
Of thy most holy Face,
Yet angel hosts adore thee,
And tremble as they gaze.

✦ The Lord of every nation
Was hung upon a tree;
His death was our salvation,
Our sins, his agony.
O Jesus, by thy Passion,
Thy Life in us increase;
Thy death for us did fashion
Our pardon and our peace.

Text: H.W. Baker, 1821-1877, alt. and St. 2, M. Farrell, S.S., 1961

Psalmody

Ant. 1   Christ was scourged and treated with contempt,
but God's right hand has raised him up.

Book 5: Psalm 110: 1-5, 7
The Messiah, king and priest

[Sit]   ✦ The Lord's revelation to my Master:
"Sit on my right:
your foes I will put beneath your feet."

✦ The Lord will wield from Zion
your scepter of power:
rule in the midst of all your foes.

✦ A prince from the day of your birth
on the holy mountains;
from the womb before the dawn I begot you.

✦ The Lord has sworn an oath he will not change.
"You are a priest for ever,
a priest like Melchizedek of old."

✦ The Master standing at your right hand
will shatter kings in the day of his great wrath.

✦ He shall drink from the stream by the wayside
and therefore he shall lift up his head.

[Bow]   ✦ Glory to the Father...

Psalm Prayer
Almighty God,...[See psalm prayer on front flap]

Ant.   Christ was scourged and treated with contempt,
but God's right hand has raised him up.

Ant. 2   The blood of Christ washes away our sins and
makes us worthy to serve the living God.

Palm Sunday
in Passiontide
[Psalter, Week II]

Book 5: Psalm 115
'Praise' of the 'true' God

✦ Not to us, Lord, not to us,
but to your name give the glory
for the sake of your love and your truth,
lest the heathen say: "Where is their God?"

✦ But our God is in the heavens;
he does whatever he wills.
Their idols are silver and gold,
the work of human hands.

✦ They have mouths but they cannot speak;
they have eyes but they cannot see;
they have ears but they cannot hear;
they have nostrils but they cannot smell.

✦ With their hands they cannot feel;
with their feet they cannot walk.
No sound comes from their throats.
Their makers will come to be like them
and so will all who trust in them.

✦ Sons of Israel, trust in the Lord;
he is their help and their shield.
Sons of Aaron, trust in the Lord;
he is their help and their shield.

✦ You who fear him, trust in the Lord;
he is their help and their shield.
He remembers us, and he will bless us;
he will bless the sons of Israel.
He will bless the sons of Aaron.

✦ The Lord will bless those who fear him,
the little no less than the great:
to you may the Lord grant increase,
to you and all your children.

✦ May you be blessed by the Lord,
the maker of heaven and earth.
The heavens belong to the Lord
but the earth he has given to men.

✦ The dead shall not praise the Lord,
nor those who go down into the silence.
But we who live bless the Lord
now and for ever. Amen.

[Bow]   ✦ Glory to the Father...

Psalm Prayer
Father, creator...[See psalm prayer on front flap]

50

Ant.   The blood of Christ washes away our sins and makes us worthy to serve the living God.

Ant. 3   Christ bore our sins in his own body on the cross so that we might die to sin and be alive to all that is good.

Canticle: 1 Peter 2: 21-24
The willing acceptance of his passion by Christ, the servant of God

+ Christ suffered for you,
  and left you an example
  to have you follow in his footsteps.

+ He did no wrong;
  no deceit was found in his mouth.
  when he was insulted,
  he returned no insult.

+ When he was made to suffer,
  he did not counter with threats.
  instead he delivered himself up
  to the One who judges justly.

+ In his own body
  he brought your sins to the cross,
  so that all of us, dead to sin,
  could live in accord with God's will.

+ By his wounds you were healed.

[Bow]   + Glory to the Father…

Ant.   Christ bore our sins in his own body on the cross so that we might die to sin and be alive to all that is good.

Reading: Acts 13: 26-30

My brothers, it was to us that this message of salvation was sent forth. The inhabitants of Jerusalem and their rulers failed to recognize him, and in condemning him they fulfilled the words of the prophets which we read sabbath after sabbath. Even though they found no charge against him which deserved death, they begged Pilate to have him executed. Once they had thus brought about all that had been written of him, they took him down from the tree and laid him in a tomb. Yet God raised him from the dead.

Responsory

℣.   We worship you, O Christ, and we praise you.
℟.   We worship you, O Christ, and we praise you.
℣.   Because by your cross you have redeemed the world.
℟.   We praise you.
[Bow] ℣.   Glory to the Father, and to the Son, and to the Holy Spirit.
℟.   We worship you, O Christ, and we praise you.

Canticle Of Mary

Ant.   It is written: I will strike the shepherd and his
[Stand]   flock shall be scattered. But when I have risen, I will go before you into Galilee. There you shall see me, says the Lord.

Magnificat: Luke 1: 46-55
My soul ✠ proclaims the… [See Prayer On Back.]

Intercessions

Introductory Formula
The Savior of mankind by dying destroyed death and by rising again restored life. Let us humbly ask him:
℟.   Sanctify your people, redeemed by your blood.

Petitions
℣.   Redeemer of the world, give us a greater share of your passion through a deeper spirit of repentance,
℟.   so that we may share the glory of your resurrection.
℣.   May your Mother, comfort of the afflicted, protect us,
℟.   may we console others as you console us.
℣.   Look with love on those who suffer because of our indifference,
℟.   come to their aid, and turn our uncaring hearts to works of justice and charity.
℣.   You humbled yourself by being obedient even to accepting death, death on a cross,
℟.   give all who serve you the gifts of obedience and patient endurance.
℣.   Transform the bodies of the dead to be like your own in glory,
℟.   and bring us at last into their fellowship.

The Lord's Prayer
Our Father… [See prayer on back flap]

Prayer

Almighty, ever-living God,
you have given the human race
Jesus Christ our Savior as a model of humility.
He fulfilled your will by becoming man and
  giving his life on the cross.
Help us to bear witness to you by following
his example of suffering and make us worthy
  to share in his resurrection.
We ask this through our Lord Jesus Christ,
  your Son,
who lives and reigns with you
  and the Holy Spirit,
one God, for ever and ever. Amen.

Closing Rite Or Dismissal [See Back Flap.]

51

Introductory Rite

[Stand] V. God, ✠ come to my assistance.
R. Lord, make haste to help me.

[Bow] Glory to the Father, and to the Son,
and to the Holy Spirit:
as it was in the beginning, is now,
and will be for ever. Amen.

Hymn

   ✦ At the Lamb's high feast we sing
Praise to our victorious King,
Who has washed us in the tide
Flowing from his wounded side;
Praise the Lord, whose love divine
Gives his sacred blood for wine,
Gives his body for the feast,
Christ the victim, Christ the priest.

   ✦ Where the Paschal blood is poured,
Death's dark angel sheathes his sword;
Israel's hosts in triumph go
Through the waves that drown the foe.
Christ the Lamb whose blood was shed,
Paschal victim, Paschal bread;
Let us with a fervent love
Taste the manna from above.

   ✦ Mighty victim from on high,
Pow'rs of hell now vanquished lie;
Sin is conquered in the fight:
You have brought us life and light;
Your resplendent banners wave,
You have risen from the grave;
Christ has opened Paradise,
And in him all men shall rise.

   ✦ Easter triumph, Easter joy,
Sin alone can this destroy;
Souls from sin and death set free
Glory in their liberty.
Hymns of glory, hymns of praise
Father unto you we raise;
Risen Lord, for joy we sing:
Let our hymns through heaven ring.

Translator: R. Campbell, 1814-1868, adapted, Geoffrey Laycock

Psalmody

Ant. 1   Mary Magdalene and the other Mary came to
see the Lord's tomb, alleluia.

   Book 5: Psalm 110: 1-5, 7
   The Messiah, king and priest

[Sit]   ✦ The Lord's revelation to my Master:
"Sit on my right:
your foes I will put beneath your feet."

   ✦ The Lord will wield from Zion

EASTER SUNDAY
Sacred Triduum

your scepter of power:
rule in the midst of all your foes.

✦ A prince from the day of your birth
on the holy mountains;
from the womb before the dawn I begot you.

✦ The Lord has sworn an oath he will not change.
"You are a priest for ever,
a priest like Melchizedek of old."

✦ The Master standing at your right hand
will shatter kings in the day of his great wrath.

✦ He shall drink from the stream by the wayside
and therefore he shall lift up his head.

[Bow] ✦ Glory to the Father, and to the Son,
and to the Holy Spirit:
as it was in the beginning, is now,
and will be for ever. Amen.

Ant.   Mary Magdalene and the other Mary came to
see the Lord's tomb, alleluia.

Ant. 2   Come and see the place where the Lord was
buried, alleluia.

   Book 2: Psalm 114
   The Israelites are delivered from the bondage of Egypt

✦ When Israel came forth from Egypt,
Jacob's sons from an alien people,
Judah became the Lord's temple,
Israel became his kingdom.

✦ The sea fled at the sight:
the Jordan turned back on its course,
the mountains leapt like rams
and the hills like yearling sheep.

✦ Why was it, sea, that you fled,
that you turned back, Jordan, on your course?
Mountains, that you leapt like rams,
hills, like yearling sheep?

✦ Tremble, O earth, before the Lord,
in the presence of the God of Jacob,
who turns the rock into a pool
and flint into a spring of water.

[Bow] ✦ Glory to the Father, and to the Son,
and to the Holy Spirit:
as it was in the beginning, is now,
and will be for ever. Amen.

Ant. Come and see the place where the Lord was buried, alleluia.

Ant. 3 Jesus said: Do not be afraid. Go and tell my brothers to set out for Galilee; there they will see me, alleluia.

Canticle based on Revelation 19: 1-7
The wedding of the Lamb

✦ Alleluia.
Salvation, glory, and power to our God:
(℟ Alleluia.)
his judgments are honest and true.
℟ Alleluia (alleluia).

✦ Alleluia.
Sing praise to our God, all you his servants,
(℟ Alleluia.)
all who worship him reverently, great and small.
℟ Alleluia (alleluia).

✦ Alleluia.
The Lord our all-powerful God is King;
(℟ Alleluia.)
let us rejoice, sing praise, and give him glory.
℟ Alleluia (alleluia).

✦ Alleluia.
The wedding feast of the Lamb has begun,
(℟ Alleluia.)
and his bride is prepared to welcome him.
℟ Alleluia (alleluia).

[Bow] ✦ Glory to the Father, and to the Son,
and to the Holy Spirit:
as it was in the beginning, is now,
and will be for ever. Amen.

Ant. Jesus said: Do not be afraid. Go and tell my brothers to set out for Galilee; there they will see me, alleluia.

Reading: Hebrews 10: 12-14
Jesus offered one sacrifice for sins and took his seat forever at the right hand of God; now he waits until his enemies are placed beneath his feet. By one offering he has forever perfected those who are being sanctified.

Responsory
This is the day the Lord has made; let us rejoice and be glad, alleluia.

Canticle Of Mary

Ant.
[Stand] On the evening of the first day of the week, the disciples were gathered together behind locked doors; suddenly, Jesus stood among them and said: Peace be with you, alleluia.

Magnificat: Luke 1: 46-55
My soul ✠ proclaims the… [See Prayer On Back Flap. Then Repeat The Antiphon Above.]

Intercessions

Introductory Formula
With joy in our hearts, let us call upon Christ the Lord, who died and rose again, and lives always to intercede for us:
℟ Victorious King, hear our prayer.

Petitions
℣ Light and salvation of all peoples,
℟ send into our hearts the fire of your Spirit, as we proclaim your resurrection.

℣ Let Israel recognize in you her longed-for Messiah,
℟ and the whole earth be filled with the knowledge of your glory.

℣ Keep us in the communion of your saints,
℟ and grant us rest from our labors in their company.

℣ You have triumphed over death, your enemy; destroy in us the power of death,
℟ that we may live only for you, victorious and immortal Lord.

℣ Savior Christ, you were obedient even to accepting death, and were raised up to the right hand of the Father,
℟ in your goodness welcome your brothers and sisters into the kingdom of your glory.

The Lord's Prayer
Our Father… [See prayer on back flap]

Prayer
God our Father,
by raising Christ your Son
you conquered the power of death
and opened for us the way to eternal life.
Let our celebration today
raise us up and renew our lives
by the Spirit that is within us.
Grant this through our Lord Jesus Christ,
   your Son,
who lives and reigns with you
   and the Holy Spirit,
one God, for ever and ever. Amen.

Closing Rite Or Dismissal
[See Closing Rite on Back Flap]

Introductory Rite

[Stand] V. God, ✠ come to my assistance.

R. Lord, make haste to help me.

[Bow] Glory to the Father, and to the Son,
and to the Holy Spirit:
as it was in the beginning, is now,
and will be for ever. Amen.

Hymn

✦ At the Lamb's high feast we sing
Praise to our victorious King,
Who has washed us in the tide
Flowing from his wounded side;
Praise the Lord, whose love divine
Gives his sacred blood for wine,
Gives his body for the feast,
Christ the victim, Christ the priest.

✦ Where the Paschal blood is poured,
Death's dark angel sheathes his sword;
Israel's hosts in triumph go
Through the waves that drown the foe.
Christ the Lamb whose blood was shed,
Paschal victim, Paschal bread;
Let us with a fervent love
Taste the manna from above.

✦ Mighty victim from on high,
Pow'rs of hell now vanquished lie;
Sin is conquered in the fight:
You have brought us life and light;
Your resplendent banners wave,
You have risen from the grave;
Christ has opened Paradise,
And in him all men shall rise.

✦ Easter triumph, Easter joy,
Sin alone can this destroy;
Souls from sin and death set free
Glory in their liberty.
Hymns of glory, hymns of praise
Father unto you we raise;
Risen Lord, for joy we sing:
Let our hymns through heaven ring.

Translator: R. Campbell, 1814-1868, adapted, Geoffrey Laycock

Psalmody

Ant. 1   Mary Magdalene and the other Mary
came to see the Lord's tomb, alleluia.

Book 5: Psalm 110: 1-5, 7
The Messiah, king and priest

[Sit] ✦ The Lord's revelation to my Master:
"Sit on my right:
your foes I will put beneath your feet."

✦ The Lord will wield from Zion

your scepter of power:
rule in the midst of all your foes.

✦ A prince from the day of your birth
on the holy mountains;
from the womb before the dawn I begot you.

✦ The Lord has sworn an oath he will not change.
"You are a priest for ever,
a priest like Melchizedek of old."

✦ The Master standing at your right hand
will shatter kings in the day of his great wrath.

✦ He shall drink from the stream by the wayside
and therefore he shall lift up his head.

[Bow] ✦ Glory to the Father, and to the Son,
and to the Holy Spirit:
as it was in the beginning, is now,
and will be for ever. Amen.

Ant.   Mary Magdalene and the other Mary
came to see the Lord's tomb, alleluia.

Ant. 2   Come and see the place where the Lord
was buried, alleluia.

Book 2: Psalm 114
The Israelites are delivered from the bondage of Egypt

✦ When Israel came forth from Egypt,
Jacob's sons from an alien people,
Judah became the Lord's temple,
Israel became his kingdom.

✦ The sea fled at the sight:
the Jordan turned back on its course,
the mountains leapt like rams
and the hills like yearling sheep.

✦ Why was it, sea, that you fled,
that you turned back, Jordan, on your course?
Mountains, that you leapt like rams,
hills, like yearling sheep?

✦ Tremble, O earth, before the Lord,
in the presence of the God of Jacob,
who turns the rock into a pool
and flint into a spring of water.

[Bow] ✦ Glory to the Father, and to the Son,
and to the Holy Spirit:
as it was in the beginning, is now,
and will be for ever. Amen.

SECOND SUNDAY
of Easter

Ant.   Come and see the place where the Lord was buried, alleluia.

Ant. 3   Jesus said: Do not be afraid. Go and tell my brothers to set out for Galilee; there they will see me, alleluia.

Canticle based on Revelation 19: 1-7
The wedding of the Lamb

✦ Alleluia.
Salvation, glory, and power to our God:
(℟ Alleluia.)
his judgments are honest and true.
℟ Alleluia (alleluia).

✦ Alleluia.
Sing praise to our God, all you his servants,
(℟ Alleluia.)
all who worship him reverently, great and small.
℟ Alleluia (alleluia).

✦ Alleluia.
The Lord our all-powerful God is King;
(℟ Alleluia.)
let us rejoice, sing praise, and give him glory.
℟ Alleluia (alleluia).

✦ Alleluia.
The wedding feast of the Lamb has begun,
(℟ Alleluia.)
and his bride is prepared to welcome him.
℟ Alleluia (alleluia).

[Bow]   ✦ Glory to the Father, and to the Son,
and to the Holy Spirit:
as it was in the beginning, is now,
and will be for ever. Amen.

Ant.   Jesus said: Do not be afraid. Go and tell my brothers to set out for Galilee; there they will see me, alleluia.

Reading: Hebrews 10: 12-14

Jesus offered one sacrifice for sins and took his seat forever at the right hand of God; now he waits until his enemies are placed beneath his feet. By one offering he has forever perfected those who are being sanctified.

Responsory

This is the day the Lord has made; let us rejoice and be glad, alleluia.

Canticle Of Mary

Ant.   Because you have seen me, Thomas, you have
[Stand]   believed; blessed are they who have not seen me and yet believe, alleluia.

Magnificat: Luke 1: 46-55
My soul ✚ proclaims the... [See Prayer On Back Flap. Then Repeat The Antiphon Above.]

Intercessions

Introductory Formula
God the Father raised Christ from the dead and exalted him at his right hand. Let us pray to the Father, saying:
℟ Through Christ in glory, watch over your people, Lord.

Petitions
℣ Righteous Father, you lifted Jesus above the earth through the triumph of the cross,
℟ may all things be lifted up in him.
℣ Through your Son in glory send the Holy Spirit upon the Church,
℟ that it may be the sacrament of unity for the whole human race.
℣ You have brought a new family into being through water and the Holy Spirit,
℟ keep them faithful to their baptism, and bring them to everlasting life.
℣ Through your exalted Son help those in distress, free those in captivity, heal the sick,
℟ and by your blessings give joy to the world.
℣ You nourished our deceased brothers and sisters with the body and blood of the risen Christ,
℟ raise them up at the last day.

The Lord's Prayer
Our Father... [See prayer on back flap]

Prayer

God of mercy,
you wash away our sins in water,
you give us new birth in the Spirit,
and redeem us in the blood of Christ.
As we celebrate Christ's resurrection
increase our awareness of these blessings,
and renew your gift of life within us.
We as this through our Lord Jesus Christ,
  your Son,
who lives and reigns with you
  and the Holy Spirit,
one God, for ever and ever. Amen.

Closing Rite Or Dismissal

[See Closing Rite on Back Flap]

Introductory Rite

[STAND] V. God, ✠ come to my assistance.

R. Lord, make haste to help me.

[BOW] Glory to the Father, and to the Son,
and to the Holy Spirit:
as it was in the beginning, is now,
and will be for ever. Amen.

Hymn

‡ Christ Jesus lay in death's strong bands
For our offenses given:
But now at God's right hand he stands
And brings us life from heaven;
Therefore let us joyful be,
And praise the Father thankfully
With songs of Alleluia.
Alleluia.

‡ How long and bitter was the strife
When life and death contended,
The victory remained with life,
The reign of death was ended:
Stripped of power, no more it reigns,
And empty form alone remains.
Death's sting is lost for ever.
Alleluia.

‡ So let us keep this festival
To which Our Lord invites us,
The Savoir who is joy of all,
The Sun that warms and lights us:
By his grace he shall impart
Eternal sunshine to the heart;
The night of sin has ended.
Alleluia.

Translator: R. Massie, 1800-1887, adapted by Anthony G. Petti

Psalmody

Ant. 1 He purified us from our sins, and is seated on
high at God's right hand, alleluia.

Book 5: Psalm 110: 1-5, 7
The Messiah, king and priest

[SIT] ‡ The Lord's revelation to my Master:
"Sit on my right:
your foes I will put beneath your feet."

‡ The Lord will wield from Zion
your scepter of power:
rule in the midst of all your foes.

‡ A prince from the day of your birth
on the holy mountains;
from the womb before the dawn I begot you.

‡ The Lord has sworn an oath he will not change.
"You are a priest for ever,
a priest like Melchizedek of old."

56

THIRD SUNDAY
of Easter

‡ The Master standing at your right hand
will shatter kings in the day of his great wrath.

‡ He shall drink from the stream by the wayside
and therefore he shall lift up his head.

[BOW] ‡ Glory to the Father, and to the Son,
and to the Holy Spirit:
as it was in the beginning, is now,
and will be for ever. Amen.

Psalm Prayer
Father, we ask you to give us victory and
peace. In Jesus Christ, our Lord and King, we
are already seated at your right hand. We look
forward to praising you in the fellowship of all
your saints in our heavenly homeland.

Ant. He purified us from our sins, and is seated on
high at God's right hand, alleluia.

Ant. 2 The Lord has redeemed his people, alleluia.

Book 5: Psalm 111
God's marvelous works

‡ I will thank the Lord with all my heart
in the meeting of the just and their assembly.
Great are the works of the Lord;
to be pondered by all who love them.

‡ Majestic and glorious his work,
his justice stands firm for ever.
He makes us remember his wonders.
The Lord is compassion and love.

‡ He gives food to those who fear him;
keeps his covenant ever in mind.
He has shown his might to his people
by giving them the lands of the nations.

‡ His works are justice and truth:
his precepts are all of them sure,
standing firm for ever and ever:
they are made in uprightness and truth.

‡ He has sent deliverance to his people
and established his covenant for ever.
Holy his name, to be feared.

‡ To fear the Lord is the first stage of wisdom;
all who do so prove themselves wise.
His praise shall last for ever!

[BOW] ‡ Glory to the Father...

Psalm Prayer

Merciful and gentle Lord, you are the crowning glory of all the saints. Give us, your children, the gift of obedience which is the beginning of wisdom, so that we may do what you command and be filled with your mercy.

Ant. The Lord has redeemed his people, alleluia.

Ant. 3 Alleluia, our Lord is king; let us rejoice and give glory to him, alleluia.

Canticle based on Revelation 19: 1-7
The wedding of the Lamb

✦ Alleluia.
Salvation, glory, and power to our God:
(℞ Alleluia.)
his judgments are honest and true.
℞ Alleluia (alleluia).

✦ Alleluia.
Sing praise to our God, all you his servants,
(℞ Alleluia.)
all who worship him reverently, great and small.
℞ Alleluia (alleluia).

✦ Alleluia.
The Lord our all-powerful God is King;
(℞ Alleluia.)
let us rejoice, sing praise, and give him glory.
℞ Alleluia (alleluia).

✦ Alleluia.
The wedding feast of the Lamb has begun,
(℞ Alleluia.)
and his bride is prepared to welcome him.
℞ Alleluia (alleluia).

[Bow] ✦ Glory to the Father…

Ant. Alleluia, our Lord is king; let us rejoice and give glory to him, alleluia.

Reading: Hebrews 10: 12-14

Jesus offered one sacrifice for sins and took his seat forever at the right hand of God; now he waits until his enemies are placed beneath his feet. By one offering he has forever perfected those who are being sanctified.

Responsory

℣ The Lord is risen, alleluia, alleluia.
℞ The Lord is risen, alleluia, alleluia.
℣ He has appeared to Simon,
℞ alleluia, alleluia.
[Bow] ℣ Glory to the Father, and to the Son, and to the Holy Spirit.
℞ The Lord is risen, alleluia, alleluia.

Canticle Of Mary

Ant.
[Stand] Jesus said to his disciples: Bring me some of the fish you have just caught. Simon Peter went aboard and hauled ashore the net, full of large fish, alleluia.

Magnificat: Luke 1: 46-55
My soul ✠ proclaims the… [See Prayer On Back Flap. Then Repeat The Antiphon Above.]

Intercessions

Introductory Formula
With joy in our hearts, let us call upon Christ the Lord, who died for us and rose again, and lives always to intercede for us:
℞ Victorious King, hear our prayer.

Petitions
℣ Light and salvation of all peoples,
℞ send into our hearts the fire of your Spirit, as we proclaim your resurrection.
℣ Let Israel recognize in you her longed-for Messiah,
℞ and the whole earth be filled with the knowledge of your glory.
℣ Keep us in the communion of your saints,
℞ and grant us rest from our labors in their company.
℣ You have triumphed over death, your enemy; destroy in us the power of death,
℞ that we may live only for you, victorious and immortal Lord.
℣ Savior Christ, you were obedient even to accepting death, and were raised up to the right hand of the Father,
℞ in your goodness welcome your brothers and sisters into the kingdom of your glory.

The Lord's Prayer
Our Father… [See prayer on back flap]

Prayer

God our Father,
may we look forward with hope
  to our resurrection,
for you have made us
  your sons and daughters,
and restored the joy of our youth.
We ask this through our Lord Jesus Christ,
  your Son,
who lives and reigns with you
  and the Holy Spirit,
one God, for ever and ever. Amen.

Closing Rite Or Dismissal

[See Closing Rite on Back Flap]

Introductory Rite

[STAND] V. God, + come to my assistance.

R. Lord, make haste to help me.

[BOW] Glory to the Father, and to the Son,
and to the Holy Spirit:
as it was in the beginning, is now,
and will be for ever. Amen.

Hymn

✦ Christ Jesus lay in death's strong bands
For our offenses given:
But now at God's right hand he stands
And brings us life from heaven;
Therefore let us joyful be,
And praise the Father thankfully
With songs of Alleluia.
Alleluia.

✦ How long and bitter was the strife
When life and death contended,
The victory remained with life,
The reign of death was ended:
Stripped of power, no more it reigns,
And empty form alone remains.
Death's sting is lost for ever.
Alleluia.

✦ So let us keep this festival
To which Our Lord invites us,
The Savoir who is joy of all,
The Sun that warms and lights us:
By his grace he shall impart
Eternal sunshine to the heart;
The night of sin has ended.
Alleluia.

Translator: R. Massie, 1800-1887, adapted by Anthony G. Petti

Psalmody

Ant. 1   Seek the things that are above where Christ is
seated at God's right hand, alleluia.

Book 5: Psalm 110: 1-5, 7
The Messiah, king and priest

[SIT] ✦ The Lord's revelation to my Master:
"Sit on my right:
your foes I will put beneath your feet."

✦ The Lord will wield from Zion
your scepter of power:
rule in the midst of all your foes.

✦ A prince from the day of your birth
on the holy mountains;
from the womb before the dawn I begot you.

✦ The Lord has sworn an oath he will not change.
"You are a priest for ever,
a priest like Melchizedek of old."

58

FOURTH SUNDAY
of Easter

[PSALTER, WEEK IV]

✦ The Master standing at your right hand
will shatter kings in the day of his great wrath.

✦ He shall drink from the stream by the wayside
and therefore he shall lift up his head.

[BOW] ✦ Glory to the Father, and to the Son,
and to the Holy Spirit:
as it was in the beginning, is now,
and will be for ever. Amen.

Psalm Prayer

Father, we ask you to give us victory and peace.
In Jesus Christ, our Lord and King, we are
already seated at your right hand. We look
forward to praising you in the fellowship of all
your saints in our heavenly homeland.

Ant.   Seek the things that are above where Christ is
seated at God's right hand, alleluia.

Ant. 2   In the darkness he dawns: a light for upright
hearts, alleluia.

Book 5: Psalm 112
The happiness of the just man

✦ Happy the man who fears the Lord,
who takes delight in all his commands.
His sons will be powerful on earth;
the children of the upright are blessed.

✦ Riches and wealth are in his house;
his justice stands firm for ever.
He is a light in the darkness for the upright:
he is generous, merciful and just.

✦ The good man takes pity and lends,
he conducts his affairs with honor.
The just man will never waver:
he will be remembered for ever.

✦ He has no fear of evil news;
with a firm heart he trusts in the Lord.
With a steadfast heart he will not fear;
he will see the downfall of his foes.

✦ Open-handed, he gives to the poor;
his justice stands firm for ever.
His head will be raised in glory.

✦ The wicked man sees and is angry,
grinds his teeth and fades away;
the desire of the wicked leads to doom.

[Bow] ♦ Glory to the Father...

Psalm Prayer

Lord God, you are the eternal light which illumines the hearts of good people. Help us to love you, to rejoice in your glory, and so to live in this world as to avoid harsh judgment in the next. May we come to see the light of your countenance.

Ant. In the darkness he dawns: a light for upright hearts, alleluia.

Ant. 3 Alleluia, salvation, glory, and power to our God, alleluia.

Canticle based on Revelation 19: 1-7

The wedding of the Lamb

♦ Alleluia.
Salvation, glory, and power to our God:
(℟ Alleluia.)
his judgments are honest and true.
℟ Alleluia (alleluia).

♦ Alleluia.
Sing praise to our God, all you his servants,
(℟ Alleluia.)
all who worship him reverently, great and small.
℟ Alleluia (alleluia).

♦ Alleluia.
The Lord our all-powerful God is King;
(℟ Alleluia.)
let us rejoice, sing praise, and give him glory.
℟ Alleluia (alleluia).

♦ Alleluia.
The wedding feast of the Lamb has begun,
(℟ Alleluia.)
and his bride is prepared to welcome him.
℟ Alleluia (alleluia).

[Bow] ♦ Glory to the Father...

Ant. Alleluia, salvation, glory, and power to our God, alleluia.

Reading: Hebrews 10: 12-14

Jesus offered one sacrifice for sins and took his seat forever at the right hand of God; now he waits until his enemies are placed beneath his feet. By one offering he has forever perfected those who are being sanctified.

Responsory

℣ The Lord is risen, alleluia, alleluia.
℟ The Lord is risen, alleluia, alleluia.
℣ He has appeared to Simon,
℟ alleluia, alleluia.

[Bow] ℣ Glory to the Father, and to the Son, and to the Holy Spirit.
℟ The Lord is risen, alleluia, alleluia.

Canticle Of Mary

Ant. My sheep will hear my voice. I, their Lord,
[Stand] know them.

Magnificat: Luke 1: 46-55
My soul ✠ proclaims the... [See Prayer On Back Flap. Then Repeat The Antiphon Above.]

Intercessions

Introductory Formula
God the Father raised Christ from the dead and exalted him at his right hand. Let us pray to the Father, saying:
℟ Through Christ in glory, watch over your people, Lord.

Petitions
℣ Righteous Father, you lifted Jesus above the earth through the triumph of the cross,
may all things be lifted up in him.
℣ Through your Son in glory send the Holy Spirit upon the Church,
℟ that it may be the sacrament of unity for the whole human race.
℣ You have brought a new family into being through water and the Holy Spirit,
℟ keep them faithful to their baptism, and bring them to everlasting life.
℣ Through your exalted Son help those in distress, free those in captivity, heal the sick,
℟ and by your blessings give joy to the world.
℣ You nourished our deceased brothers and sisters with the body and blood of the risen Christ,
℟ raise them up at the last day.

The Lord's Prayer
Our Father... [See prayer on back flap]

Prayer

Almighty and ever-living God,
give us new strength
from the courage of Christ our shepherd,
and lead us to join the saints in heaven,
where he lives and reigns with you
and the Holy Spirit,
one God, for ever and ever. Amen.

Closing Rite Or Dismissal

[See Closing Rite on Back Flap]

Introductory Rite

[STAND] V. God, ✠ come to my assistance.

R. Lord, make haste to help me.

[BOW] Glory to the Father, and to the Son,
and to the Holy Spirit:
as it was in the beginning, is now,
and will be for ever. Amen.

Hymn

✦ Christ Jesus lay in death's strong bands
For our offenses given:
But now at God's right hand he stands
And brings us life from heaven;
Therefore let us joyful be,
And praise the Father thankfully
With songs of Alleluia.
Alleluia.

✦ How long and bitter was the strife
When life and death contended,
The victory remained with life,
The reign of death was ended:
Stripped of power, no more it reigns,
And empty form alone remains.
Death's sting is lost for ever.
Alleluia.

✦ So let us keep this festival
To which Our Lord invites us,
The Savoir who is joy of all,
The Sun that warms and lights us:
By his grace he shall impart
Eternal sunshine to the heart;
The night of sin has ended.
Alleluia.

Translator: R. Massie, 1800-1887, adapted by Anthony G. Petti

Psalmody

Ant. 1 The Lord has risen and is seated at the right
hand of God, alleluia.

Book 5: Psalm 110: 1-5, 7
The Messiah, king and priest

[SIT] ✦ The Lord's revelation to my Master:
"Sit on my right:
your foes I will put beneath your feet."

✦ The Lord will wield from Zion
your scepter of power:
rule in the midst of all your foes.

✦ A prince from the day of your birth
on the holy mountains;
from the womb before the dawn I begot you.

✦ The Lord has sworn an oath he will not change.
"You are a priest for ever,
a priest like Melchizedek of old."

FIFTH SUNDAY
of Easter

[PSALTER, WEEK I]

✦ The Master standing at your right hand
will shatter kings in the day of his great wrath.

✦ He shall drink from the stream by the wayside
and therefore he shall lift up his head.

[BOW] ✦ Glory to the Father…

Psalm Prayer
Father, we ask you to give us victory and peace.
In Jesus Christ, our Lord and King, we are
already seated at your right hand. We look
forward to praising you in the fellowship of all
your saints in our heavenly homeland.

Ant. The Lord has risen and is seated at the right
hand of God, alleluia.

Ant. 2 He has rescued us from the power of darkness
and has brought us into the kingdom of his Son,
alleluia.

Book 2: Psalm 114
The Israelites are delivered from the bondage of Egypt

✦ When Israel came forth from Egypt,
Jacob's sons from an alien people,
Judah became the Lord's temple,
Israel became his kingdom.

✦ The sea fled at the sight:
the Jordan turned back on its course,
the mountains leapt like rams
and the hills like yearling sheep.

✦ Why was it, sea, that you fled,
that you turned back, Jordan, on your course?
Mountains, that you leapt like rams,
hills, like yearling sheep?

✦ Tremble, O earth, before the Lord,
in the presence of the God of Jacob,
who turns the rock into a pool
and flint into a spring of water.

[BOW] ✦ Glory to the Father…

Psalm Prayer
Almighty God, ever-living mystery of unity and
trinity, you gave life to the new Israel by birth
from water and the Spirit, and made it a chosen
race, a royal priesthood, a people set apart as
your eternal possession. May all those you have

called to walk in the splendor of the new light
render you fitting service and adoration.

Ant. He has rescued us from the power of darkness
and has brought us into the kingdom of his Son,
alleluia.

Ant. 3 Alleluia, our God is king; glory and praise to
him, alleluia.

Canticle based on Revelation 19: 1-7
The wedding of the Lamb

✦ Alleluia.
Salvation, glory, and power to our God:
(℟ Alleluia.)
his judgments are honest and true.
℟ Alleluia (alleluia).

✦ Alleluia.
Sing praise to our God, all you his servants,
(℟ Alleluia.)
all who worship him reverently, great and small.
℟ Alleluia (alleluia).

✦ Alleluia.
The Lord our all-powerful God is King;
(℟ Alleluia.)
let us rejoice, sing praise, and give him glory.
℟ Alleluia (alleluia).

✦ Alleluia.
The wedding feast of the Lamb has begun,
(℟ Alleluia.)
and his bride is prepared to welcome him.
℟ Alleluia (alleluia).

[Bow] ✦ Glory to the Father…

Ant. Alleluia, our God is king; glory and praise to
him, alleluia.

Reading: Hebrews 10: 12-14

Jesus offered one sacrifice for sins and took his
seat forever at the right hand of God; now he
waits until his enemies are placed beneath his
feet. By one offering he has forever perfected
those who are being sanctified.

Responsory

℣. The Lord is risen, alleluia, alleluia.
℟. The Lord is risen, alleluia, alleluia.
℣. He has appeared to Simon,
℟. alleluia, alleluia.
[Bow] ℣. Glory to the Father, and to the Son,
and to the Holy Spirit.
℟. The Lord is risen, alleluia, alleluia.

Canticle Of Mary

Ant.
[Stand] I give you a new commandment: love one
another as I have loved you, says the Lord,
alleluia.

Magnificat: Luke 1: 46-55
My soul ✝ proclaims the… [See Prayer On Back
Flap. Then Repeat The Antiphon Above.]

Intercessions

Introductory Formula
With joy in our hearts, let us call upon Christ
the Lord, who died and rose again, and lives
always to intercede for us:
℟. Victorious King, hear our prayer.

Petitions
℣. Light and salvation of all peoples,
℟. send into our hearts the fire of your Spirit, as
we proclaim your resurrection.
℣. Let Israel recognize in you her longed-for
Messiah,
℟. and the whole earth be filled with the
knowledge of your glory.
℣. Keep us in the communion of your saints,
℟. and grant us rest from our labors in
their company.
℣. You have triumphed over death, your enemy;
destroy in us the power of death,
℟. that we may live only for you, victorious and
immortal Lord.
℣. Savior Christ, you were obedient even to
accepting death, and were raised up to the
right hand of the Father,
℟. in your goodness welcome your brothers and
sisters into the kingdom of your glory.

The Lord's Prayer
Our Father… [See prayer on back flap]

Prayer

God our Father,
look upon us with love.
You redeem us and make us your children
in Christ.
Give us true freedom
and bring us to the inheritance you promised.
We ask this through our Lord Jesus Christ,
your Son,
who lives and reigns with you
and the Holy Spirit,
one God, for ever and ever. Amen.

Closing Rite Or Dismissal

[See Closing Rite on Back Flap]

61

Introductory Rite

[See Introductory Rite on Front Flap]

Hymn

◦ Alleluia! Alleluia! Alleluia!
The strife is o'er, the battle done;
Now is the victor's triumph won:
O let the song of praise be sung.
Alleluia!

◦ Alleluia! Alleluia! Alleluia!
On the third morn he rose again,
Glorious in majesty to reign:
O let us swell the joyful strain:
Alleluia!

◦ Alleluia! Alleluia! Alleluia!
O risen Lord, all praise to thee,
Who from our sin has set us free,
That we may live eternally:
Alleluia!

Translator: Francis Pott, 1861, alt.

Psalmody

Ant. 1   God raised up Christ from the dead and gave
him a place at his right hand in heaven, alleluia.

Book 5: Psalm 110: 1-5, 7
The Messiah, king and priest

[Sit]   ◦ The Lord's revelation to my Master:
"Sit on my right:
your foes I will put beneath your feet."

◦ The Lord will wield from Zion
your scepter of power:
rule in the midst of all your foes.

◦ A prince from the day of your birth
on the holy mountains;
from the womb before the dawn I begot you.

◦ The Lord has sworn an oath he will not change.
"You are a priest for ever,
a priest like Melchizedek of old."

◦ The Master standing at your right hand
will shatter kings in the day of his great wrath.

◦ He shall drink from the stream by the wayside
and therefore he shall lift up his head.

[Bow]   ◦ Glory to the Father…

Psalm Prayer
Almighty God, bring the kingdom of Christ,
your anointed one, to its fullness. May the
perfect offering of your Son, eternal priest of
the new Jerusalem, be offered in every place to
your name, and make all nations a holy people
for you.

SIXTH SUNDAY
of Easter
[Psalter, Week II]

Ant.   God raised up Christ from the dead and
gave him a place at his right hand in heaven,
alleluia.

Ant. 2   You have been turned from faith in idols to
the living God, alleluia.

Book 5: Psalm 115
'Praise' of the 'true' God

◦ Not to us, Lord, not to us,
but to your name give the glory
for the sake of your love and your truth,
lest the heathen say: "Where is their God?"

◦ But our God is in the heavens;
he does whatever he wills.
Their idols are silver and gold,
the work of human hands.

◦ They have mouths but they cannot speak;
they have eyes but they cannot see;
they have ears but they cannot hear;
they have nostrils but they cannot smell.

◦ With their hands they cannot feel;
with their feet they cannot walk.
No sound comes from their throats.
Their makers will come to be like them
and so will all who trust in them.

◦ Sons of Israel, trust in the Lord;
he is their help and their shield.
Sons of Aaron, trust in the Lord;
he is their help and their shield.

◦ You who fear him, trust in the Lord;
he is their help and their shield.
He remembers us, and he will bless us;
he will bless the sons of Israel.
He will bless the sons of Aaron.

◦ The Lord will bless those who fear him,
the little no less than the great:
to you may the Lord grant increase,
to you and all your children.

◦ May you be blessed by the Lord,
the maker of heaven and earth.
The heavens belong to the Lord
but the earth he has given to men.

◦ The dead shall not praise the Lord,
nor those who go down into the silence.

But we who live bless the Lord
now and for ever. Amen.

[Bow]   ✦ Glory to the Father…

Psalm Prayer
Father, creator… [See psalm prayer on front flap]

Ant.   You have been turned from faith in idols to the
living God, alleluia.

Ant. 3   Alleluia, salvation, glory, and power to our God,
alleluia.

Canticle based on Revelation 19: 1-7
The wedding of the Lamb

✦ Alleluia.
Salvation, glory, and power to our God:
(℟ Alleluia.)
his judgments are honest and true.
℟ Alleluia (alleluia).

✦ Alleluia.
Sing praise to our God, all you his servants,
(℟ Alleluia.)
all who worship him reverently, great and small.
℟ Alleluia (alleluia).

✦ Alleluia.
The Lord our all-powerful God is King;
(℟ Alleluia.)
let us rejoice, sing praise, and give him glory.
℟ Alleluia (alleluia).

✦ Alleluia.
The wedding feast of the Lamb has begun,
(℟ Alleluia.)
and his bride is prepared to welcome him.
℟ Alleluia (alleluia).

[Bow]   ✦ Glory to the Father…

Ant.   Alleluia, salvation, glory, and power to our God,
alleluia.

Reading: Hebrews 10: 12-14

Jesus offered one sacrifice for sins and took his
seat forever at the right hand of God; now he
waits until his enemies are placed beneath his
feet. By one offering he has forever perfected
those who are being sanctified.

Responsory

℣ The Lord is risen, alleluia, alleluia.
℟ The Lord is risen, alleluia, alleluia.
℣ He has appeared to Simon,
℟ alleluia, alleluia.
[Bow]   ℣ Glory to the Father, and to the Son,
and to the Holy Spirit.
℟ The Lord is risen, alleluia, alleluia.

Canticle Of Mary

Ant.   If anyone loves me he will keep my word, and
[Stand]   my Father will love him. We will come to him
and make our home with him, alleluia.

Magnificat: Luke 1: 46-55
My soul ✠ proclaims the… [See Prayer On Back
Flap. Then Repeat The Antiphon Above.]

Intercessions

Introductory Formula
God the Father raised Christ from the dead
and exalted him at his right hand. Let us pray
to the Father, saying:
℟ Through Christ in glory, watch over your
people, Lord.

Petitions
℣ Righteous Father, you lifted Jesus above the
earth through the triumph of the cross,
℟ may all things be lifted up in him.
℣ Through your Son in glory send the Holy
Spirit upon the Church,
℟ that it may be the sacrament of unity for the
whole human race.
℣ You have brought a new family into being
through water and the Holy Spirit,
℟ keep them faithful to their baptism, and bring
them to everlasting life.
℣ Through your exalted Son help those in
distress, free those in captivity, heal the sick,
℟ and by your blessings give joy to the world.
℣ You nourished our deceased brothers and
sisters with the body and blood of the
risen Christ,
℟ raise them up at the last day.

The Lord's Prayer
Our Father… [See prayer on back flap]

Prayer

Ever-living God,
help us to celebrate our joy
in the resurrection of the Lord
and to express in our lives
the love we celebrate.
Grant this through our Lord Jesus Christ,
your Son,
who lives and reigns with you
and the Holy Spirit,
one God, for ever and ever. Amen.

Closing Rite Or Dismissal

[See Closing Rite on Back Flap]

Introductory Rite

[Stand] V. God, ✠ come to my assistance.
R. Lord, make haste to help me.

[Bow] Glory to the Father, and to the Son,
and to the Holy Spirit:
as it was in the beginning, is now,
and will be for ever. Amen.

Hymn

◆ The head that once was crowned with thorns
Is crowned with glory now:
A royal diadem adorns
The mighty victor's brow.

◆ The highest place that heav'n affords
Is surely his by right:
The King of kings and Lord of lords,
And heav'n's eternal light.

◆ The joy he is of all above,
The joy to all below:
To ev'ryone he shows his love,
And grants his name to know.

◆ To them the cross, with all its shame,
With all its grace, is giv'n:
Their name and everlasting name.
Their joy the joy of heav'n.

◆ The cross he bore is life and health,
Though shame and death to him;
His people's hope, his people's wealth,
Their everlasting theme.

Text: Thomas Kelly, 1768-1854, slightly adapted

Psalmody

Ant. 1   He ascended into heaven and is seated at the
right hand of the Father, alleluia.

Book 5: Psalm 110: 1-5, 7
The Messiah, king and priest

[Sit] ◆ The Lord's revelation to my Master:
"Sit on my right:
your foes I will put beneath your feet."

◆ The Lord will wield from Zion
your scepter of power:
rule in the midst of all your foes.

◆ A prince from the day of your birth
on the holy mountains;
from the womb before the dawn I begot you.

◆ The Lord has sworn an oath he will not change.
"You are a priest for ever,
a priest like Melchizedek of old."

◆ The Master standing at your right hand
will shatter kings in the day of his great wrath.

◆ He shall drink from the stream by the wayside
and therefore he shall lift up his head.

[Bow] ◆ Glory to the Father, and to the Son,
and to the Holy Spirit:
as it was in the beginning, is now,
and will be for ever. Amen.

Ant.   He ascended into heaven and is seated at the
right hand of the Father, alleluia.

Ant. 2   God ascends to shouts of joy, the Lord to the
blast of trumpets, alleluia.

Book 2: Psalm 47
The Lord Jesus is King of all

◆ All peoples, clap your hands,
cry to God with shouts of joy!
For the Lord, the Most High, we must fear,
great king over all the earth.

◆ He subdues peoples under us
and nations under our feet.
Our inheritance, our glory, is from him,
given to Jacob out of love.

◆ God goes up with shouts of joy;
the Lord goes up with trumpet blast.
Sing praise for God, sing praise,
sing praise to our king, sing praise.

◆ God is king of all the earth.
Sing praise with all your skill.
God is king over the nations;
God reigns on his holy throne.

◆ The princes of the people are assembled
with the people of Abraham's God.
The rulers of the earth belong to God,
to God who reigns over all.

[Bow] ◆ Glory to the Father, and to the Son,
and to the Holy Spirit:
as it was in the beginning, is now,
and will be for ever. Amen.

Ant.   God ascends to shouts of joy, the Lord to the
blast of trumpets, alleluia.

Ant. 3   Now the Son of Man has been glorified and
God has been glorified in him, alleluia.

ASCENSION
of the Lord

Canticle: Revelation 11: 17-18; 12: 10b-12a
The judgment of God

✦ We praise you, the Lord God Almighty,
who is and who was.
You have assumed your great power,
you have begun your reign.

✦ The nations have raged in anger,
but then came your day of wrath
and the moment to judge the dead:
the time to reward your servants the prophets
and the holy ones who revere you,
the great and the small alike.

✦ Now have salvation and power come,
the reign of our God and the authority
of his Anointed One.
For the accuser of our brothers is cast out,
who night and day accused them before God.

✦ They defeated him by the blood of the Lamb
and by the word of their testimony;
love for life did not deter them from death.
So rejoice, you heavens,
and you that dwell therein!

[Bow] ✦ Glory to the Father, and to the Son,
and to the Holy Spirit:
as it was in the beginning, is now,
and will be for ever. Amen.

Ant. Now the Son of Man has been glorified and
God has been glorified in him, alleluia.

Reading: 1 Peter 3: 18, 21-22

The reason why Christ died for sins once for
all, the just man for the sake of the unjust,
was that he might lead us to God. He was
put to death insofar as fleshly existence goes,
but was given life in the realm of the spirit.
You are now saved by a baptismal bath which
corresponds to this exactly. This baptism is
no removal of physical stain, but the pledge to
God of an irreproachable conscience through
the resurrection of Jesus Christ. He went to
heaven and is at God's right hand, with angelic
rulers and powers subjected to him.

Responsory

℣. I am ascending to my Father and your Father,
alleluia, alleluia.
℟. I am ascending to my Father and your Father,
alleluia, alleluia.
℣. To my God and your God,
℟. alleluia, alleluia.
[Bow] ℣. Glory to the Father, and to the Son,
and to the Holy Spirit.

℟. I am ascending to my Father and your Father,
alleluia, alleluia.

Canticle Of Mary

Ant.
[STAND] O Victor King, Lord of power and might,
today you have ascended in glory above the
heavens. Do not leave us orphans, but send us
the Father's promised gift, the Spirit of truth,
alleluia.

Magnificat: Luke 1: 46-55
My soul ✠ proclaims the... [SEE PRAYER ON BACK
FLAP. THEN REPEAT THE ANTIPHON ABOVE.]

Intercessions

Introductory Formula
In joy of spirit let us acclaim Christ, who sits
at the right hand of the Father:
℟. Lord Jesus, you are the King of glory.

Petitions
℣. King of glory, you took with you our frail
humanity to be glorified in heaven; remove the
sins of the world,
℟. and restore us to the innocence which was
ours before the Fall.
℣. You came down from heaven on a pilgrimage
of love,
℟. grant that we may take the same path to
your presence.
℣. You promised to draw all things to yourself,
℟. do not allow anyone of us to be separated from
your body.
℣. Where you have gone before us in glory,
℟. may we follow you in mind and heart.
℣. True God, we await your coming as our judge,
℟. may we see the vision of your glory and your
mercy in company with all the dead.

The Lord's Prayer
Our Father... [SEE PRAYER ON BACK FLAP]

Prayer

God our Father,
make us joyful in the ascension of your Son
Jesus Christ.
May we follow him into the new creation,
for his ascension is our glory and our hope.
We ask this through our Lord Jesus Christ,
your Son,
who lives and reigns with you
and the Holy Spirit,
one God, for ever and ever. Amen.

Closing Rite Or Dismissal

[SEE CLOSING RITE ON BACK FLAP]

Introductory Rite

[STAND] ℣. God, ✠ come to my assistance.

   ℟. Lord, make haste to help me.

[BOW] Glory to the Father, and to the Son,
   and to the Holy Spirit:
   as it was in the beginning, is now,
   and will be for ever. Amen.

Hymn

   ✦ Christ Jesus lay in death's strong bands
    For our offenses given:
    But now at God's right hand he stands
    And brings us life from heaven;
    Therefore let us joyful be,
    And praise the Father thankfully
    With songs of Alleluia.
    Alleluia.

   ✦ How long and bitter was the strife
    When life and death contended,
    The victory remained with life,
    The reign of death was ended:
    Stripped of power, no more it reigns,
    And empty form alone remains.
    Death's sting is lost for ever.
    Alleluia.

   ✦ So let us keep this festival
    To which Our Lord invites us,
    The Savoir who is joy of all,
    The Sun that warms and lights us:
    By his grace he shall impart
    Eternal sunshine to the heart;
    The night of sin has ended.
    Alleluia.

    Translator: R. Massie, 1800-1887, adapted by Anthony G. Petti

Psalmody

Ant. 1 He purified us from our sins, and is seated on
   high at God's right hand, alleluia.

   Book 5: Psalm 110: 1-5, 7
   The Messiah, king and priest

[SIT] ✦ The Lord's revelation to my Master:
    "Sit on my right:
    your foes I will put beneath your feet."

   ✦ The Lord will wield from Zion
    your scepter of power:
    rule in the midst of all your foes.

   ✦ A prince from the day of your birth
    on the holy mountains;
    from the womb before the dawn I begot you.

   ✦ The Lord has sworn an oath he will not change.
    "You are a priest for ever,
    a priest like Melchizedek of old."

SEVENTH SUNDAY
of Easter
[PSALTER, WEEK III]

 ✦ The Master standing at your right hand
  will shatter kings in the day of his great wrath.

 ✦ He shall drink from the stream by the wayside
  and therefore he shall lift up his head.

[BOW] ✦ Glory to the Father, and to the Son,
  and to the Holy Spirit:
  as it was in the beginning, is now,
  and will be for ever. Amen.

 Psalm Prayer
 Father, we ask you to give us victory and
 peace. In Jesus Christ, our Lord and King, we
 are already seated at your right hand. We look
 forward to praising you in the fellowship of all
 your saints in our heavenly homeland.

Ant. He purified us from our sins, and is seated on
  high at God's right hand, alleluia.

Ant. 2 The Lord has redeemed his people, alleluia.

 Book 5: Psalm 111
 God's marvelous works

 ✦ I will thank the Lord with all my heart
  in the meeting of the just and their assembly.
  Great are the works of the Lord;
  to be pondered by all who love them.

 ✦ Majestic and glorious his work,
  his justice stands firm for ever.
  He makes us remember his wonders.
  The Lord is compassion and love.

 ✦ He gives food to those who fear him;
  keeps his covenant ever in mind.
  He has shown his might to his people
  by giving them the lands of the nations.

 ✦ His works are justice and truth:
  his precepts are all of them sure,
  standing firm for ever and ever:
  they are made in uprightness and truth.

 ✦ He has sent deliverance to his people
  and established his covenant for ever.
  Holy his name, to be feared.

 ✦ To fear the Lord is the first stage of wisdom;
  all who do so prove themselves wise.
  His praise shall last for ever!

[BOW] ✦ Glory to the Father…

Psalm Prayer

Merciful and gentle Lord, you are the crowning glory of all the saints. Give us, your children, the gift of obedience which is the beginning of wisdom, so that we may do what you command and be filled with your mercy.

Ant. The Lord has redeemed his people, alleluia.

Ant. 3 Alleluia, our Lord is king; let us rejoice and give glory to him, alleluia.

Canticle based on Revelation 19: 1-7
The wedding of the Lamb

✦ Alleluia.
Salvation, glory, and power to our God:
(℟ Alleluia.)
his judgments are honest and true.
℟ Alleluia (alleluia).

✦ Alleluia.
Sing praise to our God, all you his servants,
(℟ Alleluia.)
all who worship him reverently, great and small.
℟ Alleluia (alleluia).

✦ Alleluia.
The Lord our all-powerful God is King;
(℟ Alleluia.)
let us rejoice, sing praise, and give him glory.
℟ Alleluia (alleluia).

✦ Alleluia.
The wedding feast of the Lamb has begun,
(℟ Alleluia.)
and his bride is prepared to welcome him.
℟ Alleluia (alleluia).

[Bow] ✦ Glory to the Father…

Ant. Alleluia, our Lord is king; let us rejoice and give glory to him, alleluia.

Reading: Hebrews 10: 12-14

Jesus offered one sacrifice for sins and took his seat forever at the right hand of God; now he waits until his enemies are placed beneath his feet. By one offering he has forever perfected those who are being sanctified.

Responsory

℣ The Holy Spirit is the Paraclete, alleluia, alleluia.
℟ The Holy Spirit is the Paraclete, alleluia, alleluia.
℣ He will teach you all things,
℟ alleluia, alleluia.
[Bow] ℣ Glory to the Father, and to the Son, and to the Holy Spirit.

℟ The Holy Spirit is the Paraclete, alleluia, alleluia.

Canticle Of Mary

Ant.
[Stand] I will send you the Spirit of truth who comes from the Father. When the Paraclete comes he will bear witness to me, alleluia.

Magnificat: Luke 1: 46-55
My soul ✠ proclaims the… [See Prayer On Back Flap. Then Repeat The Antiphon Above.]

Intercessions

Introductory Formula
We do not know how to pray as we ought, but the Spirit himself prays for us with inexpressible longing. Let us then say:
℟ May the Holy Spirit pray on our behalf.

Petitions
℣ Lord Jesus, shepherd in glory, give wisdom and counsel to our shepherds,
℟ to lead your flock more surely to salvation.
℣ You are exalted in heaven, and are rich in mercy,
look with compassion on the poor and needy on earth.
℣ You were conceived by the Virgin Mary by the overshadowing of the Holy Spirit,
℟ sustain those vowed to virginity in the spirit of their self-offering.
℣ You are our priest, offering praise to the Father in the Holy Spirit,
℟ unite all mankind in your sacrifice of praise.
℣ May the dead enter into the glorious freedom of God's children,
℟ and the fullness of redemption for their bodies.

The Lord's Prayer
Our Father… [See prayer on back flap]

Prayer

Father,
help us keep in mind that Christ our Savior lives with you in glory
and promised to remain with us until the end of time.
We ask this through our Lord Jesus Christ, your Son,
who lives and reigns with you and the Holy Spirit,
one God, for ever and ever. Amen.

Closing Rite Or Dismissal

[See Closing Rite on Back Flap]

67

Introductory Rite

[Stand] V. God, ✠ come to my assistance.

R. Lord, make haste to help me.

[Bow] Glory to the Father…

Hymn

✦ Come, Holy Ghost, Creator, come
From thy bright heavenly throne,
Come, take possession of our souls
And make them all thy own.

✦ Thou who are called the Paraclete,
Best gift of God above,
The living spring, the living fire,
Sweet unction and true love.

✦ Thou who art sevenfold in thy grace,
Finger of God's right hand;
His promise, teaching little ones
To speak and understand.

✦ O guide our minds with thy blest light,
With love our hearts inflame;
And with thy strength, which ne'er decays,
Confirm our mortal frame.

✦ Far from us drive our deadly foe;
True peace unto us bring;
And from all perils lead us safe
Beneath thy sacred wing.

✦ Through thee may we the Father know,
Through thee th'eternal Son,
And thee the Spirit of them both,
Thrice-blessed Three in One.

[Bow] ✦ All glory to the Father be,
With his co-equal Son:
The same to thee, great Paraclete,
While endless ages run.

Text: Rabanus Maurus, 766-856. Translator: Anonymous

Psalmody

Ant. 1 The Spirit of the Lord has filled the whole world, alleluia.

Book 5: Psalm 110: 1-5, 7
The Messiah, king and priest

[Sit] ✦ The Lord's revelation to my Master:
"Sit on my right:
your foes I will put beneath your feet."

✦ The Lord will wield from Zion
your scepter of power:
rule in the midst of all your foes.

✦ A prince from the day of your birth
on the holy mountains;
from the womb before the dawn I begot you.

✦ The Lord has sworn an oath he will not change.
"You are a priest for ever,
a priest like Melchizedek of old."

✦ The Master standing at your right hand
will shatter kings in the day of his great wrath.

✦ He shall drink from the stream by the wayside
and therefore he shall lift up his head.

[Bow] ✦ Glory to the Father, and to the Son,
and to the Holy Spirit:
as it was in the beginning, is now and will be
for ever. Amen.

Ant. The Spirit of the Lord has filled the whole world, alleluia.

Ant. 2 Send us your strength, O God, from your holy temple in Jerusalem, and perfect your work in us, alleluia.

Book 2: Psalm 114
The Israelites are delivered from the bondage of Egypt

✦ When Israel came forth from Egypt,
Jacob's sons from an alien people,
Judah became the Lord's temple,
Israel became his kingdom.

✦ The sea fled at the sight:
the Jordan turned back on its course,
the mountains leapt like rams
and the hills like yearling sheep.

✦ Why was it, sea, that you fled,
that you turned back, Jordan, on your course?
Mountains, that you leapt like rams,
hills, like yearling sheep?

✦ Tremble, O earth, before the Lord,
in the presence of the God of Jacob,
who turns the rock into a pool
and flint into a spring of water.

[Bow] ✦ Glory to the Father…

Ant. Send us your strength, O God, from your holy temple in Jerusalem, and perfect your work in us, alleluia.

Ant. 3 All were filled with the Holy Spirit, and they began to speak, alleluia.

Canticle based on Revelation 19: 1-7
The wedding of the Lamb

+ Alleluia.
Salvation, glory, and power to our God:
(℞ Alleluia.)
his judgments are honest and true.
℞ Alleluia (alleluia).

+ Alleluia.
Sing praise to our God, all you his servants,
(℞ Alleluia.)
all who worship him reverently, great and small.
℞ Alleluia (alleluia).

+ Alleluia.
The Lord our all-powerful God is King;
(℞ Alleluia.)
let us rejoice, sing praise, and give him glory.
℞ Alleluia (alleluia).

+ Alleluia.
The wedding feast of the Lamb has begun,
(℞ Alleluia.)
and his bride is prepared to welcome him.
℞ Alleluia (alleluia).

[Bow] + Glory to the Father…

Ant. All were filled with the Holy Spirit, and they began to speak, alleluia.

Reading: Ephesians 4: 3-6
Make every effort to preserve the unity which has the Spirit as its origin and peace as its binding force. There is but one body and one Spirit, just as there is but one hope given all of you by your call. There is one Lord, one faith, one baptism; one God and Father of all, who is over all, and works through all, and is in all.

Responsory
℣ The Spirit of the Lord has filled the whole world, alleluia, alleluia.
℞ The Spirit of the Lord has filled the whole world, alleluia, alleluia.
℣ He sustains all creation and knows every word that is spoken,
℞ alleluia, alleluia.
[Bow] ℣ Glory to the Father, and to the Son, and to the Holy Spirit.
℞ The Spirit of the Lord has filled the whole world, alleluia, alleluia.

Canticle Of Mary
Ant.
[Stand] Today we celebrate the feast of Pentecost, alleluia; on this day the Holy Spirit appeared before the apostles in tongues of fire and gave them his spiritual gifts. He sent them out to preach to the whole world, and to proclaim that all who believe and are baptized shall be saved, alleluia.

Magnificat: Luke 1: 46-55
My soul ✠ proclaims the… [See Prayer On Back Flap. Then Repeat The Antiphon Above.]

Intercessions

Introductory Formula
God the Father has gathered his Church in unity through Christ. With joy in our hearts let us ask him:
℞ Send your Holy Spirit into the Church.

Petitions
℣ You desire the unity of all Christians through one baptism in the Spirit,
℞ make all who believe one in heart and soul.
℣ You desire the whole world to be filled with the Spirit,
℞ help all mankind to build a world of justice and peace.
℣ Lord God, Father of all mankind, you desire to gather together your scattered children in unity of faith,
℞ enlighten the world by the grace of the Holy Spirit.
℣ Through the Spirit you make all things new,
℞ heal the sick, comfort the distressed, give salvation to all.
℣ Through the Spirit you raised your Son from the dead,
℞ raise up the bodies of the dead into everlasting life.

The Lord's Prayer
Our Father… [See prayer on back flap]

Prayer

God our Father,
let the Spirit you sent on your Church
to begin the teaching of the gospel
continue to work in the world
through the hearts of all who believe.
We ask this through our Lord Jesus Christ,
  your Son,
who lives and reigns with you
  and the Holy Spirit,
one God, for ever and ever. Amen.

Closing Rite Or Dismissal
[See Closing Rite on Back Flap]

69

Introductory Rite

[Stand] V. God, ✠ come to my assistance.
R. Lord, make haste to help me.

[Bow] Glory to the Father, and to the Son,
and to the Holy Spirit:
as it was in the beginning, is now,
and will be for ever. Amen.

Hymn

+ Come, thou almighty King,
Help us thy name to sing;
Help us to praise:
Father, all glorious,
O'er all victorious,
Come, and reign over us,
Ancient of Days.

+ Come, thou incarnate Word,
Gird on thy mighty sword;
Our prayer attend;
Come, and thy people bless,
And give thy word success;
Spirit of holiness,
On us descend.

+ Come, holy Comforter,
Thy sacred witness bear
In this glad hour!
Thou who almighty art,
Now rule in ev'ry heart,
And ne'er from us depart,
Spirit of pow'r.

+ To the great One in Three,
Eternal praises be,
Hence evermore!
His sov'reign majesty
May we in glory see,
And to eternity
Love and adore.

Text: Anonymous, c. 1757

Psalmody

Ant. 1   O Trinity most high, eternal and true: Father,
Son and Holy Spirit.

Book 5: Psalm 110: 1-5, 7
The Messiah, king and priest

[Sit] + The Lord's revelation to my Master:
"Sit on my right:
your foes I will put beneath your feet."

+ The Lord will wield from Zion
your scepter of power:
rule in the midst of all your foes.

+ A prince from the day of your birth
on the holy mountains;
from the womb before the dawn I begot you.

TRINITY SUNDAY
after Pentecost

+ The Lord has sworn an oath he will not change.
"You are a priest for ever,
a priest like Melchizedek of old."

+ The Master standing at your right hand
will shatter kings in the day of his great wrath.

+ He shall drink from the stream by the wayside
and therefore he shall lift up his head.

[Bow] + Glory to the Father, and to the Son,
and to the Holy Spirit:
as it was in the beginning, is now and will be
for ever. Amen.

Ant.   O Trinity most high, eternal and true: Father,
Son and Holy Spirit.

Ant. 2   Save us, set us free and give us life, O blessed
Trinity.

Book 2: Psalm 114
The Israelites are delivered from the bondage of Egypt

+ When Israel came forth from Egypt,
Jacob's sons from an alien people,
Judah became the Lord's temple,
Israel became his kingdom.

+ The sea fled at the sight:
the Jordan turned back on its course,
the mountains leapt like rams
and the hills like yearling sheep.

+ Why was it, sea, that you fled,
that you turned back, Jordan, on your course?
Mountains, that you leapt like rams,
hills, like yearling sheep?

+ Tremble, O earth, before the Lord,
in the presence of the God of Jacob,
who turns the rock into a pool
and flint into a spring of water.

[Bow] + Glory to the Father…

Ant.   Save us, set us free and give us life, O blessed
Trinity.

Ant. 3   Holy, holy, holy Lord, God of power and might,
the God who is, who was, and who is to come.

Canticle based on Revelation 19: 1-7
The wedding of the Lamb

+ Alleluia.
Salvation, glory, and power to our God:

(℟ Alleluia.)
his judgments are honest and true.
℟ Alleluia (alleluia).

♦ Alleluia.
Sing praise to our God, all you his servants,
(℟ Alleluia.)
all who worship him reverently, great and
small.
℟ Alleluia (alleluia).

♦ Alleluia.
The Lord our all-powerful God is King;
(℟ Alleluia.)
let us rejoice, sing praise, and give him glory.
℟ Alleluia (alleluia).

♦ Alleluia.
The wedding feast of the Lamb has begun,
(℟ Alleluia.)
and his bride is prepared to welcome him.
℟ Alleluia (alleluia).

[Bow]   ♦ Glory to the Father…

Ant.   Holy, holy, holy Lord, God of power and
might, the God who is, who was, and who is to
come.

Reading: Ephesians 4: 3-6

Make every effort to preserve the unity which
has the Spirit as its origin and peace as its
binding force. There is but one body and one
Spirit, just as there is but one hope given all of
you by your call. There is one Lord, one faith,
one baptism; one God and Father of all, who
is over all, and works through all, and is in all.

Responsory

℣ Let us worship the Father, the Son and the
Holy Spirit; let us praise God for ever.
℟ Let us worship the Father, the Son and the
Holy Spirit; let us praise God for ever.
℣ To God alone be honor and glory;
℟ let us praise God for ever.
[Bow]   ℣ Glory to the Father, and to the Son,
and to the Holy Spirit.
℟ Let us worship the Father, the Son and the
Holy Spirit; let us praise God for ever.

Canticle Of Mary

Ant.   With our whole heart and voice we acclaim
[Stand] you, O God; we offer you our praise and
worship, unbegotten Father, only-begotten
Son, Holy Spirit, constant friend and guide;
most holy and undivided Trinity, to you be
glory for ever.

Magnificat: Luke 1: 46-55
My soul ✠ proclaims the… [See Prayer On Back
Flap. Then Repeat The Antiphon Above.]

Intercessions

Introductory Formula
The Father through the Holy Spirit has given
life to the humanity of Christ his Son, and has
made him a source of life for us; let us raise
our voices in praise to the triune God:
[Bow]   ℟ Glory to the Father, and to the Son and to the
Holy Spirit.

Petitions
℣ Father, almighty and eternal God, send the
Holy Spirit upon your Church in your
Son's name,
℟ preserve it in the unity of charity and in the
fullness of truth.
℣ Send laborers into your harvest, Lord, to teach
the truth to all nations, and to baptize them in
the name of the Father, and of the Son and of
the Holy Spirit
℟ and to confirm their faith.
℣ Father, send help to all who suffer persecution
in the name of your Son,
℟ for he promised to send the Spirit of Truth to
answer for them.
℣ Father omnipotent, may all men come to
acknowledge you, together with the Word and
the Holy Spirit, as the one true God,
℟ may they believe in you, hope in you, love you.
℣ Father of all the living, bring the dead to share
in your glory,
℟ the glory of your eternal reign with your Son
and the Holy Spirit.

The Lord's Prayer
Our Father… [See prayer on back flap]

Prayer

Father, you sent your Word to bring us truth
and your Spirit to make us holy.
Through them we come to know the mystery
of your life.
Help us to worship you, one God
in three Persons,
by proclaiming and living our faith in you.
Grant this through our Lord Jesus Christ,
your Son,
who lives and reigns with you
and the Holy Spirit,
one God, for ever and ever. Amen.

Closing Rite Or Dismissal
[See Closing Rite on Back Flap]

71

Introductory Rite

[STAND] V. God, ✠ come to my assistance.
R. Lord, make haste to help me.

[BOW] Glory to the Father, and to the Son,
and to the Holy Spirit:
as it was in the beginning, is now,
and will be for ever. Amen.

Hymn

◆ Father, we thank thee who hast planted
Thy holy Name within our hearts.
Knowledge and faith and life immortal
Jesus, thy Son, to us imparts.
Thou, Lord, didst make all for thy pleasure,
Didst give man food for all his days,
Giving in Christ the Bread eternal;
Thine is the power, be thine the praise.

◆ Watch o'er thy Church, O Lord, in mercy,
Save it from evil, guard it still;
Perfect it in thy love, unite it,
Cleansed and conformed unto thy will.
As grain, once scattered on the hill sides,
Was in this broken bread made one,
So from all lands thy Church be gathered
Into thy kingdom by thy Son.

Translator: F. Bland Tucker, 1941

Psalmody

Ant. 1 Christ the Lord is a priest for ever in the line of
Melchizedek; he offered up bread and wine.

Book 5: Psalm 110: 1-5, 7
The Messiah, king and priest

[SIT] ◆ The Lord's revelation to my Master:
"Sit on my right:
your foes I will put beneath your feet."

◆ The Lord will wield from Zion
your scepter of power:
rule in the midst of all your foes.

◆ A prince from the day of your birth
on the holy mountains;
from the womb before the dawn I begot you.

◆ The Lord has sworn an oath he will not change.
"You are a priest for ever,
a priest like Melchizedek of old."

◆ The Master standing at your right hand
will shatter kings in the day of his great wrath.

◆ He shall drink from the stream by the wayside
and therefore he shall lift up his head.

[BOW] ◆ Glory to the Father, and to the Son,
and to the Holy Spirit:

as it was in the beginning, is now and will be
for ever. Amen.

Ant. Christ the Lord is a priest for ever in the line
of Melchizedek; he offered up bread and wine.

Ant. 2 I will take up the cup of salvation, and I will
offer a sacrifice of praise.

Book 5: Psalm 116: 10-19
Thanksgiving in the Temple

◆ I trusted, even when I said:
"I am sorely afflicted,"
and when I said in my alarm:
"No man can be trusted."

◆ How can I repay the Lord
for his goodness to me?
The cup of salvation I will raise;
I will call on the Lord's name.

◆ My vows to the Lord I will fulfill
before all his people.
O precious in the eyes of the Lord
is the death of his faithful.

◆ Your servant, Lord, your servant am I;
you have loosened my bonds.
A thanksgiving sacrifice I make:
I will call on the Lord's name.

◆ My vows to the Lord I will fulfill
before all his people,
in the courts of the house of the Lord,
in your midst, O Jerusalem.

[BOW] ◆ Glory to the Father, and to the Son,
and to the Holy Spirit:
as it was in the beginning, is now and will be
for ever. Amen.

Ant. I will take up the cup of salvation, and I will
offer a sacrifice of praise.

Ant. 3 You are the way, the truth and the life of the
world, O Lord.

Canticle based on Revelation 19: 1-7
The wedding of the Lamb

◆ Alleluia.
Salvation, glory, and power to our God:
(R. Alleluia.)

his judgments are honest and true.
℟ Alleluia (alleluia).

✦ Alleluia.
Sing praise to our God, all you his servants,
(℟ Alleluia.)
all who worship him reverently, great and small.
℟ Alleluia (alleluia).

✦ Alleluia.
The Lord our all-powerful God is King;
(℟ Alleluia.)
let us rejoice, sing praise, and give him glory.
℟ Alleluia (alleluia).

✦ Alleluia.
The wedding feast of the Lamb has begun,
(℟ Alleluia.)
and his bride is prepared to welcome him.
℟ Alleluia (alleluia).

[Bow]   ✦ Glory to the Father…

Ant.   You are the way, the truth and the life of the
world, O Lord.

Reading: 1 Corinthians 11: 23-25

I received from the Lord what I handed on to
you, namely, that the Lord Jesus on the night in
which he was betrayed took bread, and after he
had given thanks, broke it and said, "This is my
body, which is for you. Do this in remembrance
of me." In the same way, after the supper,
he took the cup, saying, "This cup is the new
covenant in my blood. Do this, whenever you
drink it, in remembrance of me."

Responsory

℣ He gave them bread from heaven,
alleluia, alleluia.
℟ He gave them bread from heaven,
alleluia, alleluia.
℣ Man has eaten the bread of angels,
℟ alleluia, alleluia.
[Bow]   ℣ Glory to the Father, and to the Son,
and to the Holy Spirit.
℟ He gave them bread from heaven,
alleluia, alleluia.

Canticle Of Mary

Ant.   How holy this feast in which Christ is our
[Stand]   food; his passion is recalled; grace fills our
hearts; and we receive a pledge of the glory to
come, alleluia.

Magnificat: Luke 1: 46-55
My soul ✠ proclaims the… [See Prayer On Back Flap.
Then Repeat The Antiphon Above.]

Intercessions

Introductory Formula
Christ invites all to the supper in which he
gives his body and blood for the life of the
world. Let us ask him:
℟ Christ, the bread of heaven, grant us
everlasting life.

Petitions
℣ Christ, Son of the living God, you
commanded that this thanksgiving meal be
done in memory of you,
℟ enrich your Church through the faithful
celebration of these mysteries.
℣ Christ, eternal priest of the Most High,
you have commanded your priests to offer
your sacraments,
℟ may they help them to exemplify in their lives
the meaning of the sacred mysteries which
they celebrate.
℣ Christ, bread from heaven, you form one body
out of all who partake of the one bread,
℟ refresh all who believe in you with harmony
and peace.
℣ Christ, through your bread you offer the
remedy for immortality and the pledge of
future resurrection,
℟ restore health to the sick and living hope
to sinners.
℣ Christ, our king who is to come, you
commanded that
the mysteries which proclaim your death be
celebrated until you return,
℟ grant that all who die in you may share in
your resurrection.

The Lord's Prayer
Our Father… [See prayer on back flap]

Prayer

Lord Jesus Christ,
you gave us the eucharist
as the memorial of your suffering and death.
May our worship of this sacrament
of your body and blood
help us to experience the salvation you won
for us
and the peace of the kingdom
where you live with the Father
and the Holy Spirit,
one God, for ever and ever. Amen.

Closing Rite Or Dismissal

[See Closing Rite on Back Flap]

Introductory Rite

[STAND] V. God, ✠ come to my assistance.

R. Lord, make haste to help me.

[BOW] Glory to the Father, and to the Son,
and to the Holy Spirit:
as it was in the beginning, is now,
and will be for ever. Amen.

Hymn

◆ Love divine, all loves excelling,
Joy of heaven to earth come down,
And impart to us, here dwelling,
Grace and mercy all around.
Jesus, source of all compassion,
Pure, unbounded love you share;
Grant us many choicest blessings,
Keep us in your loving care.

◆ Come, O source of inspiration,
Pure and spotless let us be:
Let us see your true salvation,
Perfect in accord with thee.
Praising Father for all glory
With the Spirit and the Son;
Everlasting thanks we give thee,
Undivided, love, in one.

Text: C. Wesley, 1707-1788, adapted by C.T. Andrews 1968

Psalmody

Ant. 1 In eternal splendor, before the dawn of light on
earth, I have begotten you, alleluia.

Book 5: Psalm 110: 1-5, 7
The Messiah, king and priest

[SIT] ◆ The Lord's revelation to my Master:
"Sit on my right:
your foes I will put beneath your feet."

◆ The Lord will wield from Zion
your scepter of power:
rule in the midst of all your foes.

◆ A prince from the day of your birth
on the holy mountains;
from the womb before the dawn I begot you.

◆ The Lord has sworn an oath he will not change.
"You are a priest for ever,
a priest like Melchizedek of old."

◆ The Master standing at your right hand
will shatter kings in the day of his great wrath.

◆ He shall drink from the stream by the wayside
and therefore he shall lift up his head.

[BOW] ◆ Glory to the Father, and to the Son,
and to the Holy Spirit:

EIGHTH SUNDAY
in Ordinary Time
[PSALTER, WEEK IV]

as it was in the beginning, is now and will be
for ever. Amen.

Psalm Prayer
Father, we ask you to give us victory and
peace. In Jesus Christ, our Lord and King, we
are already seated at your right hand. We look
forward to praising you in the fellowship of all
your saints in our heavenly homeland.

Ant. In eternal splendor, before the dawn of light
on earth, I have begotten you, alleluia.

Ant. 2 Blessed are they who hunger and thirst for
holiness; they will be satisfied.

Book 5: Psalm 112
The happiness of the just man

◆ Happy the man who fears the Lord,
who takes delight in all his commands.
His sons will be powerful on earth;
the children of the upright are blessed.

◆ Riches and wealth are in his house;
his justice stands firm for ever.
He is a light in the darkness for the upright:
he is generous, merciful and just.

◆ The good man takes pity and lends,
he conducts his affairs with honor.
The just man will never waver:
he will be remembered for ever.

◆ He has no fear of evil news;
with a firm heart he trusts in the Lord.
With a steadfast heart he will not fear;
he will see the downfall of his foes.

◆ Open-handed, he gives to the poor;
his justice stands firm for ever.
His head will be raised in glory.

◆ The wicked man sees and is angry,
grinds his teeth and fades away;
the desire of the wicked leads to doom.

[BOW] ◆ Glory to the Father, and to the Son,
and to the Holy Spirit:
as it was in the beginning, is now and will be
for ever. Amen.

74

Psalm Prayer

Lord God, you are the eternal light which illumines the hearts of good people. Help us to love you, to rejoice in your glory, and so to live in this world as to avoid harsh judgment in the next. May we come to see the light of your countenance.

Ant. Blessed are they who hunger and thirst for holiness; they will be satisfied.

Ant. 3 Praise God, all you who serve him, both great and small, alleluia.

Canticle based on Revelation 19: 1-7
The wedding of the Lamb

✦ Alleluia.
Salvation, glory, and power to our God:
(℟ Alleluia.)
his judgments are honest and true.
℟ Alleluia (alleluia).

✦ Alleluia.
Sing praise to our God, all you his servants,
(℟ Alleluia.)
all who worship him reverently, great and small.
℟ Alleluia (alleluia).

✦ Alleluia.
The Lord our all-powerful God is King;
(℟ Alleluia.)
let us rejoice, sing praise, and give him glory.
℟ Alleluia (alleluia).

✦ Alleluia.
The wedding feast of the Lamb has begun,
(℟ Alleluia.)
and his bride is prepared to welcome him.
℟ Alleluia (alleluia).

[Bow] ✦ Glory to the Father…

Ant. Praise God, all you who serve him, both great and small, alleluia.

Reading: Hebrews 12: 22-24

You have drawn near to Mount Zion and the city of the living God, the heavenly Jerusalem, to myriads of angels in festal gathering, to the assembly of the first-born enrolled in heaven, to God the judge of all, to the spirits of just men made perfect, to Jesus, the mediator of a new covenant, and to the sprinkled blood which speaks more eloquently than that of Abel.

Responsory

℣ Our Lord is great, mighty is his power.
℟ Our Lord is great, mighty is his power.

℣ His wisdom is beyond compare,
℟ mighty is his power.

[Bow] ℣ Glory to the Father, and to the Son, and to the Holy Spirit.
℟ Our Lord is great, mighty is his power.

Canticle Of Mary

Ant. A good tree cannot bear bad fruit, nor a bad
[Stand] tree good fruit.

Magnificat: Luke 1: 46-55
My soul ✠ proclaims the… [See Prayer On Back Flap. Then Repeat The Antiphon Above.]

Intercessions

Introductory Formula
Rejoicing in the Lord, from whom all good things come, let us pray:
℟ Lord, hear our prayer.

Petitions
℣ Father and Lord of all, you sent your Son into the world, that your name might be glorified in every place,
℟ strengthen the witness of your Church among the nations.
℣ Make us obedient to the teachings of your apostles,
℟ and bound to the truth of our faith.
℣ As you love the innocent,
℟ render justice to those who are wronged.
℣ Free those in bondage and give sight to the blind,
℟ raise up the fallen and protect the stranger.
℣ Fulfill your promise to those who already sleep in your peace,
℟ through your Son grant them a blessed resurrection.

The Lord's Prayer
Our Father… [See prayer on back flap]

Prayer

Lord,
guide the course of world events
and give your Church the joy and peace
of serving you in freedom.
We ask this through our Lord Jesus Christ,
  your Son,
who lives and reigns with you
  and the Holy Spirit,
one God, for ever and ever. Amen.

Closing Rite Or Dismissal

[See Closing Rite on Back Flap]

75

Introductory Rite

[STAND] V. God, ✠ come to my assistance.
R. Lord, make haste to help me.

[BOW] Glory to the Father, and to the Son,
and to the Holy Spirit:
as it was in the beginning, is now,
and will be for ever. Amen.

Hymn

+ O Christ, you are the light and day
Which drives away the night,
The ever shining Sun of God
And pledge of future light.

+ As now the ev'ning shadows fall
Please grant us, Lord, we pray,
A quiet night to rest in you
Until the break of day.

+ Remember us, poor mortal men,
We humbly ask, O Lord,
And may your presence in our souls
Be now our great reward.
Translator: Rev. M. Quinn, O.P. et al.

Psalmody

Ant. 1 The Lord will stretch forth his mighty scepter
from Zion, and he will reign for ever, alleluia.

Book 5: Psalm 110: 1-5, 7
The Messiah, king and priest

[SIT] + The Lord's revelation to my Master:
"Sit on my right:
your foes I will put beneath your feet."

+ The Lord will wield from Zion
your scepter of power:
rule in the midst of all your foes.

+ A prince from the day of your birth
on the holy mountains;
from the womb before the dawn I begot you.

+ The Lord has sworn an oath he will not change.
"You are a priest for ever,
a priest like Melchizedek of old."

+ The Master standing at your right hand
will shatter kings in the day of his great wrath.

+ He shall drink from the stream by the wayside
and therefore he shall lift up his head.

[BOW] + Glory to the Father, and to the Son,
and to the Holy Spirit:
as it was in the beginning, is now and will be
for ever. Amen.

Psalm Prayer
Father, we ask you to give us victory and peace.
In Jesus Christ, our Lord and King, we are

76

NINTH SUNDAY
in Ordinary Time
[PSALTER, WEEK I]

already seated at your right hand. We look
forward to praising you in the fellowship of all
your saints in our heavenly homeland.

Ant. The Lord will stretch forth his mighty scepter
from Zion, and he will reign for ever, alleluia.

Ant. 2 The earth is shaken to its depths before the
glory of your face.

Book 2: Psalm 114
The Israelites are delivered from the bondage of Egypt

+ When Israel came forth from Egypt,
Jacob's sons from an alien people,
Judah became the Lord's temple,
Israel became his kingdom.

+ The sea fled at the sight:
the Jordan turned back on its course,
the mountains leapt like rams
and the hills like yearling sheep.

+ Why was it, sea, that you fled,
that you turned back, Jordan, on your course?
Mountains, that you leapt like rams,
hills, like yearling sheep?

+ Tremble, O earth, before the Lord,
in the presence of the God of Jacob,
who turns the rock into a pool
and flint into a spring of water.

[BOW] + Glory to the Father, and to the Son,
and to the Holy Spirit:
as it was in the beginning, is now and will be
for ever. Amen.

Psalm Prayer
Almighty God, ever-living mystery of unity
and trinity, you gave life to the new Israel by
birth from water and the Spirit, and made
it a chosen race, a royal priesthood, a people
set apart as your eternal possession. May all
those you have called to walk in the splendor
of the new light render you fitting service and
adoration.

Ant. The earth is shaken to its depths before the
glory of your face.

Ant. 3 All power is yours, Lord God, our mighty
King, alleluia.

Canticle based on Revelation 19: 1-7
The wedding of the Lamb

+ Alleluia.
Salvation, glory, and power to our God:
(℟ Alleluia.)
his judgments are honest and true.

℟ Alleluia (alleluia).

+ Alleluia.
Sing praise to our God, all you his servants,
(℟ Alleluia.)
all who worship him reverently, great and small.

℟ Alleluia (alleluia).

+ Alleluia.
The Lord our all-powerful God is King;
(℟ Alleluia.)
let us rejoice, sing praise, and give him glory.

℟ Alleluia (alleluia).

+ Alleluia.
The wedding feast of the Lamb has begun,
(℟ Alleluia.)
and his bride is prepared to welcome him.

℟ Alleluia (alleluia).

[Bow] + Glory to the Father, and to the Son,
and to the Holy Spirit:
as it was in the beginning, is now and will be
for ever. Amen.

Ant. All power is yours, Lord God, our mighty King,
alleluia.

Reading: 2 Corinthians 1: 3-7

Praised be God, the Father of our Lord Jesus
Christ, the Father of mercies and the God
of all consolation! He comforts us in all our
afflictions and thus enables us to comfort
those who are in trouble, with the same
consolation we have received from him. As we
have shared much in the suffering of Christ,
so through Christ do we share abundantly in
his consolation. If we are afflicted it is for your
encouragement and salvation, and when we are
consoled it is for your consolation, so that you
may endure patiently the same sufferings we
endure. Our hope for you is firm because we
know that just as you share in the sufferings, so
you will share in the consolation.

Responsory

℣ The whole creation proclaims the greatness
of your glory.

℟ The whole creation proclaims the greatness
of your glory.

℣ Eternal ages praise

℟ the greatness of your glory.

[Bow] ℣ Glory to the Father, and to the Son,
and to the Holy Spirit.

℟ The whole creation proclaims the greatness
of your glory.

Canticle Of Mary

Ant.
[Stand] Lord, I am not worthy to have you enter my
house; just say the word and my servant will
be healed.

Magnificat: Luke 1: 46-55
My soul ✠ proclaims the... [See Prayer On Back
Flap. Then Repeat The Antiphon Above.]

Intercessions

Introductory Formula
Christ the Lord is our head; we are his
members. In joy let us call out to him:

℟ Lord, may your kingdom come.

Petitions
℣ Christ our Savior, make your Church a more
vivid symbol of the unity of all mankind,

℟ make it more effectively the sacrament of
salvation for all peoples.

℣ Through your presence, guide the college of
bishops in union with the Pope,

℟ give them the gifts of unity, love and peace.

℣ Bind all Christians more closely to yourself,
their divine Head,

℟ lead them to proclaim your kingdom by the
witness of their lives.

℣ Grant peace to the world,

℟ let every land flourish in justice and security.

℣ Grant to the dead the glory of resurrection,

℟ and give us a share in their happiness.

The Lord's Prayer
Our Father... [See prayer on back flap]

Prayer

Father,
your love never fails.
Hear our call.
Keep us from danger
and provide for all our needs.
Grant this through our Lord Jesus Christ,
your Son,
who lives and reigns with you
and the Holy Spirit,
one God, for ever and ever. Amen.

Closing Rite Or Dismissal
[See Closing Rite on Back Flap]

Introductory Rite

[See Introductory Rite on Front Flap]

Hymn

♦ Love divine, all loves excelling,
Joy of heaven to earth come down,
And impart to us, here dwelling,
Grace and mercy all around.
Jesus, source of all compassion,
Pure, unbounded love you share;
Grant us many choicest blessings,
Keep us in your loving care.

♦ Come, O source of inspiration,
Pure and spotless let us be:
Let us see your true salvation,
Perfect in accord with thee.
Praising Father for all glory
With the Spirit and the Son;
Everlasting thanks we give thee,
Undivided, love, in one.

Text: C. Wesley, 1707-1788, adapted by C.T. Andrews 1968

Psalmody

Ant. 1 Christ our Lord is a priest for ever, like
Melchizedek of old, alleluia.

Book 5: Psalm 110: 1-5, 7
The Messiah, king and priest

[Sit]
♦ The Lord's revelation to my Master:
"Sit on my right:
your foes I will put beneath your feet."

♦ The Lord will wield from Zion
your scepter of power:
rule in the midst of all your foes.

♦ A prince from the day of your birth
on the holy mountains;
from the womb before the dawn I begot you.

♦ The Lord has sworn an oath he will not change.
"You are a priest for ever,
a priest like Melchizedek of old."

♦ The Master standing at your right hand
will shatter kings in the day of his great wrath.

♦ He shall drink from the stream by the wayside
and therefore he shall lift up his head.

[Bow] ♦ Glory to the Father…

Psalm Prayer
Almighty God, bring the kingdom of Christ,
your anointed one, to its fullness. May the
perfect offering of your Son, eternal priest of
the new Jerusalem, be offered in every place to
your name, and make all nations a holy people
for you.

TENTH SUNDAY
in Ordinary Time

Ant. Christ our Lord is a priest for ever, like
Melchizedek of old, alleluia.

Ant. 2 God dwells in highest heaven; he has power to
do all he wills, alleluia.

Book 5: Psalm 115
Praise of the true God

♦ Not to us, Lord, not to us,
but to your name give the glory
for the sake of your love and your truth,
lest the heathen say: "Where is their God?"

♦ But our God is in the heavens;
he does whatever he wills.
Their idols are silver and gold,
the work of human hands.

♦ They have mouths but they cannot speak;
they have eyes but they cannot see;
they have ears but they cannot hear;
they have nostrils but they cannot smell.

♦ With their hands they cannot feel;
with their feet they cannot walk.
No sound comes from their throats.
Their makers will come to be like them
and so will all who trust in them.

♦ Sons of Israel, trust in the Lord;
he is their help and their shield.
Sons of Aaron, trust in the Lord;
he is their help and their shield.

♦ You who fear him, trust in the Lord;
he is their help and their shield.
He remembers us, and he will bless us;
he will bless the sons of Israel.
He will bless the sons of Aaron.

♦ The Lord will bless those who fear him,
the little no less than the great:
to you may the Lord grant increase,
to you and all your children.

♦ May you be blessed by the Lord,
the maker of heaven and earth.
The heavens belong to the Lord
but the earth he has given to men.

♦ The dead shall not praise the Lord,
nor those who go down into the silence.

But we who live bless the Lord
now and for ever. Amen.

[Bow]   ✦ Glory to the Father…

Psalm Prayer
Father, creator… [See psalm prayer on front flap]

Ant.   God dwells in highest heaven; he has power to
do all he wills, alleluia.

Ant.   Praise God, all you who serve him, both great
and small, alleluia.

Canticle based on Revelation 19: 1-7
The wedding of the Lamb
✦ Alleluia.
Salvation, glory, and power to our God:
(℟ Alleluia.)
his judgments are honest and true.
℟ Alleluia (alleluia).

✦ Alleluia.
Sing praise to our God, all you his servants,
(℟ Alleluia.)
all who worship him reverently, great and small.
℟ Alleluia (alleluia).

✦ Alleluia.
The Lord our all-powerful God is King;
(℟ Alleluia.)
let us rejoice, sing praise, and give him glory.
℟ Alleluia (alleluia).

✦ Alleluia.
The wedding feast of the Lamb has begun,
(℟ Alleluia.)
and his bride is prepared to welcome him.
℟ Alleluia (alleluia).

[Bow]   ✦ Glory to the Father…

Ant.   Praise God, all you who serve him, both great
and small, alleluia.

Reading: 2 Thessalonians 2: 13-14

We are bound to thank God for you always,
beloved brothers in the Lord, because you are
the first fruits of those whom God has chosen
for salvation, in holiness of spirit and fidelity
to truth. He called you through our preaching
of the good news so that you might achieve the
glory of our Lord Jesus Christ.

Responsory

℣ Our Lord is great, mighty is his power.
℟ Our Lord is great, mighty is his power.
℣ His wisdom is beyond compare,
℟ mighty is his power.

[Bow]   ℣ Glory to the Father, and to the Son,
and to the Holy Spirit.
℟ Our Lord is great, mighty is his power.

Canticle Of Mary

Ant.   A great prophet has risen up among us and
[Stand]   God has visited his people.

Magnificat: Luke 1: 46-55
My soul ✠ proclaims the… [See Prayer On Back
Flap. Then Repeat The Antiphon Above.]

Intercessions

Introductory Formula
All praise and honor to Christ! He lives for
ever to intercede for us, and he is able to save
those who approach the Father in his name.
Sustained by our faith, let us call upon him:
℟ Remember your people, Lord.

Petitions
℣ As the day draws to a close, Sun of Justice, we
invoke your name upon the whole human race,
℟ so that all men may enjoy your never
failing light.
℣ Preserve the covenant which you have ratified
in your blood,
℟ cleanse and sanctify your Church.
℣ Remember your assembly, Lord,
℟ your dwelling place.
℣ Guide travelers along the path of peace
and prosperity,
℟ so that they may reach their destinations
in safety and joy.
℣ Receive the souls of the dead, Lord,
℟ grant them your favor and the gift of
eternal glory.

The Lord's Prayer
Our Father… [See prayer on back flap]

Prayer

God of wisdom and love,
source of all good,
send your Spirit to teach us your truth
and guide our actions
in your way of peace.
We ask this through our Lord Jesus Christ,
your Son,
who lives and reigns with you
and the Holy Spirit,
one God, for ever and ever. Amen.

Closing Rite Or Dismissal

[See Closing Rite on Back Flap]

79

Introductory Rite

[STAND] V. God, ✠ come to my assistance.

R. Lord, make haste to help me.

[BOW] Glory to the Father, and to the Son,
and to the Holy Spirit:
as it was in the beginning, is now,
and will be for ever. Amen.

Hymn

+ O Christ, you are the light and day
Which drives away the night,
The ever shining Sun of God
And pledge of future light.

+ As now the ev'ning shadows fall
Please grant us, Lord, we pray,
A quiet night to rest in you
Until the break of day.

+ Remember us, poor mortal men,
We humbly ask, O Lord,
And may your presence in our souls
Be now our great reward.
Translator: Rev. M. Quinn, O.P. et al.

Psalmody

Ant. 1 The Lord said to my Master: Sit at my right
hand, alleluia.

Book 5: Psalm 110: 1-5, 7
The Messiah, king and priest

[SIT] + The Lord's revelation to my Master:
"Sit on my right:
your foes I will put beneath your feet."

+ The Lord will wield from Zion
your scepter of power:
rule in the midst of all your foes.

+ A prince from the day of your birth
on the holy mountains;
from the womb before the dawn I begot you.

+ The Lord has sworn an oath he will not change.
"You are a priest for ever,
a priest like Melchizedek of old."

+ The Master standing at your right hand
will shatter kings in the day of his great wrath.

+ He shall drink from the stream by the wayside
and therefore he shall lift up his head.

[BOW] + Glory to the Father…

Psalm Prayer
Father, we ask you to give us victory and peace.
In Jesus Christ, our Lord and King, we are
already seated at your right hand. We look

ELEVENTH SUNDAY
in Ordinary Time
[PSALTER, WEEK III]

forward to praising you in the fellowship of all
your saints in our heavenly homeland.

Ant. The Lord said to my Master: Sit at my right
hand, alleluia.

Ant. 2 Our compassionate Lord has left us a
memorial of his wonderful work, alleluia.

Book 5: Psalm 111
God's marvelous works

+ I will thank the Lord with all my heart
in the meeting of the just and their assembly.
Great are the works of the Lord;
to be pondered by all who love them.

+ Majestic and glorious his work,
his justice stands firm for ever.
He makes us remember his wonders.
The Lord is compassion and love.

+ He gives food to those who fear him;
keeps his covenant ever in mind.
He has shown his might to his people
by giving them the lands of the nations.

+ His works are justice and truth:
his precepts are all of them sure,
standing firm for ever and ever:
they are made in uprightness and truth.

+ He has sent deliverance to his people
and established his covenant for ever.
Holy his name, to be feared.

+ To fear the Lord is the first stage of wisdom;
all who do so prove themselves wise.
His praise shall last for ever!

[BOW] + Glory to the Father…

Psalm Prayer
Merciful and gentle Lord, you are the
crowning glory of all the saints. Give us, your
children, the gift of obedience which is the
beginning of wisdom, so that we may do what
you command and be filled with your mercy.

Ant. Our compassionate Lord has left us a
memorial of his wonderful work, alleluia.

Ant. 3 All power is yours, Lord God, our mighty
King, alleluia.

Canticle based on Revelation 19: 1-7

The wedding of the Lamb

✛ Alleluia.
Salvation, glory, and power to our God:
(℟ Alleluia.)
his judgments are honest and true.
℟ Alleluia (alleluia).

✛ Alleluia.
Sing praise to our God, all you his servants,
(℟ Alleluia.)
all who worship him reverently, great and small.
℟ Alleluia (alleluia).

✛ Alleluia.
The Lord our all-powerful God is King;
(℟ Alleluia.)
let us rejoice, sing praise, and give him glory.
℟ Alleluia (alleluia).

✛ Alleluia.
The wedding feast of the Lamb has begun,
(℟ Alleluia.)
and his bride is prepared to welcome him.
℟ Alleluia (alleluia).

[Bow] ✛ Glory to the Father…

Ant. All power is yours, Lord God, our mighty
King, alleluia.

Reading: 1 Peter 1: 3-7

Praised be the God and Father /of our Lord
Jesus Christ, /he who in his great mercy /gave
us new birth; /a birth unto hope which draws
its life /from the resurrection of Jesus Christ
from the dead; /a birth to an imperishable
inheritance, /incapable of fading or defilement,
/which is kept in heaven for you /who are
guarded with God's power through faith; /a
birth to a salvation which stands ready /to be
revealed in the last days.

There is cause for rejoicing here. You may for
a time have to suffer the distress of many trials;
but this is so that your faith, which is more
precious than the passing splendor of fire-tried
gold, may by its genuineness lead to praise,
glory, and honor when Jesus Christ appears.

Responsory

℣ The whole creation proclaims the greatness
of your glory.
℟ The whole creation proclaims the greatness
of your glory.
℣ Eternal ages praise
℟ the greatness of your glory.

[Bow] ℣ Glory to the Father, and to the Son,
and to the Holy Spirit.
℟ The whole creation proclaims the greatness
of your glory.

Canticle Of Mary

Ant. Jesus said to the woman: Your faith has saved
[Stand] you, go in peace.

Magnificat: Luke 1: 46-55
My soul ✛ proclaims the… [See Prayer On Back
Flap. Then Repeat The Antiphon Above.]

Intercessions

Introductory Formula
The world was created by the Word of
God, re-created by his redemption, and it is
continually renewed by his love. Rejoicing in
him we call out:
℟ Renew the wonders of your love, Lord.

Petitions
℣ We give thanks to God whose power is
revealed in nature,
℟ and whose providence is revealed in history.
℣ Through your Son, the herald of
reconciliation, the victor of the cross,
℟ free us from empty fear and hopelessness.
℣ May all those who love and pursue justice,
℟ work together without deceit to build a world
of true peace.
℣ Be with the oppressed, free the captives,
console the sorrowing, feed the hungry,
strengthen the weak,
℟ in all people reveal the victory of your cross.
℣ After your Son's death and burial you raised
him up again in glory,
℟ grant that the faithful departed may live
with him.

The Lord's Prayer
Our Father… [See prayer on back flap]

Prayer

Almighty God,
our hope and our strength,
without you we falter.
Help us to follow Christ
and to live according to your will.
We ask this through our Lord Jesus Christ,
your Son,
who lives and reigns with you
and the Holy Spirit,
one God, for ever and ever. Amen.

Closing Rite Or Dismissal

[See Closing Rite on Back Flap]

Introductory Rite

[STAND] V. God, ✠ come to my assistance.
R. Lord, make haste to help me.

[BOW] Glory to the Father, and to the Son,
and to the Holy Spirit:
as it was in the beginning, is now,
and will be for ever. Amen.

Hymn

＋ Love divine, all loves excelling,
Joy of heaven to earth come down,
And impart to us, here dwelling,
Grace and mercy all around.
Jesus, source of all compassion,
Pure, unbounded love you share;
Grant us many choicest blessings,
Keep us in your loving care.

＋ Come, O source of inspiration,
Pure and spotless let us be:
Let us see your true salvation,
Perfect in accord with thee.
Praising Father for all glory
With the Spirit and the Son;
Everlasting thanks we give thee,
Undivided, love, in one.

Text: C. Wesley, 1707-1788, adapted by C.T. Andrews 1968

Psalmody

Ant. 1 In eternal splendor, before the dawn of light on earth, I have begotten you, alleluia.

Book 5: Psalm 110: 1-5, 7
The Messiah, king and priest

[SIT] ＋ The Lord's revelation to my Master:
"Sit on my right:
your foes I will put beneath your feet."

＋ The Lord will wield from Zion
your scepter of power:
rule in the midst of all your foes.

＋ A prince from the day of your birth
on the holy mountains;
from the womb before the dawn I begot you.

＋ The Lord has sworn an oath he will not change.
"You are a priest for ever,
a priest like Melchizedek of old."

＋ The Master standing at your right hand
will shatter kings in the day of his great wrath.

＋ He shall drink from the stream by the wayside
and therefore he shall lift up his head.

[BOW] ＋ Glory to the Father, and to the Son,
and to the Holy Spirit:

as it was in the beginning, is now and will be
for ever. Amen.

Psalm Prayer
Father, we ask you to give us victory and
peace. In Jesus Christ, our Lord and King, we
are already seated at your right hand. We look
forward to praising you in the fellowship of all
your saints in our heavenly homeland.

Ant. In eternal splendor, before the dawn of light
on earth, I have begotten you, alleluia.

Ant. 2 Blessed are they who hunger and thirst for
holiness; they will be satisfied.

Book 5: Psalm 112
The happiness of the just man

＋ Happy the man who fears the Lord,
who takes delight in all his commands.
His sons will be powerful on earth;
the children of the upright are blessed.

＋ Riches and wealth are in his house;
his justice stands firm for ever.
He is a light in the darkness for the upright:
he is generous, merciful and just.

＋ The good man takes pity and lends,
he conducts his affairs with honor.
The just man will never waver:
he will be remembered for ever.

＋ He has no fear of evil news;
with a firm heart he trusts in the Lord.
With a steadfast heart he will not fear;
he will see the downfall of his foes.

＋ Open-handed, he gives to the poor;
his justice stands firm for ever.
His head will be raised in glory.

＋ The wicked man sees and is angry,
grinds his teeth and fades away;
the desire of the wicked leads to doom.

[BOW] ＋ Glory to the Father, and to the Son,
and to the Holy Spirit:
as it was in the beginning, is now and will be
for ever. Amen.

Psalm Prayer

Lord God, you are the eternal light which illumines the hearts of good people. Help us to love you, to rejoice in your glory, and so to live in this world as to avoid harsh judgment in the next. May we come to see the light of your countenance.

Ant. Blessed are they who hunger and thirst for holiness; they will be satisfied.

Ant. 3 Praise God, all you who serve him, both great and small, alleluia.

Canticle based on Revelation 19: 1-7
The wedding of the Lamb

✦ Alleluia.
Salvation, glory, and power to our God:
(℟ Alleluia.)
his judgments are honest and true.
℟ Alleluia (alleluia).

✦ Alleluia.
Sing praise to our God, all you his servants,
(℟ Alleluia.)
all who worship him reverently, great and small.
℟ Alleluia (alleluia).

✦ Alleluia.
The Lord our all-powerful God is King;
(℟ Alleluia.)
let us rejoice, sing praise, and give him glory.
℟ Alleluia (alleluia).

✦ Alleluia.
The wedding feast of the Lamb has begun,
(℟ Alleluia.)
and his bride is prepared to welcome him.
℟ Alleluia (alleluia).

[Bow] ✦ Glory to the Father…

Ant. Praise God, all you who serve him, both great and small, alleluia.

Reading: Hebrews 12: 22-24

You have drawn near to Mount Zion and the city of the living God, the heavenly Jerusalem, to myriads of angels in festal gathering, to the assembly of the first-born enrolled in heaven, to God the judge of all, to the spirits of just men made perfect, to Jesus, the mediator of a new covenant, and to the sprinkled blood which speaks more eloquently than that of Abel.

Responsory

℣ Our Lord is great, mighty is his power.
℟ Our Lord is great, mighty is his power.
℣ His wisdom is beyond compare,
℟ mighty is his power.
[Bow] ℣ Glory to the Father, and to the Son, and to the Holy Spirit.
℟ Our Lord is great, mighty is his power.

Canticle Of Mary

Ant.
[Stand] Whoever wishes to come after me must deny himself, take up his cross and follow me.

Magnificat: Luke 1: 46-55
My soul ✠ proclaims the… [See Prayer On Back Flap. Then Repeat The Antiphon Above.]

Intercessions

Introductory Formula
Rejoicing in the Lord, from whom all good things come, let us pray:
℟ Lord, hear our prayer.

Petitions
℣ Father and Lord of all, you sent your Son into the world, that your name might be glorified in every place,
℟ strengthen the witness of your Church among the nations.
℣ Make us obedient to the teachings of your apostles,
℟ and bound to the truth of our faith.
℣ As you love the innocent,
℟ render justice to those who are wronged.
℣ Free those in bondage and give sight to the blind,
℟ raise up the fallen and protect the stranger.
℣ Fulfill your promise to those who already sleep in your peace,
℟ through your Son grant them a blessed resurrection.

The Lord's Prayer
Our Father… [See prayer on back flap]

Prayer

Father,
guide and protector of your people,
grant us an unfailing respect for your name,
and keep us always in your love.
Grant this through our Lord Jesus Christ,
    your Son,
who lives and reigns with you
    and the Holy Spirit,
one God, for ever and ever. Amen.

Closing Rite Or Dismissal

[See Closing Rite on Back Flap]

Introductory Rite

[Stand] V. God, ✠ come to my assistance.
 R. Lord, make haste to help me.

[Bow] Glory to the Father, and to the Son,
and to the Holy Spirit:
as it was in the beginning, is now,
and will be for ever. Amen.

Hymn

+ The great forerunner of the morn,
The herald of the Word, is born;
And faithful hearts shall never fail
With thanks and praise his light to hail.

+ With heavenly message Gabriel came,
That John should be that herald's name,
And with prophetic utterance told
His actions great and manifold.

+ John, still unborn, yet gave aright
His witness to the coming light;
And Christ, the sun of all the earth,
Fulfilled that witness at his birth.

+ Of woman-born shall never be
A greater prophet than was he,
Whose mighty deeds exalt his fame
To greater than a prophet's name.

[Bow] + All praise to God the Father be,
All praise, eternal Son, to thee,
Whom with the Spirit we adore
For ever and for evermore.

Translator: J.M. Neale 1818-1866

Psalmody

Ant. 1 There was a man sent by God whose name
was John.

Book 1: Psalm 15
Who is worthy to stand in God's presence?

[Sit] + Lord, who shall be admitted to your tent
and dwell on your holy mountain?

+ He who walks without fault;
he who acts with justice
and speaks the truth from his heart;
he who does not slander with his tongue;

+ he who does no wrong to his brother,
who casts no slur on his neighbor,
who holds the godless in disdain,
but honors those who fear the Lord;

+ he who keeps his pledge, come what may;
who takes no interest on a loan
and accepts no bribes against the innocent.
Such a man will stand firm for ever.

[Bow] + Glory to the Father, and to the Son,
and to the Holy Spirit:
as it was in the beginning, is now,
and will be for ever. Amen.

Ant. There was a man sent by God whose name
was John.

Ant. 2 He came to bear witness to the truth.

Book 5: Psalm 112
The happiness of the just man

+ Happy the man who fears the Lord,
who takes delight in all his commands.
His sons will be powerful on earth;
the children of the upright are blessed.

+ Riches and wealth are in his house;
his justice stands firm for ever.
He is a light in the darkness for the upright:
he is generous, merciful and just.

+ The good man takes pity and lends,
he conducts his affairs with honor.
The just man will never waver:
he will be remembered for ever.

+ He has no fear of evil news;
with a firm heart he trusts in the Lord.
With a steadfast heart he will not fear;
he will see the downfall of his foes.

+ Open-handed, he gives to the poor;
his justice stands firm for ever.
His head will be raised in glory.

+ The wicked man sees and is angry,
grinds his teeth and fades away;
the desire of the wicked leads to doom.

[Bow] + Glory to the Father, and to the Son,
and to the Holy Spirit:
as it was in the beginning, is now,
and will be for ever. Amen.

Ant. He came to bear witness to the truth.

Ant. 3 John was like a brilliantly shining light.

Canticle: Revelation 15: 3-4
+ Mighty and wonderful are your works,
Lord God Almighty!

Righteous and true are your ways,
O King of the nations!

✦ Who would dare refuse you honor,
or the glory due your name, O Lord?

✦ Since you alone are holy,
all nations shall come
and worship in your presence.
Your mighty deeds are clearly seen.

[Bow] ✦ Glory to the Father, and to the Son,
and to the Holy Spirit:
as it was in the beginning, is now,
and will be for ever. Amen.

Ant. John was like a brilliantly shining light.

Reading: Acts 13: 23-25

According to his promise, God has brought
forth from David's descendants Jesus, a savior
for Israel. John heralded the coming of Jesus
by proclaiming a baptism of repentance to
all the people of Israel. As John's career was
coming to an end, he would say, "What you
suppose me to be I am not. Rather, look for
the one who comes after me. I am not worthy
to unfasten the sandals on his feet."

Responsory

℣ Prepare the way of the Lord; make straight
his paths.
℟ Prepare the way of the Lord; make straight
his paths.
℣ He who is to come after me existed before me.
℟ Make straight his paths.
[Bow] ℣ Glory to the Father, and to the Son,
and to the Holy Spirit.
℟ Prepare the way of the Lord; make straight
his paths.

Canticle Of Mary

Ant. This child, born to us, is greater than any
[Stand] prophet; the Savior said of him: There is no
man born of women greater than John
the Baptist.

Magnificat: Luke 1: 46-55
My soul ✠ proclaims the... [See Prayer On Back
Flap. Then Repeat The Antiphon Above.]

Intercessions

Introductory Formula
Let us pray joyfully to God our Father who
called John the Baptist to proclaim the coming
of the kingdom of Christ:
℟ O Lord, guide our feet into the way of peace.

Petitions
℣ You called John the Baptist from his mother's
womb to prepare the way of your Son,
℟ help us to follow in that path which the
Baptist opened before the Lord Jesus.
℣ May your Church, in imitation of the Baptist,
fearlessly point out the Lamb of God,
℟ so that people in every age may acknowledge
that the Lord comes to them.
℣ John the Baptist did not exalt himself but
acknowledged his role as forerunner of
the Christ,
℟ teach us to acknowledge that you are the giver
of all our good gifts and that we must use
them in your service.
℣ You called John the Baptist to give testimony
to you by his life and even by his death,
℟ help us to imitate his unceasing witness to
your truth.
℣ Remember those who have died,
℟ give them a place of light, happiness and peace.

The Lord's Prayer
Our Father... [See prayer on back flap]

Prayer

God our Father,
you raised up John the Baptist
to prepare a perfect people
for Christ the Lord.
Give your Church joy in spirit
and guide those who believe in you
into the way of salvation and peace.
We ask this through our Lord Jesus Christ,
your Son,
who lives and reigns with you
and the Holy Spirit,
one God, for ever and ever. Amen.

Closing Rite Or Dismissal

[When Priest Or Deacon Presides]
℣ The Lord be with you.
℟ And also with you.
[Bow] May almighty God bless you, ✠ the Father,
and the Son, and the Holy Spirit.
℟ Amen.
℣ Go in peace.
℟ Thanks be to God.

[When Priest Or Deacon Do Not Preside, And In Individual Recitation]
✠ May the Lord bless us, protect us from all
evil and bring us to everlasting life.
℟ Amen.

Introductory Rite

[Stand] V. God, ✠ come to my assistance.

R. Lord, make haste to help me.

[Bow] Glory to the Father, and to the Son,
and to the Holy Spirit:
as it was in the beginning, is now,
and will be for ever. Amen.

Hymn

✦ O Christ, you are the light and day
Which drives away the night,
The ever shining Sun of God
And pledge of future light.

✦ As now the ev'ning shadows fall
Please grant us, Lord, we pray,
A quiet night to rest in you
Until the break of day.

✦ Remember us, poor mortal men,
We humbly ask, O Lord,
And may your presence in our souls
Be now our great reward.

Translator: Rev. M. Quinn, O.P. et al.

Psalmody

Ant. 1   The Lord will stretch forth his mighty scepter
from Zion, and he will reign for ever, alleluia.

Book 5: Psalm 110: 1-5, 7
The Messiah, king and priest

[Sit] ✦ The Lord's revelation to my Master:
"Sit on my right:
your foes I will put beneath your feet."

✦ The Lord will wield from Zion
your scepter of power:
rule in the midst of all your foes.

✦ A prince from the day of your birth
on the holy mountains;
from the womb before the dawn I begot you.

✦ The Lord has sworn an oath he will not change.
"You are a priest for ever,
a priest like Melchizedek of old."

✦ The Master standing at your right hand
will shatter kings in the day of his great wrath.

✦ He shall drink from the stream by the wayside
and therefore he shall lift up his head.

[Bow] ✦ Glory to the Father, and to the Son,
and to the Holy Spirit:
as it was in the beginning, is now,
and will be for ever. Amen.

THIRTEENTH SUNDAY in Ordinary Time

[Psalter, Week I]

Psalm Prayer
Father, we ask you to give us victory and peace. In Jesus Christ, our Lord and King, we are already seated at your right hand. We look forward to praising you in the fellowship of all your saints in our heavenly homeland.

Ant.   The Lord will stretch forth his mighty scepter from Zion, and he will reign for ever, alleluia.

Ant. 2   The earth is shaken to its depths before the glory of your face.

Book 2: Psalm 114
The Israelites are delivered from the bondage of Egypt

✦ When Israel came forth from Egypt,
Jacob's sons from an alien people,
Judah became the Lord's temple,
Israel became his kingdom.

✦ The sea fled at the sight:
the Jordan turned back on its course,
the mountains leapt like rams
and the hills like yearling sheep.

✦ Why was it, sea, that you fled,
that you turned back, Jordan, on your course?
Mountains, that you leapt like rams,
hills, like yearling sheep?

✦ Tremble, O earth, before the Lord,
in the presence of the God of Jacob,
who turns the rock into a pool
and flint into a spring of water.

[Bow] ✦ Glory to the Father, and to the Son,
and to the Holy Spirit:
as it was in the beginning, is now,
and will be for ever. Amen.

Psalm Prayer
Almighty God, ever-living mystery of unity and trinity, you gave life to the new Israel by birth from water and the Spirit, and made it a chosen race, a royal priesthood, a people set apart as your eternal possession. May all those you have called to walk in the splendor of the new light render you fitting service and adoration.

Ant.   The earth is shaken to its depths before the glory of your face.

Ant. 3   All power is yours, Lord God, our mighty
King, alleluia.

Canticle based on Revelation 19: 1-7
The wedding of the Lamb

✦ Alleluia.
Salvation, glory, and power to our God:
(℟ Alleluia.)
his judgments are honest and true.
℟ Alleluia (alleluia).

✦ Alleluia.
Sing praise to our God, all you his servants,
(℟ Alleluia.)
all who worship him reverently, great and small.
℟ Alleluia (alleluia).

✦ Alleluia.
The Lord our all-powerful God is King;
(℟ Alleluia.)
let us rejoice, sing praise, and give him glory.
℟ Alleluia (alleluia).

✦ Alleluia.
The wedding feast of the Lamb has begun,
(℟ Alleluia.)
and his bride is prepared to welcome him.
℟ Alleluia (alleluia).

[Bow]   ✦ Glory to the Father…

Ant.   All power is yours, Lord God, our mighty
King, alleluia.

Reading: 2 Corinthians 1: 3-7

Praised be God, the Father of our Lord Jesus
Christ, the Father of mercies and the God
of all consolation! He comforts us in all our
afflictions and thus enables us to comfort
those who are in trouble, with the same
consolation we have received from him. As we
have shared much in the suffering of Christ,
so through Christ do we share abundantly in
his consolation. If we are afflicted it is for your
encouragement and salvation, and when we are
consoled it is for your consolation, so that you
may endure patiently the same sufferings we
endure. Our hope for you is firm because we
know that just as you share in the sufferings, so
you will share in the consolation.

Responsory

℣ The whole creation proclaims the greatness
of your glory.
℟ The whole creation proclaims the greatness
of your glory.
℣ Eternal ages praise
℟ the greatness of your glory.

[Bow]   ℣ Glory to the Father, and to the Son,
and to the Holy Spirit.
℟ The whole creation proclaims the greatness
of your glory.

Canticle Of Mary

Ant.   The Son of Man did not come to condemn
[Stand]   men but to save them.

Magnificat: Luke 1: 46-55
My soul ✠ proclaims the… [See Prayer On Back
Flap. Then Repeat The Antiphon Above.]

Intercessions

Introductory Formula
Christ the Lord is our head; we are his
members. In joy let us call out to him:
℟ Lord, may your kingdom come.

Petitions
℣ Christ our Savior, make your Church a more
vivid symbol of the unity of all mankind,
℟ make it more effectively the sacrament of
salvation for all peoples.
℣ Through your presence, guide the college of
bishops in union with the Pope,
℟ give them the gifts of unity, love and peace.
℣ Bind all Christians more closely to yourself,
their divine Head,
℟ lead them to proclaim your kingdom by the
witness of their lives.
℣ Grant peace to the world,
℟ let every land flourish in justice and security.
℣ Grant to the dead the glory of resurrection,
℟ and give us a share in their happiness.

The Lord's Prayer
Our Father… [See prayer on back flap]

Prayer

Father,
you call your children
to walk in the light of Christ.
Free us from darkness
and keep us in the radiance of your truth.
We ask this through our Lord Jesus Christ,
your Son,
who lives and reigns with you
and the Holy Spirit,
one God, for ever and ever. Amen.

Closing Rite Or Dismissal

[See Closing Rite on Back Flap]

Introductory Rite

[Stand] V. God, ✠ come to my assistance.
℟. Lord, make haste to help me.

[Bow] Glory to the Father, and to the Son,
and to the Holy Spirit:
as it was in the beginning, is now,
and will be for ever. Amen.

Hymn

✦ The eternal gifts of Christ the King,
The apostles' glory, let us sing,
And all with hearts of gladness, raise
Due hymns of thankful love and praise.

✦ Their faith in Christ, the Lord, prevailed;
Their hope, a light that never failed;
Their love ablaze o'er pathways trod
To lead them to the eternal God.

✦ In them the Father's glory shone,
In them the will of God the Son,
In them exults the Holy Ghost,
Through them rejoice the heav'nly host.

✦ To thee, Redeemer, now we cry,
That thou wouldst join to them on high
Thy servants, who this grace implore,
For ever and for ever more.
Translator: J.M. Neale, d. 1866

Psalmody

Ant. 1 I have prayed for you, Peter, that your faith
may not fail; and when you have turned to
me, you must strengthen the faith of your
brothers.

Book 5: Psalm 116: 10-19
Thanksgiving in the Temple
[Sit] ✦ I trusted, even when I said:
"I am sorely afflicted,"
and when I said in my alarm:
"No man can be trusted."

✦ How can I repay the Lord
for his goodness to me?
The cup of salvation I will raise;
I will call on the Lord's name.

✦ My vows to the Lord I will fulfill
before all his people.
O precious in the eyes of the Lord
is the death of his faithful.

✦ Your servant, Lord, your servant am I;
you have loosened my bonds.
A thanksgiving sacrifice I make:
I will call on the Lord's name.

Sts. Peter & Paul
Solemnity

✦ My vows to the Lord I will fulfill
before all his people,
in the courts of the house of the Lord,
in your midst, O Jerusalem.

[Bow] ✦ Glory to the Father…

Ant. I have prayed for you, Peter, that your faith
may not fail; and when you have turned to
me, you must strengthen the faith of your
brothers.

Ant. 2 Willingly I boast of my weaknesses, that the
power of Christ may live in me.

Book 5: Psalm 126
Joyful hope in God
✦ When the Lord delivered Zion from bondage,
it seemed like a dream.
Then was our mouth filled with laughter,
on our lips there were songs.

✦ The heathens themselves said: "What marvels
the Lord worked for them!"
What marvels the Lord worked for us!
Indeed we were glad.

✦ Deliver us, O Lord, from our bondage
as streams in dry land.
Those who are sowing in tears
will sing when they reap.

✦ They go out, they go out, full of tears,
carrying seed for the sowing:
they come back, they come back, full of song,
carrying their sheaves.

[Bow] ✦ Glory to the Father…

Ant. Willingly I boast of my weaknesses, that the
power of Christ may live in me.

Ant. 3 You are shepherd of the flock, the prince of the
apostles; to you were entrusted the keys of the
kingdom of heaven.

Canticle: Ephesians 1: 3-10
✦ Praised be the God and Father
of our Lord Jesus Christ,
who bestowed on us in Christ
every spiritual blessing in the heavens.

✦ God chose us in him

before the world began,
to be holy
and blameless in his sight.

✦ He predestined us
to be his adopted sons through Jesus Christ,
such was his will and pleasure,
that all might praise the glorious favor
he has bestowed on us in his beloved.

✦ In him and through his blood, we have been
redeemed,
and our sins forgiven,
so immeasurably generous
is God's favor to us.

✦ God has given us the wisdom
to understand fully the mystery,
the plan he was pleased
to decree in Christ.

✦ A plan to be carried out
in Christ, in the fullness of time,
to bring all things into one in him,
in the heavens and on the earth.

[Bow]   ✦ Glory to the Father…

Ant.   You are shepherd of the flock, the prince of the
apostles; to you were entrusted the keys of the
kingdom of heaven.

Reading: 1 Corinthians 15: 3-5, 8a

I handed on to you first of all what I myself
received, that Christ died for our sins in
accordance with the Scriptures; that he was
buried and, in accordance with the Scriptures,
rose on the third day; that he was seen by
Cephas, then by the Twelve. Last of all he was
seen by me.

Responsory

℣. The apostles proclaimed the word of God and
preached it faithfully.
℟. The apostles proclaimed the word of God and
preached it faithfully.
℣. They testified to the resurrection of Jesus Christ.
℟. And preached it faithfully.
[Bow] ℣. Glory to the Father, and to the Son,
and to the Holy Spirit.
℟. The apostles proclaimed the word of God and
preached it faithfully.

Canticle Of Mary

Ant.   Peter the apostle and Paul the teacher of the
[Stand]   Gentiles taught us your law, O Lord.

 Magnificat: Luke 1: 46-55
My soul ✠ proclaims the… [See Prayer On Back
Flap. Then Repeat The Antiphon Above.]

Intercessions

Introductory Formula
The Lord Jesus built his holy people on the
foundation of the apostles and prophets. In
faith let us pray:
℟. Lord, come to the aid of your people.

Petitions
℣. You once called Simon, the fisherman, to
catch men,
℟. now summon new workers who will bring the
message of salvation to all peoples.
℣. You calmed the waves so that your followers
would not be drowned,
℟. guard your Church, protect it from
all dangers.
℣. You gathered your scattered flock around
Peter after the resurrection,
℟. good Shepherd, bring all your people together
as one flock.
℣. You sent Paul as apostle to preach the good
news to the Gentiles,
℟. let the word of salvation be proclaimed to
all mankind.
℣. You gave the keys of your kingdom into the
hands of your holy people,
℟. open the gates of that kingdom to all who
trusted in your mercy while on earth.

The Lord's Prayer
Our Father… [See prayer on back flap]

Prayer

God our Father,
today you give us the joy
of celebrating the feast of the apostles
Peter and Paul.
Through them your Church first received
the faith.
Keep us true to their teaching.
Grant this through our Lord Jesus Christ,
your Son,
who lives and reigns with you
and the Holy Spirit,
one God, for ever and ever. Amen.

Closing Rite Or Dismissal

[See Closing Rite on Back Flap]

Introductory Rite

[See Introductory Rite on Front Flap]

Hymn

      • Love divine, all loves excelling,
        Joy of heaven to earth come down,
        And impart to us, here dwelling,
        Grace and mercy all around.
        Jesus, source of all compassion,
        Pure, unbounded love you share;
        Grant us many choicest blessings,
        Keep us in your loving care.

      • Come, O source of inspiration,
        Pure and spotless let us be:
        Let us see your true salvation,
        Perfect in accord with thee.
        Praising Father for all glory
        With the Spirit and the Son;
        Everlasting thanks we give thee,
        Undivided, love, in one.

          Text: C. Wesley, 1707-1788, adapted by C.T. Andrews 1968

Psalmody

Ant. 1   Christ our Lord is a priest for ever, like
        Melchizedek of old, alleluia.

        Book 5: Psalm 110: 1-5, 7
        The Messiah, king and priest

[Sit]   • The Lord's revelation to my Master:
        "Sit on my right:
        your foes I will put beneath your feet."

      • The Lord will wield from Zion
        your scepter of power:
        rule in the midst of all your foes.

      • A prince from the day of your birth
        on the holy mountains;
        from the womb before the dawn I begot you.

      • The Lord has sworn an oath he will not change.
        "You are a priest for ever,
        a priest like Melchizedek of old."

      • The Master standing at your right hand
        will shatter kings in the day of his great wrath.

      • He shall drink from the stream by the wayside
        and therefore he shall lift up his head.

[Bow]   • Glory to the Father…

        Psalm Prayer
        Almighty God, bring the kingdom of Christ,
        your anointed one, to its fullness. May the
        perfect offering of your Son, eternal priest of
        the new Jerusalem, be offered in every place to
        your name, and make all nations a holy people
        for you.

FOURTEENTH SUNDAY
in Ordinary Time
[Psalter, Week II]

Ant.   Christ our Lord is a priest for ever, like
        Melchizedek of old, alleluia.

Ant. 2   God dwells in highest heaven; he has power to
        do all he wills, alleluia.

        Book 5: Psalm 115
        Praise of the true God

• Not to us, Lord, not to us,
  but to your name give the glory
  for the sake of your love and your truth,
  lest the heathen say: "Where is their God?"

• But our God is in the heavens;
  he does whatever he wills.
  Their idols are silver and gold,
  the work of human hands.

• They have mouths but they cannot speak;
  they have eyes but they cannot see;
  they have ears but they cannot hear;
  they have nostrils but they cannot smell.

• With their hands they cannot feel;
  with their feet they cannot walk.
  No sound comes from their throats.
  Their makers will come to be like them
  and so will all who trust in them.

• Sons of Israel, trust in the Lord;
  he is their help and their shield.
  Sons of Aaron, trust in the Lord;
  he is their help and their shield.

• You who fear him, trust in the Lord;
  he is their help and their shield.
  He remembers us, and he will bless us;
  he will bless the sons of Israel.
  He will bless the sons of Aaron.

• The Lord will bless those who fear him,
  the little no less than the great:
  to you may the Lord grant increase,
  to you and all your children.

• May you be blessed by the Lord,
  the maker of heaven and earth.
  The heavens belong to the Lord
  but the earth he has given to men.

• The dead shall not praise the Lord,
  nor those who go down into the silence.

But we who live bless the Lord
now and for ever. Amen.

[Bow] ✠ Glory to the Father…

Psalm Prayer
Father, creator…[See psalm prayer on front flap]

Ant. God dwells in highest heaven; he has power to
do all he wills, alleluia.

Ant. 3 Praise God, all you who serve him, both great
and small, alleluia.

Canticle based on Revelation 19: 1-7
The wedding of the Lamb

✠ Alleluia.
Salvation, glory, and power to our God:
(℟ Alleluia.)
his judgments are honest and true.
℟ Alleluia (alleluia).

✠ Alleluia.
Sing praise to our God, all you his servants,
(℟ Alleluia.)
all who worship him reverently, great and small.
℟ Alleluia (alleluia).

✠ Alleluia.
The Lord our all-powerful God is King;
(℟ Alleluia.)
let us rejoice, sing praise, and give him glory.
℟ Alleluia (alleluia).

✠ Alleluia.
The wedding feast of the Lamb has begun,
(℟ Alleluia.)
and his bride is prepared to welcome him.
℟ Alleluia (alleluia).

[Bow] ✠ Glory to the Father…

Ant. Praise God, all you who serve him, both great
and small, alleluia.

Reading: 2 Thessalonians 2: 13-14
We are bound to thank God for you always,
beloved brothers in the Lord, because you are
the first fruits of those whom God has chosen
for salvation, in holiness of spirit and fidelity
to truth. He called you through our preaching
of the good news so that you might achieve the
glory of our Lord Jesus Christ.

Responsory
℣. Our Lord is great, mighty is his power.
℟. Our Lord is great, mighty is his power.
℣. His wisdom is beyond compare,
℟. mighty is his power.

[Bow] ℣. Glory to the Father, and to the Son,
and to the Holy Spirit.
℟. Our Lord is great, mighty is his power.

Canticle Of Mary
Ant. So great a harvest, and so few to gather it in;
[Stand] pray to the Lord of the harvest; beg him to
send out laborers for his harvest.

Magnificat: Luke 1: 46-55
My soul ✠ proclaims the… [See Prayer On Back
Flap. Then Repeat The Antiphon Above.]

Intercessions

Introductory Formula
All praise and honor to Christ! He lives for
ever to intercede for us, and he is able to save
those who approach the Father in his name.
Sustained by our faith, let us call upon him:
℟ Remember your people, Lord.

Petitions
℣. As the day draws to a close, Sun of Justice, we
invoke your name upon the whole human race,
℟ so that all men may enjoy your never
failing light.
℣. Preserve the covenant which you have ratified
in your blood,
℟ cleanse and sanctify your Church.
℣. Remember your assembly, Lord,
℟ your dwelling place.
℣. Guide travelers along the path of peace
and prosperity,
℟ so that they may reach their destinations in
safety and joy.
℣. Receive the souls of the dead, Lord,
℟ grant them your favor and the gift of
eternal glory.

The Lord's Prayer
Our Father… [See prayer on back flap]

Prayer
Father,
through the obedience of Jesus,
your servant and your Son,
you raised a fallen world.
Free us from sin
and bring us the joy that lasts for ever.
We ask this through our Lord Jesus Christ,
your Son,
who lives and reigns with you
and the Holy Spirit,
one God, for ever and ever. Amen.

Closing Rite Or Dismissal
[See Closing Rite on Back Flap]

Introductory Rite

[STAND] V. God, ✠ come to my assistance.

R. Lord, make haste to help me.

[BOW] Glory to the Father, and to the Son,
and to the Holy Spirit:
as it was in the beginning, is now,
and will be for ever. Amen.

Hymn

✦ O Christ, you are the light and day
Which drives away the night,
The ever shining Sun of God
And pledge of future light.

✦ As now the ev'ning shadows fall
Please grant us, Lord, we pray,
A quiet night to rest in you
Until the break of day.

✦ Remember us, poor mortal men,
We humbly ask, O Lord,
And may your presence in our souls
Be now our great reward.

Translator: Rev. M. Quinn, O.P. et al.

Psalmody

Ant. 1 The Lord said to my Master: Sit at my right
hand, alleluia.

Book 5: Psalm 110: 1-5, 7
The Messiah, king and priest

[SIT] ✦ The Lord's revelation to my Master:
"Sit on my right:
your foes I will put beneath your feet."

✦ The Lord will wield from Zion
your scepter of power:
rule in the midst of all your foes.

✦ A prince from the day of your birth
on the holy mountains;
from the womb before the dawn I begot you.

✦ The Lord has sworn an oath he will not change.
"You are a priest for ever,
a priest like Melchizedek of old."

✦ The Master standing at your right hand
will shatter kings in the day of his great wrath.

✦ He shall drink from the stream by the wayside
and therefore he shall lift up his head.

[BOW] ✦ Glory to the Father…

Psalm Prayer
Father, we ask you to give us victory and peace.
In Jesus Christ, our Lord and King, we are
already seated at your right hand. We look

FIFTEENTH SUNDAY in Ordinary Time

forward to praising you in the fellowship of all
your saints in our heavenly homeland.

Ant. The Lord said to my Master: Sit at my right
hand, alleluia.

Ant. 2 Our compassionate Lord has left us a
memorial of his wonderful work, alleluia.

Book 5: Psalm 111
God's marvelous works

✦ I will thank the Lord with all my heart
in the meeting of the just and their assembly.
Great are the works of the Lord;
to be pondered by all who love them.

✦ Majestic and glorious his work,
his justice stands firm for ever.
He makes us remember his wonders.
The Lord is compassion and love.

✦ He gives food to those who fear him;
keeps his covenant ever in mind.
He has shown his might to his people
by giving them the lands of the nations.

✦ His works are justice and truth:
his precepts are all of them sure,
standing firm for ever and ever:
they are made in uprightness and truth.

✦ He has sent deliverance to his people
and established his covenant for ever.
Holy his name, to be feared.

✦ To fear the Lord is the first stage of wisdom;
all who do so prove themselves wise.
His praise shall last for ever!

[BOW] ✦ Glory to the Father…

Psalm Prayer
Merciful and gentle Lord, you are the
crowning glory of all the saints. Give us, your
children, the gift of obedience which is the
beginning of wisdom, so that we may do what
you command and be filled with your mercy.

Ant. Our compassionate Lord has left us a
memorial of his wonderful work, alleluia.

Ant. 3 All power is yours, Lord God, our mighty
King, alleluia.

Canticle based on Revelation 19: 1-7
The wedding of the Lamb

+ Alleluia.
  Salvation, glory, and power to our God:
  (℟ Alleluia.)
  his judgments are honest and true.
℟ Alleluia (alleluia).

+ Alleluia.
  Sing praise to our God, all you his servants,
  (℟ Alleluia.)
  all who worship him reverently, great and small.
℟ Alleluia (alleluia).

+ Alleluia.
  The Lord our all-powerful God is King;
  (℟ Alleluia.)
  let us rejoice, sing praise, and give him glory.
℟ Alleluia (alleluia).

+ Alleluia.
  The wedding feast of the Lamb has begun,
  (℟ Alleluia.)
  and his bride is prepared to welcome him.
℟ Alleluia (alleluia).

[Bow] + Glory to the Father…

Ant. All power is yours, Lord God, our mighty
  King, alleluia.

Reading: 1 Peter 1: 3-7

Praised be the God and Father /of our Lord
Jesus Christ, /he who in his great mercy /gave
us new birth; /a birth unto hope which draws
its life /from the resurrection of Jesus Christ
from the dead; /a birth to an imperishable
inheritance, /incapable of fading or defilement,
/which is kept in heaven for you /who are
guarded with God's power through faith; /a
birth to a salvation which stands ready /to be
revealed in the last days.

There is cause for rejoicing here. You may for
a time have to suffer the distress of many trials;
but this is so that your faith, which is more
precious than the passing splendor of fire-tried
gold, may by its genuineness lead to praise,
glory, and honor when Jesus Christ appears.

Responsory

℣. The whole creation proclaims the greatness
  of your glory.
℟. The whole creation proclaims the greatness
  of your glory.
℣. Eternal ages praise
℟. the greatness of your glory.
[Bow] ℣. Glory to the Father, and to the Son,
  and to the Holy Spirit.

℟. The whole creation proclaims the greatness
  of your glory.

Canticle Of Mary

Ant.
[Stand] Teacher, what is the greatest commandment
  in the law? Jesus said to him: You shall love
  the Lord your God with your whole heart.

Magnificat: Luke 1: 46-55
My soul ✠ proclaims the… [See Prayer On Back
Flap. Then Repeat The Antiphon Above.]

Intercessions

Introductory Formula
The world was created by the Word of
God, re-created by his redemption, and it is
continually renewed by his love. Rejoicing in
him we call out:
℟ Renew the wonders of your love, Lord.

Petitions
℣. We give thanks to God whose power is
  revealed in nature,
℟. and whose providence is revealed in history.
℣. Through your Son, the herald of
  reconciliation, the victor of the cross,
℟. free us from empty fear and hopelessness.
℣. May all those who love and pursue justice,
℟. work together without deceit to build a world
  of true peace.
℣. Be with the oppressed, free the captives,
  console the sorrowing, feed the hungry,
  strengthen the weak,
℟. in all people reveal the victory of your cross.
℣. After your Son's death and burial you raised
  him up again in glory,
℟. grant that the faithful departed may live
  with him.

The Lord's Prayer
Our Father… [See prayer on back flap]

Prayer

God our Father,
your light of truth
guides us to the way of Christ.
May all who follow him
reject what is contrary to the gospel.
We ask this through our Lord Jesus Christ,
  your Son,
who lives and reigns with you
  and the Holy Spirit,
one God, for ever and ever. Amen.

Closing Rite Or Dismissal

[See Closing Rite on Back Flap]

Introductory Rite

[STAND] V. God, ✠ come to my assistance.
R. Lord, make haste to help me.

[Bow] Glory to the Father, and to the Son,
and to the Holy Spirit:
as it was in the beginning, is now,
and will be for ever. Amen.

Hymn

+ Love divine, all loves excelling,
Joy of heaven to earth come down,
And impart to us, here dwelling,
Grace and mercy all around.
Jesus, source of all compassion,
Pure, unbounded love you share;
Grant us many choicest blessings,
Keep us in your loving care.

+ Come, O source of inspiration,
Pure and spotless let us be:
Let us see your true salvation,
Perfect in accord with thee.
Praising Father for all glory
With the Spirit and the Son;
Everlasting thanks we give thee,
Undivided, love, in one.

Text: C. Wesley, 1707-1788, adapted by C.T. Andrews 1968

Psalmody

Ant. 1 In eternal splendor, before the dawn of light on
earth, I have begotten you, alleluia.

Book 5: Psalm 110: 1-5, 7
The Messiah, king and priest

[SIT] + The Lord's revelation to my Master:
"Sit on my right:
your foes I will put beneath your feet."

+ The Lord will wield from Zion
your scepter of power:
rule in the midst of all your foes.

+ A prince from the day of your birth
on the holy mountains;
from the womb before the dawn I begot you.

+ The Lord has sworn an oath he will not change.
"You are a priest for ever,
a priest like Melchizedek of old."

+ The Master standing at your right hand
will shatter kings in the day of his great wrath.

+ He shall drink from the stream by the wayside
and therefore he shall lift up his head.

[Bow] + Glory to the Father, and to the Son,
and to the Holy Spirit:

as it was in the beginning, is now,
and will be for ever. Amen.

Psalm Prayer

Father, we ask you to give us victory and
peace. In Jesus Christ, our Lord and King, we
are already seated at your right hand. We look
forward to praising you in the fellowship of all
your saints in our heavenly homeland.

Ant. In eternal splendor, before the dawn of light
on earth, I have begotten you, alleluia.

Ant. 2 Blessed are they who hunger and thirst for
holiness; they will be satisfied.

Book 5: Psalm 112
The happiness of the just man

+ Happy the man who fears the Lord,
who takes delight in all his commands.
His sons will be powerful on earth;
the children of the upright are blessed.

+ Riches and wealth are in his house;
his justice stands firm for ever.
He is a light in the darkness for the upright:
he is generous, merciful and just.

+ The good man takes pity and lends,
he conducts his affairs with honor.
The just man will never waver:
he will be remembered for ever.

+ He has no fear of evil news;
with a firm heart he trusts in the Lord.
With a steadfast heart he will not fear;
he will see the downfall of his foes.

+ Open-handed, he gives to the poor;
his justice stands firm for ever.
His head will be raised in glory.

+ The wicked man sees and is angry,
grinds his teeth and fades away;
the desire of the wicked leads to doom.

[Bow] + Glory to the Father, and to the Son,
and to the Holy Spirit:
as it was in the beginning, is now,
and will be for ever. Amen.

Psalm Prayer

Lord God, you are the eternal light which illumines the hearts of good people. Help us to love you, to rejoice in your glory, and so to live in this world as to avoid harsh judgment in the next. May we come to see the light of your countenance.

Ant. Blessed are they who hunger and thirst for holiness; they will be satisfied.

Ant. 3 Praise God, all you who serve him, both great and small, alleluia.

Canticle based on Revelation 19: 1-7
The wedding of the Lamb

✦ Alleluia.
Salvation, glory, and power to our God:
(℟ Alleluia.)
his judgments are honest and true.
℟ Alleluia (alleluia).

✦ Alleluia.
Sing praise to our God, all you his servants,
(℟ Alleluia.)
all who worship him reverently, great and small.
℟ Alleluia (alleluia).

✦ Alleluia.
The Lord our all-powerful God is King;
(℟ Alleluia.)
let us rejoice, sing praise, and give him glory.
℟ Alleluia (alleluia).

✦ Alleluia.
The wedding feast of the Lamb has begun,
(℟ Alleluia.)
and his bride is prepared to welcome him.
℟ Alleluia (alleluia).

[Bow] ✦ Glory to the Father…

Ant. Praise God, all you who serve him, both great and small, alleluia.

Reading: Hebrews 12: 22-24

You have drawn near to Mount Zion and the city of the living God, the heavenly Jerusalem, to myriads of angels in festal gathering, to the assembly of the first-born enrolled in heaven, to God the judge of all, to the spirits of just men made perfect, to Jesus, the mediator of a new covenant, and to the sprinkled blood which speaks more eloquently than that of Abel.

Responsory

℣. Our Lord is great, mighty is his power.
℟. Our Lord is great, mighty is his power.

℣. His wisdom is beyond compare,
℟. mighty is his power.
[Bow] ℣. Glory to the Father, and to the Son, and to the Holy Spirit.
℟. Our Lord is great, mighty is his power.

Canticle Of Mary

Ant.
[Stand] Mary has chosen the better part, and it shall not be taken from her.

Magnificat: Luke 1: 46-55
My soul ✠ proclaims the… [See Prayer On Back Flap. Then Repeat The Antiphon Above.]

Intercessions

Introductory Formula
Rejoicing in the Lord, from whom all good things come, let us pray:
℟. Lord, hear our prayer.

Petitions
℣. Father and Lord of all, you sent your Son into the world, that your name might be glorified in every place,
℟. strengthen the witness of your Church among the nations.
℣. Make us obedient to the teachings of your apostles,
℟. and bound to the truth of our faith.
℣. As you love the innocent,
℟. render justice to those who are wronged.
℣. Free those in bondage and give sight to the blind,
℟. raise up the fallen and protect the stranger.
℣. Fulfill your promise to those who already sleep in your peace,
℟. through your Son grant them a blessed resurrection.

The Lord's Prayer
Our Father… [See prayer on back flap]

Prayer

Lord,
be merciful to your people.
Fill us with your gifts
and make us always eager to serve you
in faith, hope, and love.
Grant this through our Lord Jesus Christ,
 your Son,
who lives and reigns with you
 and the Holy Spirit,
one God, for ever and ever Amen.

Closing Rite Or Dismissal

[See Closing Rite on Back Flap]

Introductory Rite

[STAND] V. God, ✠ come to my assistance.

R. Lord, make haste to help me.

[BOW] Glory to the Father, and to the Son,
and to the Holy Spirit:
as it was in the beginning, is now,
and will be for ever. Amen.

Hymn

✦ O Christ, you are the light and day
Which drives away the night,
The ever shining Sun of God
And pledge of future light.

✦ As now the ev'ning shadows fall
Please grant us, Lord, we pray,
A quiet night to rest in you
Until the break of day.

✦ Remember us, poor mortal men,
We humbly ask, O Lord,
And may your presence in our souls
Be now our great reward.

Translator: Rev. M. Quinn, O.P. et al.

Psalmody

Ant. 1 The Lord will stretch forth his mighty scepter
from Zion, and he will reign for ever, alleluia.

Book 5: Psalm 110: 1-5, 7
The Messiah, king and priest

[SIT] ✦ The Lord's revelation to my Master:
"Sit on my right:
your foes I will put beneath your feet."

✦ The Lord will wield from Zion
your scepter of power:
rule in the midst of all your foes.

✦ A prince from the day of your birth
on the holy mountains;
from the womb before the dawn I begot you.

✦ The Lord has sworn an oath he will not change.
"You are a priest for ever,
a priest like Melchizedek of old."

✦ The Master standing at your right hand
will shatter kings in the day of his great wrath.

✦ He shall drink from the stream by the wayside
and therefore he shall lift up his head.

[BOW] ✦ Glory to the Father, and to the Son,
and to the Holy Spirit:
as it was in the beginning, is now,
and will be for ever. Amen.

Psalm Prayer
Father, we ask you to give us victory and peace.
In Jesus Christ, our Lord and King, we are

already seated at your right hand. We look
forward to praising you in the fellowship of all
your saints in our heavenly homeland.

Ant. The Lord will stretch forth his mighty scepter
from Zion, and he will reign for ever, alleluia.

Ant. 2 The earth is shaken to its depths before the
glory of your face.

Book 2: Psalm 114
The Israelites are delivered from the bondage of Egypt

✦ When Israel came forth from Egypt,
Jacob's sons from an alien people,
Judah became the Lord's temple,
Israel became his kingdom.

✦ The sea fled at the sight:
the Jordan turned back on its course,
the mountains leapt like rams
and the hills like yearling sheep.

✦ Why was it, sea, that you fled,
that you turned back, Jordan, on your course?
Mountains, that you leapt like rams,
hills, like yearling sheep?

✦ Tremble, O earth, before the Lord,
in the presence of the God of Jacob,
who turns the rock into a pool
and flint into a spring of water.

[BOW] ✦ Glory to the Father, and to the Son,
and to the Holy Spirit:
as it was in the beginning, is now,
and will be for ever. Amen.

Psalm Prayer
Almighty God, ever-living mystery of unity and
trinity, you gave life to the new Israel by birth
from water and the Spirit, and made it a chosen
race, a royal priesthood, a people set apart as
your eternal possession. May all those you have
called to walk in the splendor of the new light
render you fitting service and adoration.

Ant. The earth is shaken to its depths before the
glory of your face.

Ant. 3 All power is yours, Lord God, our mighty
King, alleluia.

Canticle based on Revelation 19: 1-7
The wedding of the Lamb

+ Alleluia.
  Salvation, glory, and power to our God:
  (℟ Alleluia.)
  his judgments are honest and true.
℟ Alleluia (alleluia).

+ Alleluia.
  Sing praise to our God, all you his servants,
  (℟ Alleluia.)
  all who worship him reverently, great and small.
℟ Alleluia (alleluia).

+ Alleluia.
  The Lord our all-powerful God is King;
  (℟ Alleluia.)
  let us rejoice, sing praise, and give him glory.
℟ Alleluia (alleluia).

+ Alleluia.
  The wedding feast of the Lamb has begun,
  (℟ Alleluia.)
  and his bride is prepared to welcome him.
℟ Alleluia (alleluia).

[Bow] + Glory to the Father, and to the Son,
  and to the Holy Spirit:
  as it was in the beginning, is now,
  and will be for ever. Amen.

Ant. All power is yours, Lord God, our mighty King, alleluia.

Reading: 2 Corinthians 1: 3-7

Praised be God, the Father of our Lord Jesus Christ, the Father of mercies and the God of all consolation! He comforts us in all our afflictions and thus enables us to comfort those who are in trouble, with the same consolation we have received from him. As we have shared much in the suffering of Christ, so through Christ do we share abundantly in his consolation. If we are afflicted it is for your encouragement and salvation, and when we are consoled it is for your consolation, so that you may endure patiently the same sufferings we endure. Our hope for you is firm because we know that just as you share in the sufferings, so you will share in the consolation.

Responsory

℣ The whole creation proclaims the greatness of your glory.
℟ The whole creation proclaims the greatness of your glory.
℣ Eternal ages praise
℟ the greatness of your glory.

[Bow] ℣ Glory to the Father, and to the Son,
  and to the Holy Spirit.
℟ The whole creation proclaims the greatness of your glory.

Canticle Of Mary

Ant. Ask and you will receive, seek and you will
[Stand] find, knock and the door will be opened to you.

Magnificat: Luke 1: 46-55
My soul ✠ proclaims the… [See Prayer On Back Flap. Then Repeat The Antiphon Above.]

Intercessions

Introductory Formula
Christ the Lord is our head; we are his members. In joy let us call out to him:
℟ Lord, may your kingdom come.

Petitions
℣ Christ our Savior, make your Church a more vivid symbol of the unity of all mankind,
℟ make it more effectively the sacrament of salvation for all peoples.
℣ Through your presence, guide the college of bishops in union with the Pope,
℟ give them the gifts of unity, love and peace.
℣ Bind all Christians more closely to yourself, their divine Head,
℟ lead them to proclaim your kingdom by the witness of their lives.
℣ Grant peace to the world,
℟ let every land flourish in justice and security.
℣ Grant to the dead the glory of resurrection,
℟ and give us a share in their happiness.

The Lord's Prayer
Our Father… [See prayer on back flap]

Prayer

God our Father and protector,
without you nothing is holy,
nothing has value.
Guide us to everlasting life
by helping us to use wisely
the blessings you have given to the world.
We ask this through our Lord Jesus Christ,
  your Son,
who lives and reigns with you
  and the Holy Spirit,
one God, for ever and ever. Amen.

Closing Rite Or Dismissal

[See Closing Rite on Back Flap]

Introductory Rite

[See Introductory Rite on Front Flap]

Hymn

 ✦ Love divine, all loves excelling,
 Joy of heaven to earth come down,
 And impart to us, here dwelling,
 Grace and mercy all around.
 Jesus, source of all compassion,
 Pure, unbounded love you share;
 Grant us many choicest blessings,
 Keep us in your loving care.

 ✦ Come, O source of inspiration,
 Pure and spotless let us be:
 Let us see your true salvation,
 Perfect in accord with thee.
 Praising Father for all glory
 With the Spirit and the Son;
 Everlasting thanks we give thee,
 Undivided, love, in one.

 Text: C. Wesley, 1707-1788, adapted by C.T. Andrews 1968

Psalmody

Ant. 1 Christ our Lord is a priest for ever, like
 Melchizedek of old, alleluia.

 Book 5: Psalm 110: 1-5, 7
 The Messiah, king and priest

[Sit] ✦ The Lord's revelation to my Master:
 "Sit on my right:
 your foes I will put beneath your feet."

 ✦ The Lord will wield from Zion
 your scepter of power:
 rule in the midst of all your foes.

 ✦ A prince from the day of your birth
 on the holy mountains;
 from the womb before the dawn I begot you.

 ✦ The Lord has sworn an oath he will not change.
 "You are a priest for ever,
 a priest like Melchizedek of old."

 ✦ The Master standing at your right hand
 will shatter kings in the day of his great wrath.

 ✦ He shall drink from the stream by the wayside
 and therefore he shall lift up his head.

[Bow] ✦ Glory to the Father…

 Psalm Prayer
 Almighty God, bring the kingdom of Christ,
 your anointed one, to its fullness. May the
 perfect offering of your Son, eternal priest of the
 new Jerusalem, be offered in every place to your
 name, and make all nations a holy people
 for you.

EIGHTEENTH SUNDAY in Ordinary Time
[Psalter, Week II]

Ant. Christ our Lord is a priest for ever, like
 Melchizedek of old, alleluia.

Ant. 2 God dwells in highest heaven; he has power to
 do all he wills, alleluia.

 Book 5: Psalm 115
 Praise of the true God

 ✦ Not to us, Lord, not to us,
 but to your name give the glory
 for the sake of your love and your truth,
 lest the heathen say: "Where is their God?"

 ✦ But our God is in the heavens;
 he does whatever he wills.
 Their idols are silver and gold,
 the work of human hands.

 ✦ They have mouths but they cannot speak;
 they have eyes but they cannot see;
 they have ears but they cannot hear;
 they have nostrils but they cannot smell.

 ✦ With their hands they cannot feel;
 with their feet they cannot walk.
 No sound comes from their throats.
 Their makers will come to be like them
 and so will all who trust in them.

 ✦ Sons of Israel, trust in the Lord;
 he is their help and their shield.
 Sons of Aaron, trust in the Lord;
 he is their help and their shield.

 ✦ You who fear him, trust in the Lord;
 he is their help and their shield.
 He remembers us, and he will bless us;
 he will bless the sons of Israel.
 He will bless the sons of Aaron.

 ✦ The Lord will bless those who fear him,
 the little no less than the great:
 to you may the Lord grant increase,
 to you and all your children.

 ✦ May you be blessed by the Lord,
 the maker of heaven and earth.
 The heavens belong to the Lord
 but the earth he has given to men.

 ✦ The dead shall not praise the Lord,
 nor those who go down into the silence.

But we who live bless the Lord
now and for ever. Amen.

[Bow]   ✦ Glory to the Father…

Psalm Prayer
Father, creator… [See psalm prayer on front flap]

Ant.   God dwells in highest heaven; he has power to
do all he wills, alleluia.

Ant. 3   Praise God, all you who serve him, both great
and small, alleluia.

Canticle based on Revelation 19: 1-7
The wedding of the Lamb
✦ Alleluia.
Salvation, glory, and power to our God:
(℟ Alleluia.)
his judgments are honest and true.
℟ Alleluia (alleluia).

✦ Alleluia.
Sing praise to our God, all you his servants,
(℟ Alleluia.)
all who worship him reverently, great and small.
℟ Alleluia (alleluia).

✦ Alleluia.
The Lord our all-powerful God is King;
(℟ Alleluia.)
let us rejoice, sing praise, and give him glory.
℟ Alleluia (alleluia).

✦ Alleluia.
The wedding feast of the Lamb has begun,
(℟ Alleluia.)
and his bride is prepared to welcome him.
℟ Alleluia (alleluia).

[Bow]   ✦ Glory to the Father…

Ant.   Praise God, all you who serve him, both great
and small, alleluia.

Reading: 2 Thessalonians 2: 13-14

We are bound to thank God for you always,
beloved brothers in the Lord, because you are
the first fruits of those whom God has chosen
for salvation, in holiness of spirit and fidelity
to truth. He called you through our preaching
of the good news so that you might achieve the
glory of our Lord Jesus Christ.

Responsory

℣   Our Lord is great, mighty is his power.
℟   Our Lord is great, mighty is his power.
℣   His wisdom is beyond compare,
℟   mighty is his power.

[Bow]   ℣   Glory to the Father, and to the Son,
and to the Holy Spirit.
℟   Our Lord is great, mighty is his power.

Canticle Of Mary

Ant.   Brothers, if you desire to be truly rich, set your
[Stand]   heart on true riches.

Magnificat: Luke 1: 46-55
My soul ✠ proclaims the… [See Prayer On Back
Flap. Then Repeat The Antiphon Above.]

Intercessions

Introductory Formula
All praise and honor to Christ! He lives for
ever to intercede for us, and he is able to save
those who approach the Father in his name.
Sustained by our faith, let us call upon him:
℟   Remember your people, Lord.

Petitions
℣   As the day draws to a close, Sun of Justice, we
invoke your name upon the whole human race,
℟   so that all men may enjoy your never
failing light.
℣   Preserve the covenant which you have ratified
in your blood,
℟   cleanse and sanctify your Church.
℣   Remember your assembly, Lord,
℟   your dwelling place.
℣   Guide travelers along the path of peace
and prosperity,
℟   so that they may reach their destinations in
safety and joy.
℣   Receive the souls of the dead, Lord,
℟   grant them your favor and the gift of
eternal glory.

The Lord's Prayer
Our Father… [See prayer on back flap]

Prayer

Father of everlasting goodness,
our origin and guide,
be close to us
and hear the prayers of all who praise you.
Forgive our sins and restore us to life.
Keep us safe in your love.
Grant this through our Lord Jesus Christ,
your Son,
who lives and reigns with you
and the Holy Spirit,
one God, for ever and ever. Amen.

Closing Rite Or Dismissal

[See Closing Rite on Back Flap]

Introductory Rite

[Stand] V. God, ✠ come to my assistance.

R. Lord, make haste to help me.

[Bow] Glory to the Father, and to the Son,
and to the Holy Spirit:
as it was in the beginning, is now,
and will be for ever. Amen.

Hymn

+ 'Tis good, Lord, to be here!
Thy glory fills the night;
Thy face and garments, like the sun,
Shine with unborrowed light.

+ 'Tis good, Lord, to be here,
Thy beauty to behold,
Where Moses and Elijah stand,
Thy messengers of old.

+ Fulfiller of the past!
Promiser of things to be!
We hail thy body glorified,
And our redemption see.

+ Before we taste of death,
We see thy kingdom come;
Before us keep thy vision bright,
And make this place our home.

Text: J. A. Robinson, 1858-1933

Psalmody

Ant. 1   Jesus took Peter, James and his brother John
and led them up a high mountain where they
could be alone, and he was transfigured before
them.

Book 5: Psalm 110: 1-5, 7
The Messiah, king and priest

[Sit] + The Lord's revelation to my Master:
"Sit on my right:
your foes I will put beneath your feet."

+ The Lord will wield from Zion
your scepter of power:
rule in the midst of all your foes.

+ A prince from the day of your birth
on the holy mountains;
from the womb before the dawn I begot you.

+ The Lord has sworn an oath he will not change.
"You are a priest for ever,
a priest like Melchizedek of old."

+ The Master standing at your right hand
will shatter kings in the day of his great wrath.

+ He shall drink from the stream by the wayside
and therefore he shall lift up his head.

[Bow] + Glory to the Father, and to the Son,
and to the Holy Spirit:
as it was in the beginning, is now,
and will be for ever. Amen.

Ant.   Jesus took Peter, James and his brother John
and led them up a high mountain where they
could be alone, and he was transfigured before
them.

Ant. 2   A bright cloud overshadowed them and
suddenly a voice spoke from the cloud: This
is my beloved Son in whom I am well pleased;
listen to him.

Book 5: Psalm 121
Guardian of his people

+ I lift up my eyes to the mountains;
from where shall come my help?
My help shall come from the Lord
who made heaven and earth.

+ May he never allow you to stumble!
Let him sleep not, your guard.
No, he sleeps not nor slumbers,
Israel's guard.

+ The Lord is your guard and your shade;
at your right side he stands.
By day the sun shall not smite you
nor the moon in the night.

+ The Lord will guard you from evil,
he will guard your soul.
The Lord will guard your going and coming
both now and for ever.

[Bow] + Glory to the Father, and to the Son,
and to the Holy Spirit:
as it was in the beginning, is now,
and will be for ever. Amen.

Ant.   A bright cloud overshadowed them and
suddenly a voice spoke from the cloud: This
is my beloved Son in whom I am well pleased;
listen to him.

Ant. 3   As they came down from the mountain Jesus
commanded them: Tell no one of the vision
until the Son of Man has risen from the dead.

Canticle based on 1 Timothy 3: 16
The mystery and glory of Christ

℟ Praise the Lord, all you nations.

✦ Christ manifested in the flesh,
Christ justified in the Spirit.

℟ Praise the Lord, all you nations.

✦ Christ contemplated by the angels,
Christ proclaimed by the pagans.

℟ Praise the Lord, all you nations.

✦ Christ believed in throughout the world,
Christ exalted in glory.

℟ Praise the Lord, all you nations.

[BOW] ✦ Glory to the Father, and to the Son,
and to the Holy Spirit:
as it was in the beginning, is now,
and will be for ever. Amen.

Ant. As they came down from the mountain Jesus
commanded them: Tell no one of the vision
until the Son of Man has risen from the dead.

Reading: Romans 8: 16-17

The Spirit himself gives witness with our
spirit that we are children of God. But if we
are children, we are heirs as well: heirs of
God, heirs with Christ, if only we suffer with
him so as to be glorified with him.

Responsory

℣ Beauty and wealth surround him,
alleluia, alleluia.

℟ Beauty and wealth surround him,
alleluia, alleluia.

℣ Richness and splendor adorn his holy place.

℟ Alleluia, alleluia.

[BOW] ℣ Glory to the Father, and to the Son,
and to the Holy Spirit.

℟ Beauty and wealth surround him,
alleluia, alleluia.

Canticle Of Mary

Ant. When they heard the voice from the cloud,
[STAND] the disciples fell on their faces, overcome with
fear; Jesus came up to them, touched them
and said: Stand up. Do not be afraid.

Magnificat: Luke 1: 46-55
My soul ✠ proclaims the... [SEE PRAYER ON BACK
FLAP. THEN REPEAT THE ANTIPHON ABOVE.]

Intercessions

Introductory Formula
In the presence of his disciples our Savior was
wonderfully transfigured on Mount Tabor. Let
us pray to him with confidence:

℟ Lord, in your light may we see light.

Petitions
℣ O Christ, before your passion and death you
revealed the resurrection to your disciples on
Mount Tabor; we pray for your Church which
labors amid the cares and anxieties of this world,

℟ that in its trials it may always be transfigured
by the joy of your victory.

℣ O Christ, you took Peter, James and John and
led them up a high mountain by themselves;
we pray for our pope and bishops,

℟ that they may inspire in your people the hope
of being transfigured at the last day.

℣ O Christ, upon the mountaintop you let the
light of your face shine over Moses and Elijah,

℟ we ask your blessing upon the Jewish people; of
old you called them to be your chosen nation.

℣ O Christ, you gave light to the world when the
glory of the Creator arose over you,

℟ we pray for men of good will that they may
walk in your light.

℣ O Christ, you will reform our lowly body and
make it like your glorious one,

℟ we pray for our brothers and sisters who have
died that they may share in your glory for ever.

The Lord's Prayer
Our Father... [SEE PRAYER ON BACK FLAP]

Prayer

God our Father,
in the transfigured glory of Christ your Son,
you strengthen our faith
by confirming the witness of your prophets,
and show us the splendor of your beloved sons
  and daughters.
As we listen to the voice of your Son,
help us to become heirs to eternal life
  with him
who lives and reigns with you
  and the Holy Spirit,
one God, for ever and ever. Amen.

Closing Rite Or Dismissal

[SEE CLOSING RITE ON BACK FLAP]

Introductory Rite

[Stand] V. God, ✠ come to my assistance.

R. Lord, make haste to help me.

[Bow] Glory to the Father, and to the Son,
and to the Holy Spirit:
as it was in the beginning, is now,
and will be for ever. Amen.

Hymn

✦ O Christ, you are the light and day
Which drives away the night,
The ever shining Sun of God
And pledge of future light.

✦ As now the ev'ning shadows fall
Please grant us, Lord, we pray,
A quiet night to rest in you
Until the break of day.

✦ Remember us, poor mortal men,
We humbly ask, O Lord,
And may your presence in our souls
Be now our great reward.

Translator: Rev. M. Quinn, O.P. et al.

Psalmody

Ant. 1   The Lord said to my Master: Sit at my right
hand, alleluia.

Book 5: Psalm 110: 1-5, 7
The Messiah, king and priest

[Sit] ✦ The Lord's revelation to my Master:
"Sit on my right:
your foes I will put beneath your feet."

✦ The Lord will wield from Zion
your scepter of power:
rule in the midst of all your foes.

✦ A prince from the day of your birth
on the holy mountains;
from the womb before the dawn I begot you.

✦ The Lord has sworn an oath he will not change.
"You are a priest for ever,
a priest like Melchizedek of old."

✦ The Master standing at your right hand
will shatter kings in the day of his great wrath.

✦ He shall drink from the stream by the wayside
and therefore he shall lift up his head.

[Bow] ✦ Glory to the Father, and to the Son,
and to the Holy Spirit:
as it was in the beginning, is now,
and will be for ever. Amen.

Psalm Prayer
Father, we ask you to give us victory and peace.
In Jesus Christ, our Lord and King, we are

NINETEENTH SUNDAY
in Ordinary Time
[Psalter, Week III]

already seated at your right hand. We look
forward to praising you in the fellowship of all
your saints in our heavenly homeland.

Ant.   The Lord said to my Master: Sit at my right
hand, alleluia.

Ant. 2   Our compassionate Lord has left us a
memorial of his wonderful work, alleluia.

Book 5: Psalm 111
God's marvelous works

✦ I will thank the Lord with all my heart
in the meeting of the just and their assembly.
Great are the works of the Lord;
to be pondered by all who love them.

✦ Majestic and glorious his work,
his justice stands firm for ever.
He makes us remember his wonders.
The Lord is compassion and love.

✦ He gives food to those who fear him;
keeps his covenant ever in mind.
He has shown his might to his people
by giving them the lands of the nations.

✦ His works are justice and truth:
his precepts are all of them sure,
standing firm for ever and ever:
they are made in uprightness and truth.

✦ He has sent deliverance to his people
and established his covenant for ever.
Holy his name, to be feared.

✦ To fear the Lord is the first stage of wisdom;
all who do so prove themselves wise.
His praise shall last for ever!

[Bow] ✦ Glory to the Father…

Psalm Prayer
Merciful and gentle Lord, you are the
crowning glory of all the saints. Give us, your
children, the gift of obedience which is the
beginning of wisdom, so that we may do what
you command and be filled with your mercy.

Ant.   Our compassionate Lord has left us a
memorial of his wonderful work, alleluia.

Ant. 3   All power is yours, Lord God, our mighty
King, alleluia.

Canticle based on Revelation 19: 1-7

The wedding of the Lamb

✦ Alleluia.
Salvation, glory, and power to our God:
(℟ Alleluia.)
his judgments are honest and true.

℟ Alleluia (alleluia).

✦ Alleluia.
Sing praise to our God, all you his servants,
(℟ Alleluia.)
all who worship him reverently, great and small.

℟ Alleluia (alleluia).

✦ Alleluia.
The Lord our all-powerful God is King;
(℟ Alleluia.)
let us rejoice, sing praise, and give him glory.

℟ Alleluia (alleluia).

✦ Alleluia.
The wedding feast of the Lamb has begun,
(℟ Alleluia.)
and his bride is prepared to welcome him.

℟ Alleluia (alleluia).

[Bow] ✦ Glory to the Father…

Ant. All power is yours, Lord God, our mighty King,
alleluia.

Reading: 1 Peter 1: 3-7

Praised be the God and Father /of our Lord
Jesus Christ, /he who in his great mercy /gave
us new birth; /a birth unto hope which draws
its life /from the resurrection of Jesus Christ
from the dead; /a birth to an imperishable
inheritance, /incapable of fading or defilement,
/which is kept in heaven for you /who are
guarded with God's power through faith; /a
birth to a salvation which stands ready /to be
revealed in the last days.

There is cause for rejoicing here. You may for
a time have to suffer the distress of many trials;
but this is so that your faith, which is more
precious than the passing splendor of fire-tried
gold, may by its genuineness lead to praise,
glory, and honor when Jesus Christ appears.

Responsory

℣ The whole creation proclaims the greatness
of your glory.

℟ The whole creation proclaims the greatness
of your glory.

℣ Eternal ages praise

℟ the greatness of your glory.

[Bow] ℣ Glory to the Father, and to the Son,
and to the Holy Spirit.

℟ The whole creation proclaims the greatness
of your glory.

Canticle Of Mary

Ant.
[Stand]
Where your treasure is, there is your heart,
says the Lord.

Magnificat: Luke 1: 46-55

My soul ✠ proclaims the… [See Prayer On Back
Flap. Then Repeat The Antiphon Above.]

Intercessions

Introductory Formula
The world was created by the Word of
God, re-created by his redemption, and it is
continually renewed by his love. Rejoicing in
him we call out:

℟ Renew the wonders of your love, Lord.

Petitions

℣ We give thanks to God whose power is
revealed in nature,

℟ and whose providence is revealed in history.

℣ Through your Son, the herald of
reconciliation, the victor of the cross,

℟ free us from empty fear and hopelessness.

℣ May all those who love and pursue justice,

℟ work together without deceit to build a world
of true peace.

℣ Be with the oppressed, free the captives,
console the sorrowing, feed the hungry,
strengthen the weak,

℟ in all people reveal the victory of your cross.

℣ After your Son's death and burial you raised
him up again in glory,

℟ grant that the faithful departed may live
with him.

The Lord's Prayer
Our Father… [See prayer on back flap]

Prayer

Almighty and ever-living God,
your Spirit made us your children,
confident to call you Father.
Increase your Spirit within us
and bring us to our promised inheritance.
Grant this through our Lord Jesus Christ,
your Son,
who lives and reigns with you
and the Holy Spirit,
one God, for ever and ever. Amen.

Closing Rite Or Dismissal

[See Closing Rite on Back Flap]

Introductory Rite

God, ☩ come to my assistance.
℟. Lord, make haste to help me.

[Bow] Glory to the Father, and to the Son,
and to the Holy Spirit:
as it was in the beginning, is now,
and will be for ever. Amen.

Hymn

⁜ Love divine, all loves excelling,
Joy of heaven to earth come down,
And impart to us, here dwelling,
Grace and mercy all around.
Jesus, source of all compassion,
Pure, unbounded love you share;
Grant us many choicest blessings,
Keep us in your loving care.

⁜ Come, O source of inspiration,
Pure and spotless let us be:
Let us see your true salvation,
Perfect in accord with thee.
Praising Father for all glory
With the Spirit and the Son;
Everlasting thanks we give thee,
Undivided, love, in one.

Text: C. Wesley, 1707-1788, adapted by C.T. Andrews 1968

Psalmody

Ant. 1 In eternal splendor, before the dawn of light on
earth, I have begotten you, alleluia.

Book 5: Psalm 110: 1-5, 7
The Messiah, king and priest

⁜ The Lord's revelation to my Master:
"Sit on my right:
your foes I will put beneath your feet."

⁜ The Lord will wield from Zion
your scepter of power:
rule in the midst of all your foes.

⁜ A prince from the day of your birth
on the holy mountains;
from the womb before the dawn I begot you.

⁜ The Lord has sworn an oath he will not change.
"You are a priest for ever,
a priest like Melchizedek of old."

⁜ The Master standing at your right hand
will shatter kings in the day of his great wrath.

⁜ He shall drink from the stream by the wayside
and therefore he shall lift up his head.

[Bow] ⁜ Glory to the Father, and to the Son,
and to the Holy Spirit:

Twentieth Sunday *in Ordinary Time*

[Psalter, Week IV]

as it was in the beginning, is now,
and will be for ever. Amen.

Psalm Prayer

Father, we ask you to give us victory and
peace. In Jesus Christ, our Lord and King, we
are already seated at your right hand. We look
forward to praising you in the fellowship of all
your saints in our heavenly homeland.

Ant. In eternal splendor, before the dawn of light
on earth, I have begotten you, alleluia.

Ant. 2 Blessed are they who hunger and thirst for
holiness; they will be satisfied.

Book 5: Psalm 112
The happiness of the just man

⁜ Happy the man who fears the Lord,
who takes delight in all his commands.
His sons will be powerful on earth;
the children of the upright are blessed.

⁜ Riches and wealth are in his house;
his justice stands firm for ever.
He is a light in the darkness for the upright:
he is generous, merciful and just.

⁜ The good man takes pity and lends,
he conducts his affairs with honor.
The just man will never waver:
he will be remembered for ever.

⁜ He has no fear of evil news;
with a firm heart he trusts in the Lord.
With a steadfast heart he will not fear;
he will see the downfall of his foes.

⁜ Open-handed, he gives to the poor;
his justice stands firm for ever.
His head will be raised in glory.

⁜ The wicked man sees and is angry,
grinds his teeth and fades away;
the desire of the wicked leads to doom.

[Bow] ⁜ Glory to the Father, and to the Son,
and to the Holy Spirit:
as it was in the beginning, is now,
and will be for ever. Amen.

Psalm Prayer

Lord God, you are the eternal light which illumines the hearts of good people. Help us to love you, to rejoice in your glory, and so to live in this world as to avoid harsh judgment in the next. May we come to see the light of your countenance.

Ant. Blessed are they who hunger and thirst for holiness; they will be satisfied.

Ant. 3 Praise God, all you who serve him, both great and small, alleluia.

Canticle based on Revelation 19: 1-7
The wedding of the Lamb

✦ Alleluia.
Salvation, glory, and power to our God:
(℟ Alleluia.)
his judgments are honest and true.
℟ Alleluia (alleluia).

✦ Alleluia.
Sing praise to our God, all you his servants,
(℟ Alleluia.)
all who worship him reverently, great and small.
℟ Alleluia (alleluia).

✦ Alleluia.
The Lord our all-powerful God is King;
(℟ Alleluia.)
let us rejoice, sing praise, and give him glory.
℟ Alleluia (alleluia).

✦ Alleluia.
The wedding feast of the Lamb has begun,
(℟ Alleluia.)
and his bride is prepared to welcome him.
℟ Alleluia (alleluia).

[Bow] ✦ Glory to the Father…

Ant. Praise God, all you who serve him, both great and small, alleluia.

Reading: Hebrews 12: 22-24

You have drawn near to Mount Zion and the city of the living God, the heavenly Jerusalem, to myriads of angels in festal gathering, to the assembly of the first-born enrolled in heaven, to God the judge of all, to the spirits of just men made perfect, to Jesus, the mediator of a new covenant, and to the sprinkled blood which speaks more eloquently than that of Abel.

Responsory

℣ Our Lord is great, mighty is his power.
℟ Our Lord is great, mighty is his power.
℣ His wisdom is beyond compare,
℟ mighty is his power.
[Bow] ℣ Glory to the Father, and to the Son, and to the Holy Spirit.
℟ Our Lord is great, mighty is his power.

Canticle Of Mary

Ant. I have come to cast fire upon the earth; how I
[Stand] long to see the flame leap up!

Magnificat: Luke 1: 46-55
My soul ✠ proclaims the… [See Prayer On Back Flap. Then Repeat The Antiphon Above.]

Intercessions

Introductory Formula
Rejoicing in the Lord, from whom all good things come, let us pray:
℟ Lord, hear our prayer.

Petitions
℣ Father and Lord of all, you sent your Son into the world, that your name might be glorified in every place,
℟ strengthen the witness of your Church among the nations.
℣ Make us obedient to the teachings of your apostles,
℟ and bound to the truth of our faith.
℣ As you love the innocent,
℟ render justice to those who are wronged.
℣ Free those in bondage and give sight to the blind,
℟ raise up the fallen and protect the stranger.
℣ Fulfill your promise to those who already sleep in your peace,
℟ through your Son grant them a blessed resurrection.

The Lord's Prayer
Our Father… [See prayer on back flap]

Prayer

God our Father,
may we love you in all things and above all things
and reach the joy you have prepared for us beyond all our imagining.
We ask this through our Lord Jesus Christ, your Son,
who lives and reigns with you and the Holy Spirit,
one God, for ever and ever. Amen.

Closing Rite Or Dismissal

[See Closing Rite on Back Flap]

Introductory Rite

[STAND] V. God, ✠ come to my assistance.

R. Lord, make haste to help me.

[BOW] Glory to the Father, and to the Son,
and to the Holy Spirit:
as it was in the beginning, is now,
and will be for ever. Amen.

Hymn

+ Hail, holy Queen of Heavens.
Hail, holy Queen of the Angels.
Hail, Root of Jesse.
Hail, Gate of Heaven.
By you the Light has entered the world.
Rejoice, glorious Virgin,
Beautiful among all women.
Hail, radiant Splendor,
Intercede with Christ for us.

Text: Lucien Deiss, C.S. Sp., 1965

Psalmody

Ant. 1 Mary has been taken up to heaven; the angels
rejoice. They bless the Lord and sing his
praises.

Book 5: Psalm 122
Holy city Jerusalem

[SIT] + I rejoiced when I heard them say:
"Let us go to God's house."
And now our feet are standing
within your gates, O Jerusalem.

+ Jerusalem is built as a city
strongly compact.
It is there that the tribes go up,
the tribes of the Lord.

+ For Israel's law it is,
there to praise the Lord's name.
There were set the thrones of judgment
of the house of David.

+ For the peace of Jerusalem pray:
"Peace be to your homes!
May peace reign in your walls,
in your palaces, peace!"

+ For love of my brethren and friends
I say: "Peace upon you!"
For love of the house of the Lord
I will ask for your good.

[BOW] + Glory to the Father, and to the Son,
and to the Holy Spirit:
as it was in the beginning, is now and will be
for ever. Amen.

THE ASSUMPTION
of the Blessed Virgin Mary

Ant. Mary has been taken up to heaven; the angels
rejoice. They bless the Lord and sing his praises.

Ant. 2 The Virgin Mary was taken up to the heavenly
bridal chamber where the King of kings is seated
on a starry throne.

Book 5: Psalm 127
Apart from God our labors are worthless

+ If the Lord does not build the house,
in vain do its builders labor;
if the Lord does not watch over the city,
in vain does the watchman keep vigil.

+ In vain is your earlier rising,
your going later to rest,
you who toil for the bread you eat:
when he pours gifts on his beloved while they
slumber.

+ Truly sons are a gift from the Lord,
a blessing, the fruit of the womb.
Indeed the sons of youth
are like arrows in the hand of a warrior.

+ O the happiness of the man
who has filled his quiver with these arrows!
He will have no cause for shame
when he disputes with his foes in the gateways.

[BOW] + Glory to the Father, and to the Son,
and to the Holy Spirit:
as it was in the beginning, is now,
and will be for ever. Amen.

Ant. The Virgin Mary was taken up to the heavenly
bridal chamber where the King of kings is seated
on a starry throne.

Ant. 3 We share the fruit of life through you, O
daughter blessed by the Lord.

Canticle: Ephesians 1: 3-10
God our Savior

+ Praised be the God and Father
of our Lord Jesus Christ,
who bestowed on us in Christ
every spiritual blessing in the heavens.

+ God chose us in him
before the world began,

to be holy
and blameless in his sight.

♦ He predestined us
to be his adopted sons through Jesus Christ,
such was his will and pleasure,
that all might praise the glorious favor
he has bestowed on us in his beloved.

♦ In him and through his blood, we have been
   redeemed,
and our sins forgiven,
so immeasurably generous
is God's favor to us.

♦ God has given us the wisdom
to understand fully the mystery,
the plan he was pleased
to decree in Christ.

♦ A plan to be carried out
in Christ, in the fullness of time,
to bring all things into one in him,
in the heavens and on the earth.

[Bow]   ♦ Glory to the Father, and to the Son,
and to the Holy Spirit:
as it was in the beginning, is now,
and will be for ever. Amen.

Ant.   We share the fruit of life through you, O
daughter blessed by the Lord.

Reading: 1 Corinthians 15: 22-23

Just as in Adam all die, so in Christ all will
come to life again, but each one in proper
order: Christ the first fruits and then, at his
coming, all those who belong to him.

Responsory

℣. The Virgin Mary is exalted above the choirs
of angels.
℟. The Virgin Mary is exalted above the choirs
of angels.
℣. Blessed is the Lord who has raised her up.
℟. Above the choirs of angels.
[Bow] ℣. Glory to the Father, and to the Son,
and to the Holy Spirit.
℟. The Virgin Mary is exalted above the choirs
of angels.

Canticle Of Mary

Ant.   Today the Virgin Mary was taken up to
[Stand]   heaven; rejoice, for she reigns with Christ for
ever.

Magnificat: Luke 1: 46-55
My soul ✠ proclaims the... [See Prayer On Back
Flap. Then Repeat The Antiphon Above.]

Intercessions

Introductory Formula
Let us praise God our almighty Father,
who wished that Mary, his Son's mother, be
celebrated by each generation. Now in need
we ask:
℟. Mary, full of grace, intercede for us.

Petitions
℣. O God, worker of miracles, you made the
immaculate Virgin Mary share, body and
soul, in your Son's glory in heaven,
℟. direct the hearts of your children to that
same glory.
℣. You made Mary our mother. Through her
intercession grant strength to the weak,
comfort to the sorrowing, pardon to sinners,
℟. salvation and peace to all.
℣. You made Mary full of grace,
℟. grant all men the joyful abundance of
your grace.
℣. Make your Church of one mind and one heart
in love,
℟. and help all those who believe to be one in
prayer with Mary, the mother of Jesus.
℣. You crowned Mary queen of heaven,
℟. may all the dead rejoice in your kingdom with
the saints for ever.

The Lord's Prayer
Our Father... [See prayer on back flap]

Prayer

All-powerful and ever-living God,
you raised the sinless Virgin Mary,
mother of your Son,
body and soul to the glory of heaven.
May we see heaven as our final goal
and come to share her glory.
We ask this through our Lord Jesus Christ,
   your Son,
who lives and reigns with you
   and the Holy Spirit,
one God, for ever and ever. Amen.

Closing Rite Or Dismissal
[See Closing Rite on Back Flap]

107

Introductory Rite

[STAND] V. God, ✠ come to my assistance.

R. Lord, make haste to help me.

[Bow] Glory to the Father, and to the Son,
and to the Holy Spirit:
as it was in the beginning, is now,
and will be for ever. Amen.

Hymn

+ O Christ, you are the light and day
Which drives away the night,
The ever shining Sun of God
And pledge of future light.

+ As now the ev'ning shadows fall
Please grant us, Lord, we pray,
A quiet night to rest in you
Until the break of day.

+ Remember us, poor mortal men,
We humbly ask, O Lord,
And may your presence in our souls
Be now our great reward.

Translator: Rev. M. Quinn, O.P. et al.

Psalmody

Ant. 1 The Lord will stretch forth his mighty scepter
from Zion, and he will reign for ever, alleluia.

Book 5: Psalm 110: 1-5, 7
The Messiah, king and priest

[SIT] + The Lord's revelation to my Master:
"Sit on my right:
your foes I will put beneath your feet."

+ The Lord will wield from Zion
your scepter of power:
rule in the midst of all your foes.

+ A prince from the day of your birth
on the holy mountains;
from the womb before the dawn I begot you.

+ The Lord has sworn an oath he will not change.
"You are a priest for ever,
a priest like Melchizedek of old."

+ The Master standing at your right hand
will shatter kings in the day of his great wrath.

+ He shall drink from the stream by the wayside
and therefore he shall lift up his head.

[Bow] + Glory to the Father, and to the Son,
and to the Holy Spirit:
as it was in the beginning, is now and will be
for ever. Amen.

Twenty-first Sunday in Ordinary Time

[PSALTER, WEEK I]

Psalm Prayer
Father, we ask you to give us victory and peace.
In Jesus Christ, our Lord and King, we are
already seated at your right hand. We look
forward to praising you in the fellowship of all
your saints in our heavenly homeland.

Ant. The Lord will stretch forth his mighty scepter
from Zion, and he will reign for ever, alleluia.

Ant. 2 The earth is shaken to its depths before the
glory of your face.

Book 2: Psalm 114
The Israelites are delivered from the bondage of Egypt

+ When Israel came forth from Egypt,
Jacob's sons from an alien people,
Judah became the Lord's temple,
Israel became his kingdom.

+ The sea fled at the sight:
the Jordan turned back on its course,
the mountains leapt like rams
and the hills like yearling sheep.

+ Why was it, sea, that you fled,
that you turned back, Jordan, on your course?
Mountains, that you leapt like rams,
hills, like yearling sheep?

+ Tremble, O earth, before the Lord,
in the presence of the God of Jacob,
who turns the rock into a pool
and flint into a spring of water.

[Bow] + Glory to the Father, and to the Son,
and to the Holy Spirit:
as it was in the beginning, is now and will be
for ever. Amen.

Psalm Prayer
Almighty God, ever-living mystery of unity and
trinity, you gave life to the new Israel by birth
from water and the Spirit, and made it a chosen
race, a royal priesthood, a people set apart as
your eternal possession. May all those you have
called to walk in the splendor of the new light
render you fitting service and adoration.

Ant. The earth is shaken to its depths before the
glory of your face.

Ant. 3   All power is yours, Lord God, our mighty King, alleluia.

Canticle based on Revelation 19: 1-7
The wedding of the Lamb

✦ Alleluia.
Salvation, glory, and power to our God:
(℟ Alleluia.)
his judgments are honest and true.
℟ Alleluia (alleluia).

✦ Alleluia.
Sing praise to our God, all you his servants,
(℟ Alleluia.)
all who worship him reverently, great and small.
℟ Alleluia (alleluia).

✦ Alleluia.
The Lord our all-powerful God is King;
(℟ Alleluia.)
let us rejoice, sing praise, and give him glory.
℟ Alleluia (alleluia).

✦ Alleluia.
The wedding feast of the Lamb has begun,
(℟ Alleluia.)
and his bride is prepared to welcome him.
℟ Alleluia (alleluia).

[Bow]   ✦ Glory to the Father…

Ant.   All power is yours, Lord God, our mighty King, alleluia.

Reading: 2 Corinthians 1: 3-7

Praised be God, the Father of our Lord Jesus Christ, the Father of mercies and the God of all consolation! He comforts us in all our afflictions and thus enables us to comfort those who are in trouble, with the same consolation we have received from him. As we have shared much in the suffering of Christ, so through Christ do we share abundantly in his consolation. If we are afflicted it is for your encouragement and salvation, and when we are consoled it is for your consolation, so that you may endure patiently the same sufferings we endure. Our hope for you is firm because we know that just as you share in the sufferings, so you will share in the consolation.

Responsory

℣. The whole creation proclaims the greatness of your glory.
℟. The whole creation proclaims the greatness of your glory.
℣. Eternal ages praise
℟. the greatness of your glory.

[Bow]   ℣. Glory to the Father, and to the Son, and to the Holy Spirit.
℟. The whole creation proclaims the greatness of your glory.

Canticle Of Mary

Ant.
[Stand]   Many shall come from the east and the west, and they shall sit down with Abraham and Isaac and Jacob in the kingdom of heaven.

Magnificat: Luke 1: 46-55
My soul ✠ proclaims the… [See Prayer On Back Flap. Then Repeat The Antiphon Above.]

Intercessions

Introductory Formula
Christ the Lord is our head; we are his members. In joy let us call out to him:
℟. Lord, may your kingdom come.

Petitions
℣. Christ our Savior, make your Church a more vivid symbol of the unity of all mankind,
℟. make it more effectively the sacrament of salvation for all peoples.
℣. Through your presence, guide the college of bishops in union with the Pope,
℟. give them the gifts of unity, love and peace.
℣. Bind all Christians more closely to yourself, their divine Head,
℟. lead them to proclaim your kingdom by the witness of their lives.
℣. Grant peace to the world,
℟. let every land flourish in justice and security.
℣. Grant to the dead the glory of resurrection,
℟. and give us a share in their happiness.

The Lord's Prayer
Our Father… [See prayer on back flap]

Prayer

Father,
help us to seek the values
that will bring us lasting joy in this
  changing world.
In our desire for what you promise
make us one in mind and heart.
Grant this through our Lord Jesus Christ,
  your Son,
who lives and reigns with you
  and the Holy Spirit,
one God, for ever and ever. Amen.

Closing Rite Or Dismissal
[See Closing Rite on Back Flap]

Introductory Rite

[See Introductory Rite on Front Flap]

Hymn

+ Love divine, all loves excelling,
Joy of heaven to earth come down,
And impart to us, here dwelling,
Grace and mercy all around.
Jesus, source of all compassion,
Pure, unbounded love you share;
Grant us many choicest blessings,
Keep us in your loving care.

+ Come, O source of inspiration,
Pure and spotless let us be:
Let us see your true salvation,
Perfect in accord with thee.
Praising Father for all glory
With the Spirit and the Son;
Everlasting thanks we give thee,
Undivided, love, in one.

Text: C. Wesley, 1707-1788, adapted by C.T. Andrews 1968

Psalmody

Ant. 1 Christ our Lord is a priest for ever, like
Melchizedek of old, alleluia.

Book 5: Psalm 110: 1-5, 7
The Messiah, king and priest

[Sit] + The Lord's revelation to my Master:
"Sit on my right:
your foes I will put beneath your feet."

+ The Lord will wield from Zion
your scepter of power:
rule in the midst of all your foes.

+ A prince from the day of your birth
on the holy mountains;
from the womb before the dawn I begot you.

+ The Lord has sworn an oath he will not change.
"You are a priest for ever,
a priest like Melchizedek of old."

+ The Master standing at your right hand
will shatter kings in the day of his great wrath.

+ He shall drink from the stream by the wayside
and therefore he shall lift up his head.

[Bow] + Glory to the Father…

Psalm Prayer
Almighty God,…[See psalm prayer on front flap]

Ant. Christ our Lord is a priest for ever, like
Melchizedek of old, alleluia.

Ant. 2 God dwells in highest heaven; he has power to
do all he wills, alleluia.

Twenty-second Sunday in Ordinary Time

Book 5: Psalm 115
Praise of the true God

+ Not to us, Lord, not to us,
but to your name give the glory
for the sake of your love and your truth,
lest the heathen say: "Where is their God?"

+ But our God is in the heavens;
he does whatever he wills.
Their idols are silver and gold,
the work of human hands.

+ They have mouths but they cannot speak;
they have eyes but they cannot see;
they have ears but they cannot hear;
they have nostrils but they cannot smell.

+ With their hands they cannot feel;
with their feet they cannot walk.
No sound comes from their throats.
Their makers will come to be like them
and so will all who trust in them.

+ Sons of Israel, trust in the Lord;
he is their help and their shield.
Sons of Aaron, trust in the Lord;
he is their help and their shield.

+ You who fear him, trust in the Lord;
he is their help and their shield.
He remembers us, and he will bless us;
he will bless the sons of Israel.
He will bless the sons of Aaron.

+ The Lord will bless those who fear him,
the little no less than the great:
to you may the Lord grant increase,
to you and all your children.

+ May you be blessed by the Lord,
the maker of heaven and earth.
The heavens belong to the Lord
but the earth he has given to men.

+ The dead shall not praise the Lord,
nor those who go down into the silence.
But we who live bless the Lord
now and for ever. Amen.

[Bow] + Glory to the Father…

Psalm Prayer
Father, creator… [SEE PSALM PRAYER ON FRONT FLAP]

Ant.   God dwells in highest heaven; he has power to do all he wills, alleluia.

Ant. 3   Praise God, all you who serve him, both great and small, alleluia.

Canticle based on Revelation 19: 1-7
The wedding of the Lamb

+ Alleluia.
Salvation, glory, and power to our God:
(℟ Alleluia.)
his judgments are honest and true.
℟ Alleluia (alleluia).

+ Alleluia.
Sing praise to our God, all you his servants,
(℟ Alleluia.)
all who worship him reverently, great and small.
℟ Alleluia (alleluia).

+ Alleluia.
The Lord our all-powerful God is King;
(℟ Alleluia.)
let us rejoice, sing praise, and give him glory.
℟ Alleluia (alleluia).

+ Alleluia.
The wedding feast of the Lamb has begun,
(℟ Alleluia.)
and his bride is prepared to welcome him.
℟ Alleluia (alleluia).

[BOW]   + Glory to the Father…

Ant.   Praise God, all you who serve him, both great and small, alleluia.

Reading: 2 Thessalonians 2: 13-14
We are bound to thank God for you always, beloved brothers in the Lord, because you are the first fruits of those whom God has chosen for salvation, in holiness of spirit and fidelity to truth. He called you through our preaching of the good news so that you might achieve the glory of our Lord Jesus Christ.

Responsory
℣ Our Lord is great, mighty is his power.
℟ Our Lord is great, mighty is his power.
℣ His wisdom is beyond compare,
℟ mighty is his power.
[BOW] ℣ Glory to the Father, and to the Son, and to the Holy Spirit.
℟ Our Lord is great, mighty is his power.

Canticle Of Mary
Ant.   When you are invited to a wedding, go to the
[STAND]   lowest place, so that the one who invited you can say: Friend, go up higher. Then you will be honored in the eyes of all who are at table with you.

Magnificat: Luke 1: 46-55
My soul ✠ proclaims the… [SEE PRAYER ON BACK FLAP. THEN REPEAT THE ANTIPHON ABOVE.]

Intercessions

Introductory Formula
All praise and honor to Christ! He lives for ever to intercede for us, and he is able to save those who approach the Father in his name. Sustained by our faith, let us call upon him:
℟ Remember your people, Lord.

Petitions
℣ As the day draws to a close, Sun of Justice, we invoke your name upon the whole human race,
℟ so that all men may enjoy your never failing light.
℣ Preserve the covenant which you have ratified in your blood,
℟ cleanse and sanctify your Church.
℣ Remember your assembly, Lord,
℟ your dwelling place.
℣ Guide travelers along the path of peace and prosperity,
℟ so that they may reach their destinations in safety and joy.
℣ Receive the souls of the dead, Lord,
℟ grant them your favor and the gift of eternal glory.

The Lord's Prayer
Our Father… [SEE PRAYER ON BACK FLAP]

Prayer
Almighty God,
every good thing comes from you.
Fill our hearts with love for you,
increase our faith,
and by your constant care
protect the good you have given us.
We ask this through our Lord Jesus Christ,
  your Son,
who lives and reigns with you
  and the Holy Spirit,
one God, for ever and ever. Amen.

Closing Rite Or Dismissal
[SEE CLOSING RITE ON BACK FLAP]

Introductory Rite

[STAND] V. God, ✝ come to my assistance.

R. Lord, make haste to help me.

[BOW] Glory to the Father, and to the Son,
and to the Holy Spirit:
as it was in the beginning, is now,
and will be for ever. Amen.

Hymn

✦ O Christ, you are the light and day
Which drives away the night,
The ever shining Sun of God
And pledge of future light.

✦ As now the ev'ning shadows fall
Please grant us, Lord, we pray,
A quiet night to rest in you
Until the break of day.

✦ Remember us, poor mortal men,
We humbly ask, O Lord,
And may your presence in our souls
Be now our great reward.

Translator: Rev. M. Quinn, O.P. et al.

Psalmody

Ant. 1 The Lord said to my Master: Sit at my right
hand, alleluia.

Book 5: Psalm 110: 1-5, 7
The Messiah, king and priest

[SIT] ✦ The Lord's revelation to my Master:
"Sit on my right:
your foes I will put beneath your feet."

✦ The Lord will wield from Zion
your scepter of power:
rule in the midst of all your foes.

✦ A prince from the day of your birth
on the holy mountains;
from the womb before the dawn I begot you.

✦ The Lord has sworn an oath he will not change.
"You are a priest for ever,
a priest like Melchizedek of old."

✦ The Master standing at your right hand
will shatter kings in the day of his great wrath.

✦ He shall drink from the stream by the wayside
and therefore he shall lift up his head.

[BOW] ✦ Glory to the Father…

Psalm Prayer
Father, we ask you to give us victory and peace.
In Jesus Christ, our Lord and King, we are
already seated at your right hand. We look
forward to praising you in the fellowship of all
your saints in our heavenly homeland.

112

TWENTY-THIRD SUNDAY
in Ordinary Time
[PSALTER, WEEK III]

Ant. The Lord said to my Master: Sit at my right
hand, alleluia.

Ant. 2 Our compassionate Lord has left us a
memorial of his wonderful work, alleluia.

Book 5: Psalm 111
God's marvelous works

✦ I will thank the Lord with all my heart
in the meeting of the just and their assembly.
Great are the works of the Lord;
to be pondered by all who love them.

✦ Majestic and glorious his work,
his justice stands firm for ever.
He makes us remember his wonders.
The Lord is compassion and love.

✦ He gives food to those who fear him;
keeps his covenant ever in mind.
He has shown his might to his people
by giving them the lands of the nations.

✦ His works are justice and truth:
his precepts are all of them sure,
standing firm for ever and ever:
they are made in uprightness and truth.

✦ He has sent deliverance to his people
and established his covenant for ever.
Holy his name, to be feared.

✦ To fear the Lord is the first stage of wisdom;
all who do so prove themselves wise.
His praise shall last for ever!

[BOW] ✦ Glory to the Father…

Psalm Prayer
Merciful and gentle Lord, you are the
crowning glory of all the saints. Give us, your
children, the gift of obedience which is the
beginning of wisdom, so that we may do what
you command and be filled with your mercy.

Ant. Our compassionate Lord has left us a
memorial of his wonderful work, alleluia.

Ant. 3 All power is yours, Lord God, our mighty
King, alleluia.

Canticle based on Revelation 19: 1-7
The wedding of the Lamb

✛ Alleluia.
Salvation, glory, and power to our God:
(℟ Alleluia.)
his judgments are honest and true.
℟ Alleluia (alleluia).

✛ Alleluia.
Sing praise to our God, all you his servants,
(℟ Alleluia.)
all who worship him reverently, great and small.
℟ Alleluia (alleluia).

✛ Alleluia.
The Lord our all-powerful God is King;
(℟ Alleluia.)
let us rejoice, sing praise, and give him glory.
℟ Alleluia (alleluia).

✛ Alleluia.
The wedding feast of the Lamb has begun,
(℟ Alleluia.)
and his bride is prepared to welcome him.
℟ Alleluia (alleluia).

[Bow] ✛ Glory to the Father…

Ant. All power is yours, Lord God, our mighty King, alleluia.

Reading: 1 Peter 1: 3-7

Praised be the God and Father /of our Lord Jesus Christ, /he who in his great mercy /gave us new birth; /a birth unto hope which draws its life /from the resurrection of Jesus Christ from the dead; /a birth to an imperishable inheritance, /incapable of fading or defilement, /which is kept in heaven for you /who are guarded with God's power through faith; /a birth to a salvation which stands ready /to be revealed in the last days.

There is cause for rejoicing here. You may for a time have to suffer the distress of many trials; but this is so that your faith, which is more precious than the passing splendor of fire-tried gold, may by its genuineness lead to praise, glory, and honor when Jesus Christ appears.

Responsory

℣ The whole creation proclaims the greatness of your glory.
℟ The whole creation proclaims the greatness of your glory.
℣ Eternal ages praise
℟ the greatness of your glory.
[Bow] ℣ Glory to the Father, and to the Son, and to the Holy Spirit.

℟ The whole creation proclaims the greatness of your glory.

Canticle Of Mary

Ant.
[Stand] Whoever refuses to take up his cross and follow me cannot be my disciple, says the Lord.

Magnificat: Luke 1: 46-55
My soul ✛ proclaims the… [See Prayer On Back Flap. Then Repeat The Antiphon Above.]

Intercessions

Introductory Formula
The world was created by the Word of God, re-created by his redemption, and it is continually renewed by his love. Rejoicing in him we call out:
℟ Renew the wonders of your love, Lord.

Petitions
℣ We give thanks to God whose power is revealed in nature,
℟ and whose providence is revealed in history.
℣ Through your Son, the herald of reconciliation, the victor of the cross,
℟ free us from empty fear and hopelessness.
℣ May all those who love and pursue justice,
℟ work together without deceit to build a world of true peace.
℣ Be with the oppressed, free the captives, console the sorrowing, feed the hungry, strengthen the weak,
℟ in all people reveal the victory of your cross.
℣ After your Son's death and burial you raised him up again in glory,
℟ grant that the faithful departed may live with him.

The Lord's Prayer
Our Father… [See prayer on back flap]

Prayer

God our Father,
you redeem us
and make us your children in Christ.
Look upon us,
give us true freedom
and bring us to the inheritance you promised.
Grant this through our Lord Jesus Christ,
   your Son,
who lives and reigns with you
   and the Holy Spirit,
one God, for ever and ever. Amen.

Closing Rite Or Dismissal

[See Closing Rite on Back Flap]

113

Introductory Rite

[Stand] V. God, ✠ come to my assistance.
R. Lord, make haste to help me.

[Bow] Glory to the Father, and to the Son,
and to the Holy Spirit:
as it was in the beginning, is now,
and will be for ever. Amen.

Hymn

✦ Love divine, all loves excelling,
Joy of heaven to earth come down,
And impart to us, here dwelling,
Grace and mercy all around.
Jesus, source of all compassion,
Pure, unbounded love you share;
Grant us many choicest blessings,
Keep us in your loving care.

✦ Come, O source of inspiration,
Pure and spotless let us be:
Let us see your true salvation,
Perfect in accord with thee.
Praising Father for all glory
With the Spirit and the Son;
Everlasting thanks we give thee,
Undivided, love, in one.

Text: C. Wesley, 1707-1788, adapted by C.T. Andrews 1968

Psalmody

Ant. 1 In eternal splendor, before the dawn of light on
earth, I have begotten you, alleluia.

Book 5: Psalm 110: 1-5, 7
The Messiah, king and priest

[Sit] ✦ The Lord's revelation to my Master:
"Sit on my right:
your foes I will put beneath your feet."

✦ The Lord will wield from Zion
your scepter of power:
rule in the midst of all your foes.

✦ A prince from the day of your birth
on the holy mountains;
from the womb before the dawn I begot you.

✦ The Lord has sworn an oath he will not change.
"You are a priest for ever,
a priest like Melchizedek of old."

✦ The Master standing at your right hand
will shatter kings in the day of his great wrath.

✦ He shall drink from the stream by the wayside
and therefore he shall lift up his head.

[Bow] ✦ Glory to the Father, and to the Son,
and to the Holy Spirit:

Twenty-fourth Sunday in Ordinary Time

as it was in the beginning, is now and will be
for ever. Amen.

Psalm Prayer

Father, we ask you to give us victory and
peace. In Jesus Christ, our Lord and King, we
are already seated at your right hand. We look
forward to praising you in the fellowship of all
your saints in our heavenly homeland.

Ant. In eternal splendor, before the dawn of light
on earth, I have begotten you, alleluia.

Ant. 2 Blessed are they who hunger and thirst for
holiness; they will be satisfied.

Book 5: Psalm 112
The happiness of the just man

✦ Happy the man who fears the Lord,
who takes delight in all his commands.
His sons will be powerful on earth;
the children of the upright are blessed.

✦ Riches and wealth are in his house;
his justice stands firm for ever.
He is a light in the darkness for the upright:
he is generous, merciful and just.

✦ The good man takes pity and lends,
he conducts his affairs with honor.
The just man will never waver:
he will be remembered for ever.

✦ He has no fear of evil news;
with a firm heart he trusts in the Lord.
With a steadfast heart he will not fear;
he will see the downfall of his foes.

✦ Open-handed, he gives to the poor;
his justice stands firm for ever.
His head will be raised in glory.

✦ The wicked man sees and is angry,
grinds his teeth and fades away;
the desire of the wicked leads to doom.

[Bow] ✦ Glory to the Father, and to the Son,
and to the Holy Spirit:
as it was in the beginning, is now and will be
for ever. Amen.

Psalm Prayer

Lord God, you are the eternal light which illumines the hearts of good people. Help us to love you, to rejoice in your glory, and so to live in this world as to avoid harsh judgment in the next. May we come to see the light of your countenance.

Ant. Blessed are they who hunger and thirst for holiness; they will be satisfied.

Ant. 3 Praise God, all you who serve him, both great and small, alleluia.

Canticle based on Revelation 19: 1-7
The wedding of the Lamb

✦ Alleluia.
Salvation, glory, and power to our God:
(℟ Alleluia.)
his judgments are honest and true.
℟ Alleluia (alleluia).

✦ Alleluia.
Sing praise to our God, all you his servants,
(℟ Alleluia.)
all who worship him reverently, great and small.
℟ Alleluia (alleluia).

✦ Alleluia.
The Lord our all-powerful God is King;
(℟ Alleluia.)
let us rejoice, sing praise, and give him glory.
℟ Alleluia (alleluia).

✦ Alleluia.
The wedding feast of the Lamb has begun,
(℟ Alleluia.)
and his bride is prepared to welcome him.
℟ Alleluia (alleluia).

[Bow] ✦ Glory to the Father…

Ant. Praise God, all you who serve him, both great and small, alleluia.

Reading: Hebrews 12: 22-24

You have drawn near to Mount Zion and the city of the living God, the heavenly Jerusalem, to myriads of angels in festal gathering, to the assembly of the first-born enrolled in heaven, to God the judge of all, to the spirits of just men made perfect, to Jesus, the mediator of a new covenant, and to the sprinkled blood which speaks more eloquently than that of Abel.

Responsory

℣ Our Lord is great, mighty is his power.
℟ Our Lord is great, mighty is his power.
℣ His wisdom is beyond compare,
℟ mighty is his power.
[Bow] ℣ Glory to the Father, and to the Son, and to the Holy Spirit.
℟ Our Lord is great, mighty is his power.

Canticle Of Mary

Ant. I say to you: there is great rejoicing among the
[Stand] angels of God over one repentant sinner.

Magnificat: Luke 1: 46-55
My soul ✠ proclaims the… [See Prayer On Back Flap. Then Repeat The Antiphon Above.]

Intercessions

Introductory Formula
Rejoicing in the Lord, from whom all good things come, let us pray:
℟ Lord, hear our prayer.

Petitions
℣ Father and Lord of all, you sent your Son into the world, that your name might be glorified in every place,
℟ strengthen the witness of your Church among the nations.
℣ Make us obedient to the teachings of your apostles,
℟ and bound to the truth of our faith.
℣ As you love the innocent,
℟ render justice to those who are wronged.
℣ Free those in bondage and give sight to the blind,
℟ raise up the fallen and protect the stranger.
℣ Fulfill your promise to those who already sleep in your peace,
℟ through your Son grant them a blessed resurrection.

The Lord's Prayer
Our Father… [See prayer on back flap]

Prayer

Almighty God,
our creator and guide,
may we serve you with all our heart
and know your forgiveness in our lives.
We ask this through our Lord Jesus Christ,
your Son,
who lives and reigns with you
and the Holy Spirit,
one God, for ever and ever. Amen.

Closing Rite Or Dismissal

[See Closing Rite on Back Flap]

115

Introductory Rite

[Stand] V. God, ✝ come to my assistance.
R. Lord, make haste to help me.

[Bow] Glory to the Father, and to the Son,
and to the Holy Spirit:
as it was in the beginning, is now,
and will be for ever. Amen.

Hymn

✦ Hail, Redeemer, King divine!
Priest and Lamb, the throne is thine;
King whose reign shall never cease,
Prince of everlasting peace.

Refrain: ✦ *Angels, saints, and nations sing:*
"Praised be Jesus Christ, our King;
Lord of earth and sky and sea,
King of love on Calvary."

✦ Christ, thou King of truth and might,
Be to us eternal right,
Till in peace each nation rings
With thy praises, King of kings.

Refrain *Angels, saints, and nations sing. . .*
Text: P. Brennan, C. SS. R., alt.

Psalmody

Ant. 1 What a great work of charity! Death itself died
when life was slain on the tree.

Book 5: Psalm 110: 1-5, 7
The Messiah, king and priest
[Sit] ✦ The Lord's revelation to my Master:
"Sit on my right:
your foes I will put beneath your feet."

✦ The Lord will wield from Zion
your scepter of power:
rule in the midst of all your foes.

✦ A prince from the day of your birth
on the holy mountains;
from the womb before the dawn I begot you.

✦ The Lord has sworn an oath he will not change.
"You are a priest for ever,
a priest like Melchizedek of old."

✦ The Master standing at your right hand
will shatter kings in the day of his great wrath.

✦ He shall drink from the stream by the wayside
and therefore he shall lift up his head.

[Bow] ✦ Glory to the Father, and to the Son,
and to the Holy Spirit:
as it was in the beginning, is now,
and will be for ever. Amen.

THE EXALTATION
of the Holy Cross

Ant. What a great work of charity! Death itself
died when life was slain on the tree.

Ant. 2 We worship your cross, O Lord, and we
commemorate your glorious passion. You
suffered for us; have mercy on us.

Book 5: Psalm 116: 10-19
Thanksgiving in the Temple
✦ I trusted, even when I said:
"I am sorely afflicted,"
and when I said in my alarm:
"No man can be trusted."

✦ How can I repay the Lord
for his goodness to me?
The cup of salvation I will raise;
I will call on the Lord's name.

✦ My vows to the Lord I will fulfill
before all his people.
O precious in the eyes of the Lord
is the death of his faithful.

✦ Your servant, Lord, your servant am I;
you have loosened my bonds.
A thanksgiving sacrifice I make:
I will call on the Lord's name.

✦ My vows to the Lord I will fulfill
before all his people,
in the courts of the house of the Lord,
in your midst, O Jerusalem.

[Bow] ✦ Glory to the Father, and to the Son,
and to the Holy Spirit:
as it was in the beginning, is now,
and will be for ever. Amen.

Ant. We worship your cross, O Lord, and we
commemorate your glorious passion. You
suffered for us; have mercy on us.

Ant. 3 We adore you, O Christ, and we bless you,
for by your holy cross you have redeemed the
world.

Canticle: Revelation 4: 11; 5: 9, 10, 12
Redemption hymn
✦ O Lord our God, you are worthy
to receive glory and honor and power.

✦ For you have created all things;
by your will they came to be and were made.

✦ Worthy are you, O Lord,
to receive the scroll and break open its seals.

✦ For you were slain;
with your blood you purchased for God
men of every race and tongue,
of every people and nation.

✦ You made of them a kingdom,
and priests to serve our God,
and they shall reign on the earth.

✦ Worthy is the Lamb that was slain
to receive power and riches,
wisdom and strength,
honor and glory and praise.

[Bow] ✦ Glory to the Father, and to the Son,
and to the Holy Spirit:
as it was in the beginning, is now,
and will be for ever. Amen.

Ant. We adore you, O Christ, and we bless you,
for by your holy cross you have redeemed the
world.

Reading: 1 Corinthians 1: 23-24

We preach Christ crucified—a stumbling
block to Jews, and an absurdity to Gentiles;
but to those who are called, Jews and Greeks
alike, Christ the power of God and the
wisdom of God.

Responsory

℣ O glorious cross, on you the King of angels
was victorious.
℟ O glorious cross, on you the King of angels
was victorious.
℣ And he has washed away our sins in his own
blood.
℟ On you the King of angels was victorious.
[Bow] ℣ Glory to the Father, and to the Son,
and to the Holy Spirit.
℟ O glorious cross, on you the King of angels
was victorious.

Canticle Of Mary

Ant. O cross, you are the glorious sign of our
[Stand] victory. Through your power may we share
in the triumph of Christ Jesus.

Magnificat: Luke 1: 46-55
My soul ✠ proclaims the... [See Prayer On Back
Flap. Then Repeat The Antiphon Above.]

Intercessions

Introductory Formula
Let us pray with confidence to Christ who
endured the cross to save us:
℟ Lord, through your cross bring us to the glory
of your kingdom.

Petitions
℣ O Christ, you emptied yourself, taking the
form of a servant and being made like us,
℟ grant that your people may follow the
example of your humility.
℣ O Christ, you humbled yourself and became
obedient unto death, even death on a cross,
℟ grant that your servants may imitate your
obedience and willing acceptance of trials.
℣ O Christ, you were raised up by the Father
and given the name that is above all
other names,
℟ may your people, strengthened in the hope of
a heavenly resurrection, persevere to the end.
℣ O Christ, at your name every knee in heaven,
on earth and under the earth will bend
in adoration,
℟ pour out your love upon all men that they may
join together in proclaiming your glory.
℣ O Christ, every tongue shall confess that you
are Lord to the glory of God the Father,
℟ welcome our brothers and sisters who have
died into the unfailing joy of your kingdom.

The Lord's Prayer
Our Father... [See prayer on back flap]

Prayer

God our Father,
in obedience to you
your only Son accepted death on the cross
for the salvation of mankind.
We acknowledge the mystery of the cross
on earth.
May we receive the gift of redemption
in heaven.
We ask this through our Lord Jesus Christ,
your Son,
who lives and reigns with you
and the Holy Spirit,
one God, for ever and ever. Amen.

Closing Rite Or Dismissal

[See Closing Rite on Back Flap]

Introductory Rite

[STAND] V. God, ✠ come to my assistance.

R. Lord, make haste to help me.

[BOW] Glory to the Father, and to the Son,
and to the Holy Spirit:
as it was in the beginning, is now,
and will be for ever. Amen.

Hymn

✦ O Christ, you are the light and day
Which drives away the night,
The ever shining Sun of God
And pledge of future light.

✦ As now the ev'ning shadows fall
Please grant us, Lord, we pray,
A quiet night to rest in you
Until the break of day.

✦ Remember us, poor mortal men,
We humbly ask, O Lord,
And may your presence in our souls
Be now our great reward.

Translator: Rev. M. Quinn, O.P. et al.

Psalmody

Ant. 1 The Lord will stretch forth his mighty scepter
from Zion, and he will reign for ever, alleluia.

Book 5: Psalm 110: 1-5, 7
The Messiah, king and priest

[SIT] ✦ The Lord's revelation to my Master:
"Sit on my right:
your foes I will put beneath your feet."

✦ The Lord will wield from Zion
your scepter of power:
rule in the midst of all your foes.

✦ A prince from the day of your birth
on the holy mountains;
from the womb before the dawn I begot you.

✦ The Lord has sworn an oath he will not change.
"You are a priest for ever,
a priest like Melchizedek of old."

✦ The Master standing at your right hand
will shatter kings in the day of his great wrath.

✦ He shall drink from the stream by the wayside
and therefore he shall lift up his head.

[BOW] ✦ Glory to the Father, and to the Son,
and to the Holy Spirit:
as it was in the beginning, is now,
and will be for ever. Amen.

TWENTY-FIFTH SUNDAY in Ordinary Time

[PSALTER, WEEK I]

Psalm Prayer

Father, we ask you to give us victory and peace. In Jesus Christ, our Lord and King, we are already seated at your right hand. We look forward to praising you in the fellowship of all your saints in our heavenly homeland.

Ant. The Lord will stretch forth his mighty scepter from Zion, and he will reign for ever, alleluia.

Ant. 2 The earth is shaken to its depths before the glory of your face.

Book 2: Psalm 114
The Israelites are delivered from the bondage of Egypt

✦ When Israel came forth from Egypt,
Jacob's sons from an alien people,
Judah became the Lord's temple,
Israel became his kingdom.

✦ The sea fled at the sight:
the Jordan turned back on its course,
the mountains leapt like rams
and the hills like yearling sheep.

✦ Why was it, sea, that you fled,
that you turned back, Jordan, on your course?
Mountains, that you leapt like rams,
hills, like yearling sheep?

✦ Tremble, O earth, before the Lord,
in the presence of the God of Jacob,
who turns the rock into a pool
and flint into a spring of water.

[BOW] ✦ Glory to the Father, and to the Son,
and to the Holy Spirit:
as it was in the beginning, is now,
and will be for ever. Amen.

Psalm Prayer

Almighty God, ever-living mystery of unity and trinity, you gave life to the new Israel by birth from water and the Spirit, and made it a chosen race, a royal priesthood, a people set apart as your eternal possession. May all those you have called to walk in the splendor of the new light render you fitting service and adoration.

Ant. The earth is shaken to its depths before the glory of your face.

Ant. 3 All power is yours, Lord God, our mighty
King, alleluia.

Canticle based on Revelation 19: 1-7
The wedding of the Lamb

✢ Alleluia.
Salvation, glory, and power to our God:
(℟ Alleluia.)
his judgments are honest and true.
℟ Alleluia (alleluia).

✢ Alleluia.
Sing praise to our God, all you his servants,
(℟ Alleluia.)
all who worship him reverently, great and small.
℟ Alleluia (alleluia).

✢ Alleluia.
The Lord our all-powerful God is King;
(℟ Alleluia.)
let us rejoice, sing praise, and give him glory.
℟ Alleluia (alleluia).

✢ Alleluia.
The wedding feast of the Lamb has begun,
(℟ Alleluia.)
and his bride is prepared to welcome him.
℟ Alleluia (alleluia).

[Bow] ✢ Glory to the Father…

Ant. All power is yours, Lord God, our mighty
King, alleluia.

Reading: 2 Corinthians 1: 3-7

Praised be God, the Father of our Lord Jesus
Christ, the Father of mercies and the God
of all consolation! He comforts us in all our
afflictions and thus enables us to comfort
those who are in trouble, with the same
consolation we have received from him. As we
have shared much in the suffering of Christ,
so through Christ do we share abundantly in
his consolation. If we are afflicted it is for your
encouragement and salvation, and when we are
consoled it is for your consolation, so that you
may endure patiently the same sufferings we
endure. Our hope for you is firm because we
know that just as you share in the sufferings, so
you will share in the consolation.

Responsory

℣. The whole creation proclaims the greatness
of your glory.
℟. The whole creation proclaims the greatness
of your glory.
℣. Eternal ages praise
℟. the greatness of your glory.

[Bow] ℣. Glory to the Father, and to the Son,
and to the Holy Spirit.
℟. The whole creation proclaims the greatness
of your glory.

Canticle Of Mary

Ant. No servant can obey two masters: you cannot
[Stand] serve God and the love of money at the same
time.

Magnificat: Luke 1: 46-55
My soul ✢ proclaims the… [See Prayer On Back
Flap. Then Repeat The Antiphon Above.]

Intercessions

Introductory Formula
Christ the Lord is our head; we are his
members. In joy let us call out to him:
℟. Lord, may your kingdom come.

Petitions
℣. Christ our Savior, make your Church a more
vivid symbol of the unity of all mankind,
℟. make it more effectively the sacrament of
salvation for all peoples.
℣. Through your presence, guide the college of
bishops in union with the Pope,
℟. give them the gifts of unity, love and peace.
℣. Bind all Christians more closely to yourself,
their divine Head,
℟. lead them to proclaim your kingdom by the
witness of their lives.
℣. Grant peace to the world,
℟. let every land flourish in justice and security.
℣. Grant to the dead the glory of resurrection,
℟. and give us a share in their happiness.

The Lord's Prayer
Our Father… [See prayer on back flap]

Prayer

Father,
guide us, as you guide creation
according to your law of love.
May we love one another
and come to perfection
in the eternal life prepared for us.
Grant this through our Lord Jesus Christ,
your Son,
who lives and reigns with you
and the Holy Spirit,
one God, for ever and ever. Amen.

Closing Rite Or Dismissal

[See Closing Rite on Back Flap]

Introductory Rite

[SEE INTRODUCTORY RITE ON FRONT FLAP]

Hymn

⁜ Love divine, all loves excelling,
Joy of heaven to earth come down,
And impart to us, here dwelling,
Grace and mercy all around.
Jesus, source of all compassion,
Pure, unbounded love you share;
Grant us many choicest blessings,
Keep us in your loving care.

⁜ Come, O source of inspiration,
Pure and spotless let us be:
Let us see your true salvation,
Perfect in accord with thee.
Praising Father for all glory
With the Spirit and the Son;
Everlasting thanks we give thee,
Undivided, love, in one.

Text: C. Wesley, 1707-1788, adapted by C.T. Andrews 1968

Psalmody

Ant. 1 Christ our Lord is a priest for ever, like
Melchizedek of old, alleluia.

Book 5: Psalm 110: 1-5, 7
The Messiah, king and priest

[Sit] ⁜ The Lord's revelation to my Master:
"Sit on my right:
your foes I will put beneath your feet."

⁜ The Lord will wield from Zion
your scepter of power:
rule in the midst of all your foes.

⁜ A prince from the day of your birth
on the holy mountains;
from the womb before the dawn I begot you.

⁜ The Lord has sworn an oath he will not change.
"You are a priest for ever,
a priest like Melchizedek of old."

⁜ The Master standing at your right hand
will shatter kings in the day of his great wrath.

⁜ He shall drink from the stream by the wayside
and therefore he shall lift up his head.

[Bow] ⁜ Glory to the Father…

Psalm Prayer
Almighty God,…[SEE PSALM PRAYER ON FRONT FLAP]

Ant. Christ our Lord is a priest for ever, like
Melchizedek of old, alleluia.

Ant. 2 God dwells in highest heaven; he has power to
do all he wills, alleluia.

TWENTY-SIXTH SUNDAY in Ordinary Time

[PSALTER, WEEK II]

Book 5: Psalm 115
Praise of the true God

⁜ Not to us, Lord, not to us,
but to your name give the glory
for the sake of your love and your truth,
lest the heathen say: "Where is their God?"

⁜ But our God is in the heavens;
he does whatever he wills.
Their idols are silver and gold,
the work of human hands.

⁜ They have mouths but they cannot speak;
they have eyes but they cannot see;
they have ears but they cannot hear;
they have nostrils but they cannot smell.

⁜ With their hands they cannot feel;
with their feet they cannot walk.
No sound comes from their throats.
Their makers will come to be like them
and so will all who trust in them.

⁜ Sons of Israel, trust in the Lord;
he is their help and their shield.
Sons of Aaron, trust in the Lord;
he is their help and their shield.

⁜ You who fear him, trust in the Lord;
he is their help and their shield.
He remembers us, and he will bless us;
he will bless the sons of Israel.
He will bless the sons of Aaron.

⁜ The Lord will bless those who fear him,
the little no less than the great:
to you may the Lord grant increase,
to you and all your children.

⁜ May you be blessed by the Lord,
the maker of heaven and earth.
The heavens belong to the Lord
but the earth he has given to men.

⁜ The dead shall not praise the Lord,
nor those who go down into the silence.
But we who live bless the Lord
now and for ever. Amen.

[Bow] ⁜ Glory to the Father…

Psalm Prayer
Father, creator… [See psalm prayer on front flap]

Ant.   God dwells in highest heaven; he has power to do all he wills, alleluia.

Ant. 3   Praise God, all you who serve him, both great and small, alleluia.

Canticle based on Revelation 19: 1-7
The wedding of the Lamb

✦ Alleluia.
Salvation, glory, and power to our God:
(℟ Alleluia.)
his judgments are honest and true.
℟ Alleluia (alleluia).

✦ Alleluia.
Sing praise to our God, all you his servants,
(℟ Alleluia.)
all who worship him reverently, great and small.
℟ Alleluia (alleluia).

✦ Alleluia.
The Lord our all-powerful God is King;
(℟ Alleluia.)
let us rejoice, sing praise, and give him glory.
℟ Alleluia (alleluia).

✦ Alleluia.
The wedding feast of the Lamb has begun,
(℟ Alleluia.)
and his bride is prepared to welcome him.
℟ Alleluia (alleluia).

[Bow]   ✦ Glory to the Father…

Ant.   Praise God, all you who serve him, both great and small, alleluia.

Reading: 2 Thessalonians 2: 13-14
We are bound to thank God for you always, beloved brothers in the Lord, because you are the first fruits of those whom God has chosen for salvation, in holiness of spirit and fidelity to truth. He called you through our preaching of the good news so that you might achieve the glory of our Lord Jesus Christ.

Responsory
℣. Our Lord is great, mighty is his power.
℟. Our Lord is great, mighty is his power.
℣. His wisdom is beyond compare,
℟. mighty is his power.
[Bow]   ℣. Glory to the Father, and to the Son, and to the Holy Spirit.
℟. Our Lord is great, mighty is his power.

Canticle Of Mary
Ant.
[Stand]   Son, remember the good things you received in your lifetime and the bad things Lazarus received in his.

Magnificat: Luke 1: 46-55
My soul ✠ proclaims the… [See Prayer On Back Flap. Then Repeat The Antiphon Above.]

Intercessions

Introductory Formula
All praise and honor to Christ! He lives for ever to intercede for us, and he is able to save those who approach the Father in his name. Sustained by our faith, let us call upon him:
℟ Remember your people, Lord.

Petitions
℣. As the day draws to a close, Sun of Justice, we invoke your name upon the whole human race,
℟. so that all men may enjoy your never failing light.
℣. Preserve the covenant which you have ratified in your blood,
℟. cleanse and sanctify your Church.
℣. Remember your assembly, Lord,
℟. your dwelling place.
℣. Guide travelers along the path of peace and prosperity,
℟. so that they may reach their destinations in safety and joy.
℣. Receive the souls of the dead, Lord,
℟. grant them your favor and the gift of eternal glory.

The Lord's Prayer
Our Father… [See prayer on back flap]

Prayer
Father,
you show your almighty power
in your mercy and forgiveness.
Continue to fill us with your gifts of love.
Help us to hurry toward the eternal life
  you promise
and come to share in the joys of your kingdom.
Grant this through our Lord Jesus Christ,
  your Son,
who lives and reigns with you
  and the Holy Spirit,
one God, for ever and ever. Amen.

Closing Rite Or Dismissal
[See Closing Rite on Back Flap]

Introductory Rite

[STAND] V. God, ✠ come to my assistance.
R. Lord, make haste to help me.

[BOW] Glory to the Father…

Hymn

✦ O Christ, you are the light and day
Which drives away the night,
The ever shining Sun of God
And pledge of future light.

✦ As now the ev'ning shadows fall
Please grant us, Lord, we pray,
A quiet night to rest in you
Until the break of day.

✦ Remember us, poor mortal men,
We humbly ask, O Lord,
And may your presence in our souls
Be now our great reward.

Translator: Rev. M. Quinn, O.P. et al.

Psalmody

Ant. 1   The Lord said to my Master: Sit at my right hand, alleluia.

Book 5: Psalm 110: 1-5, 7
The Messiah, king and priest

[SIT] ✦ The Lord's revelation to my Master:
"Sit on my right:
your foes I will put beneath your feet."

✦ The Lord will wield from Zion
your scepter of power:
rule in the midst of all your foes.

✦ A prince from the day of your birth
on the holy mountains;
from the womb before the dawn I begot you.

✦ The Lord has sworn an oath he will not change.
"You are a priest for ever,
a priest like Melchizedek of old."

✦ The Master standing at your right hand
will shatter kings in the day of his great wrath.

✦ He shall drink from the stream by the wayside
and therefore he shall lift up his head.

[BOW] ✦ Glory to the Father…

Psalm Prayer
Father, we ask you to give us victory and peace. In Jesus Christ, our Lord and King, we are already seated at your right hand. We look forward to praising you in the fellowship of all your saints in our heavenly homeland.

Ant.   The Lord said to my Master: Sit at my right hand, alleluia.

TWENTY-SEVENTH SUNDAY *in Ordinary Time*
[PSALTER, WEEK III]

Ant. 2   Our compassionate Lord has left us a memorial of his wonderful work, alleluia.

Book 5: Psalm 111
God's marvelous works

✦ I will thank the Lord with all my heart
in the meeting of the just and their assembly.
Great are the works of the Lord;
to be pondered by all who love them.

✦ Majestic and glorious his work,
his justice stands firm for ever.
He makes us remember his wonders.
The Lord is compassion and love.

✦ He gives food to those who fear him;
keeps his covenant ever in mind.
He has shown his might to his people
by giving them the lands of the nations.

✦ His works are justice and truth:
his precepts are all of them sure,
standing firm for ever and ever:
they are made in uprightness and truth.

✦ He has sent deliverance to his people
and established his covenant for ever.
Holy his name, to be feared.

✦ To fear the Lord is the first stage of wisdom;
all who do so prove themselves wise.
His praise shall last for ever!

[BOW] ✦ Glory to the Father…

Psalm Prayer
Merciful and gentle Lord, you are the crowning glory of all the saints. Give us, your children, the gift of obedience which is the beginning of wisdom, so that we may do what you command and be filled with your mercy.

Ant.   Our compassionate Lord has left us a memorial of his wonderful work, alleluia.

Ant. 3   All power is yours, Lord God, our mighty King, alleluia.

Canticle based on Revelation 19: 1-7
The wedding of the Lamb

✦ Alleluia.
Salvation, glory, and power to our God:

(℟. Alleluia.)
his judgments are honest and true.
℟. Alleluia (alleluia).

♦ Alleluia.
Sing praise to our God, all you his servants,
(℟. Alleluia.)
all who worship him reverently, great and small.
℟. Alleluia (alleluia).

♦ Alleluia.
The Lord our all-powerful God is King;
(℟. Alleluia.)
let us rejoice, sing praise, and give him glory.
℟. Alleluia (alleluia).

♦ Alleluia.
The wedding feast of the Lamb has begun,
(℟. Alleluia.)
and his bride is prepared to welcome him.
℟. Alleluia (alleluia).

[Bow] ♦ Glory to the Father…

Ant. All power is yours, Lord God, our mighty King, alleluia.

Reading: 1 Peter 1: 3-7

Praised be the God and Father /of our Lord Jesus Christ, /he who in his great mercy /gave us new birth; /a birth unto hope which draws its life /from the resurrection of Jesus Christ from the dead; /a birth to an imperishable inheritance, /incapable of fading or defilement, /which is kept in heaven for you /who are guarded with God's power through faith; /a birth to a salvation which stands ready /to be revealed in the last days.

There is cause for rejoicing here. You may for a time have to suffer the distress of many trials; but this is so that your faith, which is more precious than the passing splendor of fire-tried gold, may by its genuineness lead to praise, glory, and honor when Jesus Christ appears.

Responsory

℣. The whole creation proclaims the greatness of your glory.
℟. The whole creation proclaims the greatness of your glory.
℣. Eternal ages praise
℟. the greatness of your glory.
[Bow] ℣. Glory to the Father, and to the Son, and to the Holy Spirit.
℟. The whole creation proclaims the greatness of your glory.

Canticle Of Mary

Ant.
[Stand]
Tell yourselves: We are useless servants, for we did only what we should have done.

Magnificat: Luke 1: 46-55
My soul ✠ proclaims the… [See Prayer On Back Flap. Then Repeat The Antiphon Above.]

Intercessions

Introductory Formula
The world was created by the Word of God, re-created by his redemption, and it is continually renewed by his love. Rejoicing in him we call out:
℟. Renew the wonders of your love, Lord.

Petitions
℣. We give thanks to God whose power is revealed in nature,
℟. and whose providence is revealed in history.
℣. Through your Son, the herald of reconciliation, the victor of the cross,
℟. free us from empty fear and hopelessness.
℣. May all those who love and pursue justice,
℟. work together without deceit to build a world of true peace.
℣. Be with the oppressed, free the captives, console the sorrowing, feed the hungry, strengthen the weak,
℟. in all people reveal the victory of your cross.
℣. After your Son's death and burial you raised him up again in glory,
℟. grant that the faithful departed may live with him.

The Lord's Prayer
Our Father… [See prayer on back flap]

Prayer

Father,
your love for us
surpasses all our hopes and desires.
Forgive our failings,
keep us in your peace
and lead us in the way of salvation.
We ask this through our Lord Jesus Christ,
your Son,
who lives and reigns with you
and the Holy Spirit,
one God, for ever and ever. Amen.

Closing Rite Or Dismissal

[See Closing Rite on Back Flap]

Introductory Rite

[Stand] V. God, ✠ come to my assistance.
  R. Lord, make haste to help me.

[Bow]   Glory to the Father, and to the Son,
  and to the Holy Spirit:
  as it was in the beginning, is now,
  and will be for ever. Amen.

Hymn

  ✦ Love divine, all loves excelling,
  Joy of heaven to earth come down,
  And impart to us, here dwelling,
  Grace and mercy all around.
  Jesus, source of all compassion,
  Pure, unbounded love you share;
  Grant us many choicest blessings,
  Keep us in your loving care.

  ✦ Come, O source of inspiration,
  Pure and spotless let us be:
  Let us see your true salvation,
  Perfect in accord with thee.
  Praising Father for all glory
  With the Spirit and the Son;
  Everlasting thanks we give thee,
  Undivided, love, in one.

  Text: C. Wesley, 1707-1788, adapted by C.T. Andrews 1968

Psalmody

Ant. 1   In eternal splendor, before the dawn of light on
  earth, I have begotten you, alleluia.

  Book 5: Psalm 110: 1-5, 7
  The Messiah, king and priest

[Sit]   ✦ The Lord's revelation to my Master:
  "Sit on my right:
  your foes I will put beneath your feet."

  ✦ The Lord will wield from Zion
  your scepter of power:
  rule in the midst of all your foes.

  ✦ A prince from the day of your birth
  on the holy mountains;
  from the womb before the dawn I begot you.

  ✦ The Lord has sworn an oath he will not change.
  "You are a priest for ever,
  a priest like Melchizedek of old."

  ✦ The Master standing at your right hand
  will shatter kings in the day of his great wrath.

  ✦ He shall drink from the stream by the wayside
  and therefore he shall lift up his head.

[Bow]   ✦ Glory to the Father, and to the Son,
  and to the Holy Spirit:

Twenty-eighth Sunday in Ordinary Time

[Psalter, Week IV]

  as it was in the beginning, is now,
  and will be for ever. Amen.

Psalm Prayer
Father, we ask you to give us victory and
peace. In Jesus Christ, our Lord and King, we
are already seated at your right hand. We look
forward to praising you in the fellowship of all
your saints in our heavenly homeland.

Ant.   In eternal splendor, before the dawn of light
  on earth, I have begotten you, alleluia.

Ant. 2   Blessed are they who hunger and thirst for
  holiness; they will be satisfied.

  Book 5: Psalm 112
  The happiness of the just man

  ✦ Happy the man who fears the Lord,
  who takes delight in all his commands.
  His sons will be powerful on earth;
  the children of the upright are blessed.

  ✦ Riches and wealth are in his house;
  his justice stands firm for ever.
  He is a light in the darkness for the upright:
  he is generous, merciful and just.

  ✦ The good man takes pity and lends,
  he conducts his affairs with honor.
  The just man will never waver:
  he will be remembered for ever.

  ✦ He has no fear of evil news;
  with a firm heart he trusts in the Lord.
  With a steadfast heart he will not fear;
  he will see the downfall of his foes.

  ✦ Open-handed, he gives to the poor;
  his justice stands firm for ever.
  His head will be raised in glory.

  ✦ The wicked man sees and is angry,
  grinds his teeth and fades away;
  the desire of the wicked leads to doom.

[Bow]   ✦ Glory to the Father, and to the Son,
  and to the Holy Spirit:
  as it was in the beginning, is now,
  and will be for ever. Amen.

Psalm Prayer

Lord God, you are the eternal light which illumines the hearts of good people. Help us to love you, to rejoice in your glory, and so to live in this world as to avoid harsh judgment in the next. May we come to see the light of your countenance.

Ant. Blessed are they who hunger and thirst for holiness; they will be satisfied.

Ant. 3 Praise God, all you who serve him, both great and small, alleluia.

Canticle based on Revelation 19: 1-7
The wedding of the Lamb

✦ Alleluia.
Salvation, glory, and power to our God:
(℟ Alleluia.)
his judgments are honest and true.
℟ Alleluia (alleluia).

✦ Alleluia.
Sing praise to our God, all you his servants,
(℟ Alleluia.)
all who worship him reverently, great and small.
℟ Alleluia (alleluia).

✦ Alleluia.
The Lord our all-powerful God is King;
(℟ Alleluia.)
let us rejoice, sing praise, and give him glory.
℟ Alleluia (alleluia).

✦ Alleluia.
The wedding feast of the Lamb has begun,
(℟ Alleluia.)
and his bride is prepared to welcome him.
℟ Alleluia (alleluia).

[Bow] ✦ Glory to the Father…

Ant. Praise God, all you who serve him, both great and small, alleluia.

Reading: Hebrews 12: 22-24

You have drawn near to Mount Zion and the city of the living God, the heavenly Jerusalem, to myriads of angels in festal gathering, to the assembly of the first-born enrolled in heaven, to God the judge of all, to the spirits of just men made perfect, to Jesus, the mediator of a new covenant, and to the sprinkled blood which speaks more eloquently than that of Abel.

Responsory

℣ Our Lord is great, mighty is his power.
℟ Our Lord is great, mighty is his power.

℣ His wisdom is beyond compare,
℟ mighty is his power.

[Bow] ℣ Glory to the Father, and to the Son, and to the Holy Spirit.
℟ Our Lord is great, mighty is his power.

Canticle Of Mary

Ant. One of them, realizing that he had been cured, [Stand] returned praising God in a loud voice, alleluia.

Magnificat: Luke 1: 46-55
My soul ✠ proclaims the… [See Prayer On Back Flap. Then Repeat The Antiphon Above.]

Intercessions

Introductory Formula
Rejoicing in the Lord, from whom all good things come, let us pray:
℟ Lord, hear our prayer.

Petitions
℣ Father and Lord of all, you sent your Son into the world, that your name might be glorified in every place,
℟ strengthen the witness of your Church among the nations.
℣ Make us obedient to the teachings of your apostles,
℟ and bound to the truth of our faith.
℣ As you love the innocent,
℟ render justice to those who are wronged.
℣ Free those in bondage and give sight to the blind,
℟ raise up the fallen and protect the stranger.
℣ Fulfill your promise to those who already sleep in your peace,
℟ through your Son grant them a blessed resurrection.

The Lord's Prayer
Our Father… [See prayer on back flap]

Prayer

Lord,
our help and guide,
make your love the foundation of our lives.
May our love for you express itself
in our eagerness to do good for others.
Grant this through our Lord Jesus Christ,
    your Son,
who lives and reigns with you
    and the Holy Spirit,
one God, for ever and ever. Amen.

Closing Rite Or Dismissal

[See Closing Rite on Back Flap]

125

Introductory Rite

[STAND] V. God, ✠ come to my assistance.

R. Lord, make haste to help me.

[BOW] Glory to the Father, and to the Son,
and to the Holy Spirit:
as it was in the beginning, is now,
and will be for ever. Amen.

Hymn

‹ O Christ, you are the light and day
Which drives away the night,
The ever shining Sun of God
And pledge of future light.

‹ As now the ev'ning shadows fall
Please grant us, Lord, we pray,
A quiet night to rest in you
Until the break of day.

‹ Remember us, poor mortal men,
We humbly ask, O Lord,
And may your presence in our souls
Be now our great reward.

Translator: Rev. M. Quinn, O.P. et al.

Psalmody

Ant. 1 The Lord will stretch forth his mighty scepter
from Zion, and he will reign for ever, alleluia.

Book 5: Psalm 110: 1-5, 7
The Messiah, king and priest

[SIT] ‹ The Lord's revelation to my Master:
"Sit on my right:
your foes I will put beneath your feet."

‹ The Lord will wield from Zion
your scepter of power:
rule in the midst of all your foes.

‹ A prince from the day of your birth
on the holy mountains;
from the womb before the dawn I begot you.

‹ The Lord has sworn an oath he will not change.
"You are a priest for ever,
a priest like Melchizedek of old."

‹ The Master standing at your right hand
will shatter kings in the day of his great wrath.

‹ He shall drink from the stream by the wayside
and therefore he shall lift up his head.

[BOW] ‹ Glory to the Father, and to the Son,
and to the Holy Spirit:
as it was in the beginning, is now,
and will be for ever. Amen.

TWENTY-NINTH SUNDAY in Ordinary Time

[PSALTER, WEEK I]

Psalm Prayer

Father, we ask you to give us victory and peace.
In Jesus Christ, our Lord and King, we are
already seated at your right hand. We look
forward to praising you in the fellowship of all
your saints in our heavenly homeland.

Ant. The Lord will stretch forth his mighty scepter
from Zion, and he will reign for ever, alleluia.

Ant. 2 The earth is shaken to its depths before the
glory of your face.

Book 2: Psalm 114
The Israelites are delivered from the bondage of Egypt

‹ When Israel came forth from Egypt,
Jacob's sons from an alien people,
Judah became the Lord's temple,
Israel became his kingdom.

‹ The sea fled at the sight:
the Jordan turned back on its course,
the mountains leapt like rams
and the hills like yearling sheep.

‹ Why was it, sea, that you fled,
that you turned back, Jordan, on your course?
Mountains, that you leapt like rams,
hills, like yearling sheep?

‹ Tremble, O earth, before the Lord,
in the presence of the God of Jacob,
who turns the rock into a pool
and flint into a spring of water.

[BOW] ‹ Glory to the Father, and to the Son,
and to the Holy Spirit:
as it was in the beginning, is now,
and will be for ever. Amen.

Psalm Prayer

Almighty God, ever-living mystery of unity and
trinity, you gave life to the new Israel by birth
from water and the Spirit, and made it a chosen
race, a royal priesthood, a people set apart as
your eternal possession. May all those you have
called to walk in the splendor of the new light
render you fitting service and adoration.

126

Ant. The earth is shaken to its depths before the glory of your face.

Ant. 3 All power is yours, Lord God, our mighty King, alleluia.

Canticle based on Revelation 19: 1-7
The wedding of the Lamb

✦ Alleluia.
Salvation, glory, and power to our God:
(℟ Alleluia.)
his judgments are honest and true.
℟ Alleluia (alleluia).

✦ Alleluia.
Sing praise to our God, all you his servants,
(℟ Alleluia.)
all who worship him reverently, great and small.
℟ Alleluia (alleluia).

✦ Alleluia.
The Lord our all-powerful God is King;
(℟ Alleluia.)
let us rejoice, sing praise, and give him glory.
℟ Alleluia (alleluia).

✦ Alleluia.
The wedding feast of the Lamb has begun,
(℟ Alleluia.)
and his bride is prepared to welcome him.
℟ Alleluia (alleluia).

[Bow] ✦ Glory to the Father, and to the Son,
and to the Holy Spirit:
as it was in the beginning, is now,
and will be for ever. Amen.

Ant. All power is yours, Lord God, our mighty King, alleluia.

Reading: 2 Corinthians 1: 3-7
Praised be God, the Father of our Lord Jesus Christ, the Father of mercies and the God of all consolation! He comforts us in all our afflictions and thus enables us to comfort those who are in trouble, with the same consolation we have received from him. As we have shared much in the suffering of Christ, so through Christ do we share abundantly in his consolation. If we are afflicted it is for your encouragement and salvation, and when we are consoled it is for your consolation, so that you may endure patiently the same sufferings we endure. Our hope for you is firm because we know that just as you share in the sufferings, so you will share in the consolation.

Responsory
℣. The whole creation proclaims the greatness of your glory.
℟ The whole creation proclaims the greatness of your glory.
℣. Eternal ages praise
℟ the greatness of your glory.
[Bow] ℣. Glory to the Father, and to the Son, and to the Holy Spirit.
℟ The whole creation proclaims the greatness of your glory.

Canticle Of Mary
Ant.
[Stand] When the Son of Man comes to earth, do you think he will find faith in men's hearts?

Magnificat: Luke 1: 46-55
My soul ✝ proclaims the… [See Prayer On Back Flap. Then Repeat The Antiphon Above.]

Intercessions

Introductory Formula
Christ the Lord is our head; we are his members. In joy let us call out to him:
℟ Lord, may your kingdom come.

Petitions
℣. Christ our Savior, make your Church a more vivid symbol of the unity of all mankind,
℟ make it more effectively the sacrament of salvation for all peoples.
℣. Through your presence, guide the college of bishops in union with the Pope,
℟ give them the gifts of unity, love and peace.
℣. Bind all Christians more closely to yourself, their divine Head,
℟ lead them to proclaim your kingdom by the witness of their lives.
℣. Grant peace to the world,
℟ let every land flourish in justice and security.
℣. Grant to the dead the glory of resurrection,
℟ and give us a share in their happiness.

The Lord's Prayer
Our Father… [See prayer on back flap]

Prayer
Almighty and ever-living God,
our source of power and inspiration,
give us strength and joy
in serving you as followers of Christ,
who lives and reigns with you
and the Holy Spirit,
one God, for ever and ever. Amen.

Closing Rite Or Dismissal [See Back Flap.]

Introductory Rite

[SEE INTRODUCTORY RITE ON FRONT FLAP]

Hymn

+ Love divine, all loves excelling,
Joy of heaven to earth come down,
And impart to us, here dwelling,
Grace and mercy all around.
Jesus, source of all compassion,
Pure, unbounded love you share;
Grant us many choicest blessings,
Keep us in your loving care.

+ Come, O source of inspiration,
Pure and spotless let us be:
Let us see your true salvation,
Perfect in accord with thee.
Praising Father for all glory
With the Spirit and the Son;
Everlasting thanks we give thee,
Undivided, love, in one.

Text: C. Wesley, 1707-1788, adapted by C.T. Andrews 1968

Psalmody

Ant. 1   Christ our Lord is a priest for ever, like
Melchizedek of old, alleluia.

Book 5: Psalm 110: 1-5, 7
The Messiah, king and priest

[SIT]   + The Lord's revelation to my Master:
"Sit on my right:
your foes I will put beneath your feet."

+ The Lord will wield from Zion
your scepter of power:
rule in the midst of all your foes.

+ A prince from the day of your birth
on the holy mountains;
from the womb before the dawn I begot you.

+ The Lord has sworn an oath he will not change.
"You are a priest for ever,
a priest like Melchizedek of old."

+ The Master standing at your right hand
will shatter kings in the day of his great wrath.

+ He shall drink from the stream by the wayside
and therefore he shall lift up his head.

[BOW]   + Glory to the Father...

Psalm Prayer
Almighty God,... [SEE PSALM PRAYER ON FRONT FLAP]

Ant.   Christ our Lord is a priest for ever, like
Melchizedek of old, alleluia.

Ant. 2   God dwells in highest heaven; he has power to
do all he wills, alleluia.

THIRTIETH SUNDAY in Ordinary Time

[PSALTER, WEEK II]

Book 5: Psalm 115
Praise of the true God

+ Not to us, Lord, not to us,
but to your name give the glory
for the sake of your love and your truth,
lest the heathen say: "Where is their God?"

+ But our God is in the heavens;
he does whatever he wills.
Their idols are silver and gold,
the work of human hands.

+ They have mouths but they cannot speak;
they have eyes but they cannot see;
they have ears but they cannot hear;
they have nostrils but they cannot smell.

+ With their hands they cannot feel;
with their feet they cannot walk.
No sound comes from their throats.
Their makers will come to be like them
and so will all who trust in them.

+ Sons of Israel, trust in the Lord;
he is their help and their shield.
Sons of Aaron, trust in the Lord;
he is their help and their shield.

+ You who fear him, trust in the Lord;
he is their help and their shield.
He remembers us, and he will bless us;
he will bless the sons of Israel.
He will bless the sons of Aaron.

+ The Lord will bless those who fear him,
the little no less than the great:
to you may the Lord grant increase,
to you and all your children.

+ May you be blessed by the Lord,
the maker of heaven and earth.
The heavens belong to the Lord
but the earth he has given to men.

+ The dead shall not praise the Lord,
nor those who go down into the silence.
But we who live bless the Lord
now and for ever. Amen.

[BOW]   + Glory to the Father...

Psalm Prayer

Father, creator…[See psalm prayer on front flap]

Ant.   God dwells in highest heaven; he has power to do all he wills, alleluia.

Ant. 3   Praise God, all you who serve him, both great and small, alleluia.

Canticle based on Revelation 19: 1-7
The wedding of the Lamb

✦ Alleluia.
Salvation, glory, and power to our God:
(℟ Alleluia.)
his judgments are honest and true.
℟ Alleluia (alleluia).

✦ Alleluia.
Sing praise to our God, all you his servants,
(℟ Alleluia.)
all who worship him reverently, great and small.
℟ Alleluia (alleluia).

✦ Alleluia.
The Lord our all-powerful God is King;
(℟ Alleluia.)
let us rejoice, sing praise, and give him glory.
℟ Alleluia (alleluia).

✦ Alleluia.
The wedding feast of the Lamb has begun,
(℟ Alleluia.)
and his bride is prepared to welcome him.
℟ Alleluia (alleluia).

[Bow]   ✦ Glory to the Father…

Ant.   Praise God, all you who serve him, both great and small, alleluia.

Reading: 2 Thessalonians 2: 13-14

We are bound to thank God for you always, beloved brothers in the Lord, because you are the first fruits of those whom God has chosen for salvation, in holiness of spirit and fidelity to truth. He called you through our preaching of the good news so that you might achieve the glory of our Lord Jesus Christ.

Responsory

℣. Our Lord is great, mighty is his power.
℟. Our Lord is great, mighty is his power.
℣. His wisdom is beyond compare,
℟. mighty is his power.
[Bow]   ℣. Glory to the Father, and to the Son, and to the Holy Spirit.
℟. Our Lord is great, mighty is his power.

Canticle Of Mary

Ant.
[Stand]   The publican went home at peace with God, for everyone who exalts himself shall be humbled, and whoever humbles himself shall be exalted.

Magnificat: Luke 1: 46-55
My soul ✠ proclaims the… [See Prayer On Back Flap. Then Repeat The Antiphon Above.]

Intercessions

Introductory Formula
All praise and honor to Christ! He lives for ever to intercede for us, and he is able to save those who approach the Father in his name. Sustained by our faith, let us call upon him:
℟. Remember your people, Lord.

Petitions
℣. As the day draws to a close, Sun of Justice, we invoke your name upon the whole human race,
℟. so that all men may enjoy your never failing light.
℣. Preserve the covenant which you have ratified in your blood,
℟. cleanse and sanctify your Church.
℣. Remember your assembly, Lord,
℟. your dwelling place.
℣. Guide travelers along the path of peace and prosperity,
℟. so that they may reach their destinations in safety and joy.
℣. Receive the souls of the dead, Lord,
℟. grant them your favor and the gift of eternal glory.

The Lord's Prayer
Our Father… [See prayer on back flap]

Prayer

Almighty and ever-living God,
strengthen our faith, hope, and love.
May we do with loving hearts
what you ask of us
and come to share the life you promise.
We ask this through our Lord Jesus Christ,
  your Son,
who lives and reigns with you
  and the Holy Spirit,
one God, for ever and ever. Amen.

Closing Rite Or Dismissal

[See Closing Rite on Back Flap]

Introductory Rite

[STAND] ℣. God, ✠ come to my assistance.

℟. Lord, make haste to help me.

[BOW]   Glory to the Father, and to the Son,
and to the Holy Spirit:
as it was in the beginning, is now,
and will be for ever. Amen.

Hymn

✦ O Christ, you are the light and day
Which drives away the night,
The ever shining Sun of God
And pledge of future light.

✦ As now the ev'ning shadows fall
Please grant us, Lord, we pray,
A quiet night to rest in you
Until the break of day.

✦ Remember us, poor mortal men,
We humbly ask, O Lord,
And may your presence in our souls
Be now our great reward.

Translator: Rev. M. Quinn, O.P. et al.

Psalmody

Ant. 1   The Lord said to my Master: Sit at my right
hand, alleluia.

Book 5: Psalm 110: 1-5, 7
The Messiah, king and priest

[SIT]   ✦ The Lord's revelation to my Master:
"Sit on my right:
your foes I will put beneath your feet."

✦ The Lord will wield from Zion
your scepter of power:
rule in the midst of all your foes.

✦ A prince from the day of your birth
on the holy mountains;
from the womb before the dawn I begot you.

✦ The Lord has sworn an oath he will not change.
"You are a priest for ever,
a priest like Melchizedek of old."

✦ The Master standing at your right hand
will shatter kings in the day of his great wrath.

✦ He shall drink from the stream by the wayside
and therefore he shall lift up his head.

[BOW]   ✦ Glory to the Father…

Psalm Prayer
Father, we ask you to give us victory and peace.
In Jesus Christ, our Lord and King, we are
already seated at your right hand. We look
forward to praising you in the fellowship of all
your saints in our heavenly homeland.

130

THIRTY-FIRST SUNDAY
in Ordinary Time
[PSALTER, WEEK III]

Ant.   The Lord said to my Master: Sit at my right
hand, alleluia.

Ant. 2   Our compassionate Lord has left us a
memorial of his wonderful work, alleluia.

Book 5: Psalm 111
God's marvelous works

✦ I will thank the Lord with all my heart
in the meeting of the just and their assembly.
Great are the works of the Lord;
to be pondered by all who love them.

✦ Majestic and glorious his work,
his justice stands firm for ever.
He makes us remember his wonders.
The Lord is compassion and love.

✦ He gives food to those who fear him;
keeps his covenant ever in mind.
He has shown his might to his people
by giving them the lands of the nations.

✦ His works are justice and truth:
his precepts are all of them sure,
standing firm for ever and ever:
they are made in uprightness and truth.

✦ He has sent deliverance to his people
and established his covenant for ever.
Holy his name, to be feared.

✦ To fear the Lord is the first stage of wisdom;
all who do so prove themselves wise.
His praise shall last for ever!

[BOW]   ✦ Glory to the Father…

Psalm Prayer
Merciful and gentle Lord, you are the
crowning glory of all the saints. Give us, your
children, the gift of obedience which is the
beginning of wisdom, so that we may do what
you command and be filled with your mercy.

Ant.   Our compassionate Lord has left us a
memorial of his wonderful work, alleluia.

Ant. 3   All power is yours, Lord God, our mighty
King, alleluia.

Canticle based on Revelation 19: 1-7
The wedding of the Lamb

+ Alleluia.
Salvation, glory, and power to our God:
(℟ Alleluia.)
his judgments are honest and true.

℟ Alleluia (alleluia).

+ Alleluia.
Sing praise to our God, all you his servants,
(℟ Alleluia.)
all who worship him reverently, great and small.

℟ Alleluia (alleluia).

+ Alleluia.
The Lord our all-powerful God is King;
(℟ Alleluia.)
let us rejoice, sing praise, and give him glory.

℟ Alleluia (alleluia).

+ Alleluia.
The wedding feast of the Lamb has begun,
(℟ Alleluia.)
and his bride is prepared to welcome him.

℟ Alleluia (alleluia).

[Bow] + Glory to the Father…

Ant. All power is yours, Lord God, our mighty King, alleluia.

Reading: 1 Peter 1: 3-7

Praised be the God and Father /of our Lord Jesus Christ, /he who in his great mercy /gave us new birth; /a birth unto hope which draws its life /from the resurrection of Jesus Christ from the dead; /a birth to an imperishable inheritance, /incapable of fading or defilement, /which is kept in heaven for you /who are guarded with God's power through faith; /a birth to a salvation which stands ready /to be revealed in the last days.

There is cause for rejoicing here. You may for a time have to suffer the distress of many trials; but this is so that your faith, which is more precious than the passing splendor of fire-tried gold, may by its genuineness lead to praise, glory, and honor when Jesus Christ appears.

Responsory

℣ The whole creation proclaims the greatness of your glory.

℟ The whole creation proclaims the greatness of your glory.

℣ Eternal ages praise

℟ the greatness of your glory.

[Bow] ℣ Glory to the Father, and to the Son, and to the Holy Spirit.

℟ The whole creation proclaims the greatness of your glory.

Canticle Of Mary

Ant. The Son of Man came to seek out and to save
[Stand] those who were lost.

Magnificat: Luke 1: 46-55
My soul ✝ proclaims the… [See Prayer On Back Flap. Then Repeat The Antiphon Above.]

Intercessions

Introductory Formula
The world was created by the Word of God, re-created by his redemption, and it is continually renewed by his love. Rejoicing in him we call out:

℟ Renew the wonders of your love, Lord.

Petitions
℣ We give thanks to God whose power is revealed in nature,
and whose providence is revealed in history.

℣ Through your Son, the herald of reconciliation, the victor of the cross,
℟ free us from empty fear and hopelessness.

℣ May all those who love and pursue justice,
℟ work together without deceit to build a world of true peace.

℣ Be with the oppressed, free the captives, console the sorrowing, feed the hungry, strengthen the weak,
℟ in all people reveal the victory of your cross.

℣ After your Son's death and burial you raised him up again in glory,
℟ grant that the faithful departed may live with him.

The Lord's Prayer
Our Father… [See prayer on back flap]

Prayer

God of power and mercy,
only with your help
can we offer you fitting service and praise.
May we live the faith we profess
and trust your promise of eternal life.
Grant this through our Lord Jesus Christ,
your Son,
who lives and reigns with you
and the Holy Spirit,
one God, for ever and ever. Amen.

Closing Rite Or Dismissal
[See Closing Rite on Back Flap]

131

Introductory Rite

[Stand] V. God, ✠ come to my assistance.

R. Lord, make haste to help me.

[Bow] Glory to the Father, and to the Son,
and to the Holy Spirit:
as it was in the beginning, is now,
and will be for ever. Amen.

Hymn

+ For all the saints who from their labors rest,
Who thee by faith before the world confessed,
Thy name, O Jesus, be for ever blest:
Alleluia, alleluia!

+ Thou wast their rock, their fortress and
their might;
Thou, Lord, their captain in the well-fought fight;
Thou in the darkness drear their one true light:
Alleluia, alleluia!

+ O blest communion, fellowship divine!
We feebly struggle, they in glory shine;
Yet all are one in thee, for all are thine:
Alleluia, alleluia!

+ But, lo, there breaks a yet more glorious day;
The saints triumphant rise in bright array:
The King of glory passes on his way:
Alleluia, alleluia!

Text: William W. How, 1823-1897

Psalmody

Ant. 1 I saw a vast crowd of countless numbers from
every nation, standing before the throne.

Book 5: Psalm 110: 1-5, 7
The Messiah, king and priest

[Sit] + The Lord's revelation to my Master:
"Sit on my right:
your foes I will put beneath your feet."

+ The Lord will wield from Zion
your scepter of power:
rule in the midst of all your foes.

+ A prince from the day of your birth
on the holy mountains;
from the womb before the dawn I begot you.

+ The Lord has sworn an oath he will not change.
"You are a priest for ever,
a priest like Melchizedek of old."

+ The Master standing at your right hand
will shatter kings in the day of his great wrath.

+ He shall drink from the stream by the wayside
and therefore he shall lift up his head.

ALL SAINTS
Solemnity

[Bow] + Glory to the Father, and to the Son,
and to the Holy Spirit:
as it was in the beginning, is now,
and will be for ever. Amen.

Ant. I saw a vast crowd of countless numbers from
every nation, standing before the throne.

Ant. 2 God tried them and found them worthy of
himself; they shall receive a crown of glory
from the Lord.

Book 5: Psalm 116: 10-19
Thanksgiving in the Temple

+ I trusted, even when I said:
"I am sorely afflicted,"
and when I said in my alarm:
"No man can be trusted."

+ How can I repay the Lord
for his goodness to me?
The cup of salvation I will raise;
I will call on the Lord's name.

+ My vows to the Lord I will fulfill
before all his people.
O precious in the eyes of the Lord
is the death of his faithful.

+ Your servant, Lord, your servant am I;
you have loosened my bonds.
A thanksgiving sacrifice I make:
I will call on the Lord's name.

+ My vows to the Lord I will fulfill
before all his people,
in the courts of the house of the Lord,
in your midst, O Jerusalem.

[Bow] + Glory to the Father, and to the Son,
and to the Holy Spirit:
as it was in the beginning, is now,
and will be for ever. Amen.

Ant. God tried them and found them worthy of
himself; they shall receive a crown of glory
from the Lord.

Ant. 3 By your own blood, Lord, you brought us
back to God; from every tribe and tongue, and
people and nation, you made us a kingdom for
our God.

Canticle: Revelation 4: 11; 5: 9, 10, 12

✦ O Lord our God, you are worthy
    to receive glory and honor and power.

✦ For you have created all things;
    by your will they came to be and were made.

✦ Worthy are you, O Lord,
    to receive the scroll and break open its seals.

✦ For you were slain;
    with your blood you purchased for God
    men of every race and tongue,
    of every people and nation.

✦ You made of them a kingdom,
    and priests to serve our God,
    and they shall reign on the earth.

✦ Worthy is the Lamb that was slain
    to receive power and riches,
    wisdom and strength,
    honor and glory and praise.

[Bow] ✦ Glory to the Father, and to the Son,
    and to the Holy Spirit:
    as it was in the beginning, is now,
    and will be for ever. Amen.

Ant. By your own blood, Lord, you brought us
    back to God; from every tribe and tongue, and
    people and nation, you made us a kingdom for
    our God.

Reading: 2 Corinthians 6: 16b; 7: 1

You are the temple of the living God, just as
God has said:
   "I will dwell with them and walk among
them. /I will be their God /and they shall be
my people."
   Since we have these promises, beloved, let us
purify ourselves from every defilement of flesh
and spirit, and in the fear of God strive to
fulfill our consecration perfectly.

Responsory

℣. Let the saints rejoice in the Lord.
℞. Let the saints rejoice in the Lord.
℣. God has chosen you as his own;
℞. rejoice in the Lord.
[Bow] ℣. Glory to the Father, and to the Son,
    and to the Holy Spirit.
℞. Let the saints rejoice in the Lord.

Canticle Of Mary

Ant.
[Stand]
How glorious is that kingdom where all the
saints rejoice with Christ; clothed in white
robes, they follow the Lamb wherever he goes.

Magnificat: Luke 1: 46-55
My soul ✠ proclaims the... [See Prayer On Back
Flap. Then Repeat The Antiphon Above.]

Intercessions

Introductory Formula
God is the reward of all the saints. Let us
joyfully call upon him:
℞. Lord, save your people.

Petitions
℣. O God, through your Son Jesus Christ
you built your Church on the foundation
of the apostles,
℞. keep their teaching secure among your
faithful people.
℣. You made the martyrs powerful witnesses
even to the point of giving up their lives,
℞. help all Christians to give faithful witness
to your Son.
℣. You gave holy virgins the gift of imitating
the virginity of Christ,
℞. may those consecrated to virginity be steadfast
witnesses to the coming of your kingdom.
℣. Your saints now see you face to face,
℞. keep alive in our hearts the hope of coming at
last into your presence.
℣. Bring all who have died into the company of
heaven with Mary, Joseph and all your saints,
℞. and give us also a place in the unending
fellowship of your kingdom.

The Lord's Prayer
Our Father... [See prayer on back flap]

Prayer

Father, all-powerful and ever-living God,
today we rejoice in the holy men and women
of every time and place.
May their prayers bring us your forgiveness
  and love.
We ask this through our Lord Jesus Christ,
  your Son,
who lives and reigns with you
  and the Holy Spirit,
one God, for ever and ever. Amen.

Closing Rite Or Dismissal

[See Closing Rite on Back Flap]

Introductory Rite

[STAND] V. God, ✠ come to my assistance.

R. Lord, make haste to help me.

[BOW] Glory to the Father, and to the Son,
and to the Holy Spirit:
as it was in the beginning, is now,
and will be for ever. Amen.

Hymn

✦ May flights of angels lead you on your way
To paradise, and heav'n's eternal day!
May martyrs greet you after death's dark night,
And bid you enter into Zion's light!
May choirs of angels sing you to your rest
With once poor Laz'rus, now for ever blest!

Text: James Quinn, S.J., 1969

Psalmody

Ant. 1   The Lord will keep you from all evil. He will guard your soul.

Book 5: Psalm 121
Guardian of his people

[SIT] ✦ I lift up my eyes to the mountains:
from where shall come my help?
My help shall come from the Lord
who made heaven and earth.

✦ May he never allow you to stumble!
Let him sleep not, your guard.
No, he sleeps not nor slumbers,
Israel's guard.

✦ The Lord is your guard and your shade;
at your right side he stands.
By day the sun shall not smite you
nor the moon in the night.

✦ The Lord will guard you from evil,
he will guard your soul.
The Lord will guard your going and coming
both now and for ever.

[BOW] ✦ Glory to the Father, and to the Son,
and to the Holy Spirit:
as it was in the beginning, is now,
and will be for ever. Amen.

Ant.   The Lord will keep you from all evil. He will guard your soul.

Ant. 2   If you kept a record of our sins, Lord, who could escape condemnation?

Book 5: Psalm 130
A cry from the depths

✦ Out of the depths I cry to you, O Lord,
Lord, hear my voice!

COMMEMORATION OF THE
Faithful Departed

O let your ears be attentive
to the voice of my pleading.

✦ If you, O Lord, should mark our guilt,
Lord, who would survive?
But with you is found forgiveness:
for this we revere you.

✦ My soul is waiting for the Lord.
I count on his word.
My soul is longing for the Lord
more than watchman for daybreak.
Let the watchman count on daybreak
and Israel on the Lord.

✦ Because with the Lord there is mercy
and fullness of redemption,
Israel indeed he will redeem
from all its iniquity.

[BOW] ✦ Glory to the Father, and to the Son,
and to the Holy Spirit:
as it was in the beginning, is now,
and will be for ever. Amen.

Ant.   If you kept a record of our sins, Lord, who could escape condemnation?

Ant. 3   As the Father raises the dead and gives them life, so the Son gives life to whom he wills.

Canticle: Philippians 2: 6-11
✦ Though he was in the form of God,
Jesus did not deem equality with God
something to be grasped at.

✦ Rather, he emptied himself
and took the form of a slave,
being born in the likeness of men.

✦ He was known to be of human estate,
and it was thus that he humbled himself,
obediently accepting even death,
death on a cross!

✦ Because of this,
God highly exalted him
and bestowed on him the name
above every other name,

so that at Jesus' name
every knee must bend
in the heavens, on the earth,
and under the earth,
and every tongue proclaim
to the glory of God the Father:
JESUS CHRIST IS LORD!

[Bow] ✦ Glory to the Father, and to the Son,
and to the Holy Spirit:
as it was in the beginning, is now,
and will be for ever. Amen.

Ant. As the Father raises the dead and gives them
life, so the Son gives life to whom he wills.

Reading: 1 Corinthians 15: 55-57

O death, where is your victory? O death,
where is your sting? But thanks be to God
who has given us the victory through our Lord
Jesus Christ.

Responsory

℣. Lord, in your steadfast love, give them
eternal rest.
℟. Lord, in your steadfast love, give them
eternal rest.
℣. You will come to judge the living and the dead.
℟. Give them eternal rest.
[Bow] ℣. Glory to the Father, and to the Son,
and to the Holy Spirit.
℟. Lord, in your steadfast love, give them
eternal rest.

Canticle Of Mary

Ant. All that the Father gives me will come to me,
[Stand] and whoever comes to me I shall not turn
away.

Magnificat: Luke 1: 46-55
My soul ✝ proclaims the... [See Prayer On Back
Flap. Then Repeat The Antiphon Above.]

Intercessions

Introductory Formula
We acknowledge Christ the Lord through
whom we hope that our lowly bodies will be
made like his in glory, and we say:
℟. Lord, you are our life and resurrection.

Petitions
℣. Christ, Son of the living God, who raised up
Lazarus, your friend, from the dead,
℟. raise up to life and glory the dead whom you
have redeemed by your precious blood.

℣. Christ, consoler of those who mourn, you
dried the tears of the family of Lazarus, of the
widow's son, and the daughter of Jairus,
℟. comfort those who mourn for the dead.
℣. Christ, Savior, destroy the reign of sin in our
earthly bodies, so that just as through sin we
deserved punishment,
℟. so through you we may gain eternal life.
℣. Christ, Redeemer, look on those who have no
hope because they do not know you,
℟. may they receive faith in the resurrection and
in the life of the world to come.
℣. You revealed yourself to the blind man who
begged for light of his eyes,
℟. show your face to the dead who are still
deprived of your light.
℣. When at last our earthly home is dissolved,
℟. give us a home, not of earthly making, but
built of eternity in heaven.

The Lord's Prayer
Our Father... [See prayer on back flap]

Prayer

Merciful Father,
hear our prayers and console us.
As we renew our faith in your Son,
whom you raised from the dead,
strengthen our hope that all our departed
brothers and sisters
will share in his resurrection,
who lives and reigns with you
and the Holy Spirit,
one God, for ever and ever. Amen.

Closing Rite Or Dismissal

[When Priest Or Deacon Presides]
℣. The Lord be with you.
℟. And also with you.
[Bow] May almighty God bless you, + the Father,
and the Son, and the Holy Spirit.
℟. Amen.
℣. Go in peace.
℟. Thanks be to God.

[When Priest Or Deacon Do Not Preside, And In Individual Recitation]
+ May the Lord bless us, protect us from all evil
and bring us to everlasting life.
℟. Amen.

135

Introductory Rite

[Stand] V. God, ✠ come to my assistance.

R. Lord, make haste to help me.

[Bow] Glory to the Father, and to the Son,
and to the Holy Spirit:
as it was in the beginning, is now,
and will be for ever. Amen.

Hymn

✦ Love divine, all loves excelling,
Joy of heaven to earth come down,
And impart to us, here dwelling,
Grace and mercy all around.
Jesus, source of all compassion,
Pure, unbounded love you share;
Grant us many choicest blessings,
Keep us in your loving care.

✦ Come, O source of inspiration,
Pure and spotless let us be:
Let us see your true salvation,
Perfect in accord with thee.
Praising Father for all glory
With the Spirit and the Son;
Everlasting thanks we give thee,
Undivided, love, in one.

Text: C. Wesley, 1707-1788, adapted by C.T. Andrews 1968

Psalmody

Ant. 1 In eternal splendor, before the dawn of light on
earth, I have begotten you, alleluia.

Book 5: Psalm 110: 1-5, 7
The Messiah, king and priest

[Sit] ✦ The Lord's revelation to my Master:
"Sit on my right:
your foes I will put beneath your feet."

✦ The Lord will wield from Zion
your scepter of power:
rule in the midst of all your foes.

✦ A prince from the day of your birth
on the holy mountains;
from the womb before the dawn I begot you.

✦ The Lord has sworn an oath he will not change.
"You are a priest for ever,
a priest like Melchizedek of old."

✦ The Master standing at your right hand
will shatter kings in the day of his great wrath.

✦ He shall drink from the stream by the wayside
and therefore he shall lift up his head.

[Bow] ✦ Glory to the Father, and to the Son,
and to the Holy Spirit:

THIRTY-SECOND SUNDAY in Ordinary Time

[Psalter, Week IV]

as it was in the beginning, is now,
and will be for ever. Amen.

Psalm Prayer

Father, we ask you to give us victory and
peace. In Jesus Christ, our Lord and King, we
are already seated at your right hand. We look
forward to praising you in the fellowship of all
your saints in our heavenly homeland.

Ant. In eternal splendor, before the dawn of light
on earth, I have begotten you, alleluia.

Ant. 2 Blessed are they who hunger and thirst for
holiness; they will be satisfied.

Book 5: Psalm 112
The happiness of the just man

✦ Happy the man who fears the Lord,
who takes delight in all his commands.
His sons will be powerful on earth;
the children of the upright are blessed.

✦ Riches and wealth are in his house;
his justice stands firm for ever.
He is a light in the darkness for the upright:
he is generous, merciful and just.

✦ The good man takes pity and lends,
he conducts his affairs with honor.
The just man will never waver:
he will be remembered for ever.

✦ He has no fear of evil news;
with a firm heart he trusts in the Lord.
With a steadfast heart he will not fear;
he will see the downfall of his foes.

✦ Open-handed, he gives to the poor;
his justice stands firm for ever.
His head will be raised in glory.

✦ The wicked man sees and is angry,
grinds his teeth and fades away;
the desire of the wicked leads to doom.

[Bow] ✦ Glory to the Father, and to the Son,
and to the Holy Spirit:
as it was in the beginning, is now,
and will be for ever. Amen.

Psalm Prayer

Lord God, you are the eternal light which illumines the hearts of good people. Help us to love you, to rejoice in your glory, and so to live in this world as to avoid harsh judgment in the next. May we come to see the light of your countenance.

Ant. Blessed are they who hunger and thirst for holiness; they will be satisfied.

Ant. 3 Praise God, all you who serve him, both great and small, alleluia.

Canticle based on Revelation 19: 1-7
The wedding of the Lamb

✦ Alleluia.
Salvation, glory, and power to our God:
(℞ Alleluia.)
his judgments are honest and true.
℞ Alleluia (alleluia).

✦ Alleluia.
Sing praise to our God, all you his servants,
(℞ Alleluia.)
all who worship him reverently, great and small.
℞ Alleluia (alleluia).

✦ Alleluia.
The Lord our all-powerful God is King;
(℞ Alleluia.)
let us rejoice, sing praise, and give him glory.
℞ Alleluia (alleluia).

✦ Alleluia.
The wedding feast of the Lamb has begun,
(℞ Alleluia.)
and his bride is prepared to welcome him.
℞ Alleluia (alleluia).

[Bow] ✦ Glory to the Father…

Ant. Praise God, all you who serve him, both great and small, alleluia.

Reading: Hebrews 12: 22-24

You have drawn near to Mount Zion and the city of the living God, the heavenly Jerusalem, to myriads of angels in festal gathering, to the assembly of the first-born enrolled in heaven, to God the judge of all, to the spirits of just men made perfect, to Jesus, the mediator of a new covenant, and to the sprinkled blood which speaks more eloquently than that of Abel.

Responsory

℣ Our Lord is great, mighty is his power.
℞ Our Lord is great, mighty is his power.
℣ His wisdom is beyond compare,
℞ mighty is his power.
[Bow] ℣ Glory to the Father, and to the Son, and to the Holy Spirit.
℞ Our Lord is great, mighty is his power.

Canticle Of Mary

Ant.
[Stand] He is not a God of the dead, but of the living: for to him all things are alive, alleluia.

Magnificat: Luke 1: 46-55
My soul ✠ proclaims the… [See Prayer On Back Flap. Then Repeat The Antiphon Above.]

Intercessions

Introductory Formula
Rejoicing in the Lord, from whom all good things come, let us pray:
℞ Lord, hear our prayer.

Petitions
℣ Father and Lord of all, you sent your Son into the world, that your name might be glorified in every place,
℞ strengthen the witness of your Church among the nations.
℣ Make us obedient to the teachings of your apostles,
℞ and bound to the truth of our faith.
℣ As you love the innocent,
℞ render justice to those who are wronged.
℣ Free those in bondage and give sight to the blind,
℞ raise up the fallen and protect the stranger.
℣ Fulfill your promise to those who already sleep in your peace,
℞ through your Son grant them a blessed resurrection.

The Lord's Prayer
Our Father… [See prayer on back flap]

Prayer

God of power and mercy,
protect us from all harm.
Give us freedom of spirit
and health in mind and body
to do your work on earth.
We ask this through our Lord Jesus Christ,
  your Son,
who lives and reigns with you
  and the Holy Spirit,
one God, for ever and ever. Amen.

Closing Rite Or Dismissal

[See Closing Rite on Back Flap]

Introductory Rite

[See Introductory Rite on Front Flap]

THE DEDICATION
of St. John Lateran

Hymn

◆ Christ is made our sure foundation,
  Christ is head and Cornerstone;
  Chosen of the Lord and precious,
  Binding all the Church in one,
  Holy Zion's help for ever,
  And her confidence alone.

◆ To this temple, we implore you,
  Come, great Lord of hosts, today;
  Come with all your loving kindness,
  Hear your servants as they pray,
  And your fullest benediction
  Shed in all its brightest ray.

◆ Grant, we pray, to all your people,
  All the grace they ask to gain;
  What they gain from you for ever
  With the blessed to retain,
  And hereafter in your glory
  Evermore with you to reign.

[Bow] ◆ Praise and honor to the Father,
  Praise and honor to the Son,
  Praise and honor to the Spirit,
  Ever Three and ever One:
  Unified in power and glory,
  While unending ages run.

Translator: J.M. Neale, 1816-1866, alt. by Anthony G. Petti

Psalmody

Ant. 1   This is God's dwelling place and he has made it holy; it will stand for ever firm.

Book 2: Psalm 46
God our refuge and our strength

[Sit] ◆ God is for us a refuge and strength,
  a helper close at hand, in time of distress:
  so we shall not fear though the earth
    should rock,
  though the mountains fall into the depths
    of the sea,
  even though its waters rage and foam,
  even though the mountains be shaken
    by its waves.

◆ The Lord of hosts is with us:
  the God of Jacob is our stronghold.

◆ The waters of a river give joy to God's city,
  the holy place where the Most High dwells.
  God is within, it cannot be shaken;
  God will help it at the dawning of the day.
  Nations are in tumult, kingdoms are shaken:
  he lifts his voice, the earth shrinks away.

◆ The Lord of hosts is with us:
  the God of Jacob is our stronghold.

◆ Come, consider the works of the Lord,
  the redoubtable deeds he has done on the earth.
  He puts an end to wars over all the earth;
  the bow he breaks, the spear he snaps.
  He burns the shields with fire.
  "Be still and know that I am God,
  supreme among the nations, supreme
    on the earth!"

◆ The Lord of hosts is with us:
  the God of Jacob is our stronghold.

[Bow] ◆ Glory to the Father…

Ant.   This is God's dwelling place and he has made it holy; it will stand for ever firm.

Ant. 2   Let us go up with rejoicing to the house of the Lord.

Book 5: Psalm 122
Holy city Jerusalem

◆ I rejoiced when I heard them say:
  "Let us go to God's house."
  And now our feet are standing
  within your gates, O Jerusalem.

◆ Jerusalem is built as a city
  strongly compact.
  It is there that the tribes go up,
  the tribes of the Lord.

◆ For Israel's law it is,
  there to praise the Lord's name.
  There were set the thrones of judgment
  of the house of David.

◆ For the peace of Jerusalem pray:
  "Peace be to your homes!
  May peace reign in your walls,
  in your palaces, peace!"

◆ For love of my brethren and friends
  I say: "Peace upon you!"
  For love of the house of the Lord
  I will ask for your good.

[Bow] ◆ Glory to the Father…

Ant.   Let us go up with rejoicing to the house of the Lord.

Ant. 3   All you his saints, sing out the praises of our God.

Canticle based on Revelation 19: 1-7
The wedding of the Lamb

✦ Alleluia.
Salvation, glory, and power to our God:
(℟ Alleluia.)
his judgments are honest and true.
℟ Alleluia (alleluia).

✦ Alleluia.
Sing praise to our God, all you his servants,
(℟ Alleluia.)
all who worship him reverently, great and small.
℟ Alleluia (alleluia).

✦ Alleluia.
The Lord our all-powerful God is King;
(℟ Alleluia.)
let us rejoice, sing praise, and give him glory.
℟ Alleluia (alleluia).

✦ Alleluia.
The wedding feast of the Lamb has begun,
(℟ Alleluia.)
and his bride is prepared to welcome him.
℟ Alleluia (alleluia).

[Bow]   ✦ Glory to the Father…

Ant.   All you his saints, sing out the praises of our God.

Reading: Revelation 21: 2-3, 22, 27

I saw a new Jerusalem, the holy city, coming down out of heaven from God, beautiful as a bride prepared to meet her husband. I heard a loud voice from the throne cry out: "This is God's dwelling among men. He shall dwell with them and they shall be his people and he shall be their God who is always with them." I saw no temple in the city. The Lord, God the Almighty, is its temple—he and the Lamb. But nothing profane shall enter it, nor anyone who is a liar or has done a detestable act. Only those shall enter whose names are inscribed in the book of the living kept by the Lamb.

Responsory

℣ Blessed are they who dwell in your house, O Lord.
℟ Blessed are they who dwell in your house, O Lord.
℣ They will praise you for ever,
℟ in your house, O Lord.
[Bow]   ℣ Glory to the Father, and to the Son, and to the Holy Spirit.

℟ Blessed are they who dwell in your house, O Lord.

Canticle Of Mary

Ant.
[Stand]   This is God's dwelling place and he has made it holy; here we call on his name, for Scripture says: There you will find me.

Magnificat: Luke 1: 46-55
My soul ✚ proclaims the… [See Prayer On Back Flap.]

Intercessions

Introductory Formula
Our Savior laid down his life so that all God's scattered children might be gathered together. In our need we cry out:
℟ Remember your Church, Lord.

Petitions
℣ Lord Jesus, you built your house upon a rock,
℟ strengthen your Church with solid and lasting faith.
℣ Lord Jesus, blood and water flowed from your side,
℟ give new life to your Church through the sacraments of your new and unending covenant.
℣ Lord Jesus, you are in the midst of those who gather in your name,
℟ hear the prayers of your universal Church.
℣ Lord Jesus, you prepare a dwelling-place in your Father's house for all who love you,
℟ help your Church to grow in divine love.
℣ Lord Jesus, you never cast out anyone who comes to you,
℟ open your Father's house to all those who have died.

The Lord's Prayer
Our Father… [See prayer on back flap]

Prayer

God our Father,
from living stones, your chosen people,
you built an eternal temple to your glory.
Increase the spiritual gifts you have given to your Church
that your faithful people may continue to grow
into the new and eternal Jerusalem.
We ask this through our Lord Jesus Christ, your Son,
who lives and reigns with you and the Holy Spirit,
one God, for ever and ever. Amen.

Closing Rite Or Dismissal

[See Closing Rite on Back Flap]

139

Introductory Rite

[Stand] V. God, ✠ come to my assistance.

R. Lord, make haste to help me.

[Bow] Glory to the Father, and to the Son,
and to the Holy Spirit:
as it was in the beginning, is now,
and will be for ever. Amen.

Hymn

❖ O Christ, you are the light and day
Which drives away the night,
The ever shining Sun of God
And pledge of future light.

❖ As now the ev'ning shadows fall
Please grant us, Lord, we pray,
A quiet night to rest in you
Until the break of day.

❖ Remember us, poor mortal men,
We humbly ask, O Lord,
And may your presence in our souls
Be now our great reward.

Translator: Rev. M. Quinn, O.P. et al.

Psalmody

Ant. 1   The Lord will stretch forth his mighty scepter
from Zion, and he will reign for ever, alleluia.

Book 5: Psalm 110: 1-5, 7
The Messiah, king and priest

[Sit] ❖ The Lord's revelation to my Master:
"Sit on my right:
your foes I will put beneath your feet."

❖ The Lord will wield from Zion
your scepter of power:
rule in the midst of all your foes.

❖ A prince from the day of your birth
on the holy mountains;
from the womb before the dawn I begot you.

❖ The Lord has sworn an oath he will not change.
"You are a priest for ever,
a priest like Melchizedek of old."

❖ The Master standing at your right hand
will shatter kings in the day of his great wrath.

❖ He shall drink from the stream by the wayside
and therefore he shall lift up his head.

[Bow] ❖ Glory to the Father, and to the Son,
and to the Holy Spirit:
as it was in the beginning, is now,
and will be for ever. Amen.

Thirty-third Sunday in Ordinary Time

[Psalter, Week I]

Psalm Prayer

Father, we ask you to give us victory and peace. In Jesus Christ, our Lord and King, we are already seated at your right hand. We look forward to praising you in the fellowship of all your saints in our heavenly homeland.

Ant.   The Lord will stretch forth his mighty scepter from Zion, and he will reign for ever, alleluia.

Ant. 2   The earth is shaken to its depths before the glory of your face.

Book 2: Psalm 114
The Israelites are delivered from the bondage of Egypt

❖ When Israel came forth from Egypt,
Jacob's sons from an alien people,
Judah became the Lord's temple,
Israel became his kingdom.

❖ The sea fled at the sight:
the Jordan turned back on its course,
the mountains leapt like rams
and the hills like yearling sheep.

❖ Why was it, sea, that you fled,
that you turned back, Jordan, on your course?
Mountains, that you leapt like rams,
hills, like yearling sheep?

❖ Tremble, O earth, before the Lord,
in the presence of the God of Jacob,
who turns the rock into a pool
and flint into a spring of water.

[Bow] ❖ Glory to the Father, and to the Son,
and to the Holy Spirit:
as it was in the beginning, is now,
and will be for ever. Amen.

Psalm Prayer

Almighty God, ever-living mystery of unity and trinity, you gave life to the new Israel by birth from water and the Spirit, and made it a chosen race, a royal priesthood, a people set apart as your eternal possession. May all those you have called to walk in the splendor of the new light render you fitting service and adoration.

Ant.   The earth is shaken to its depths before the glory of your face.

Ant. 3   All power is yours, Lord God, our mighty King, alleluia.

> **Canticle based on Revelation 19: 1-7**
> *The wedding of the Lamb*
>
> ✦ Alleluia.
> Salvation, glory, and power to our God:
> (℟ Alleluia.)
> his judgments are honest and true.
> ℟ Alleluia (alleluia).
>
> ✦ Alleluia.
> Sing praise to our God, all you his servants,
> (℟ Alleluia.)
> all who worship him reverently, great and small.
> ℟ Alleluia (alleluia).
>
> ✦ Alleluia.
> The Lord our all-powerful God is King;
> (℟ Alleluia.)
> let us rejoice, sing praise, and give him glory.
> ℟ Alleluia (alleluia).
>
> ✦ Alleluia.
> The wedding feast of the Lamb has begun,
> (℟ Alleluia.)
> and his bride is prepared to welcome him.
> ℟ Alleluia (alleluia).

[Bow]   ✦ Glory to the Father…

Ant.   All power is yours, Lord God, our mighty King, alleluia.

Reading: 2 Corinthians 1: 3-7

Praised be God, the Father of our Lord Jesus Christ, the Father of mercies and the God of all consolation! He comforts us in all our afflictions and thus enables us to comfort those who are in trouble, with the same consolation we have received from him. As we have shared much in the suffering of Christ, so through Christ do we share abundantly in his consolation. If we are afflicted it is for your encouragement and salvation, and when we are consoled it is for your consolation, so that you may endure patiently the same sufferings we endure. Our hope for you is firm because we know that just as you share in the sufferings, so you will share in the consolation.

Responsory

℣   The whole creation proclaims the greatness of your glory.

℟   The whole creation proclaims the greatness of your glory.

℣   Eternal ages praise

℟   the greatness of your glory.

[Bow]   ℣   Glory to the Father, and to the Son, and to the Holy Spirit.

℟   The whole creation proclaims the greatness of your glory.

Canticle Of Mary

Ant.   By your trusting acceptance of trials, you will
[Stand]   gain your life, says the Lord.

> **Magnificat: Luke 1: 46-55**
> My soul ✠ proclaims the… [See Prayer On Back Flap. Then Repeat The Antiphon Above.]

Intercessions

Introductory Formula
Christ the Lord is our head; we are his members. In joy let us call out to him:

℟   Lord, may your kingdom come.

Petitions

℣   Christ our Savior, make your Church a more vivid symbol of the unity of all mankind,

℟   make it more effectively the sacrament of salvation for all peoples.

℣   Through your presence, guide the college of bishops in union with the Pope,

℟   give them the gifts of unity, love and peace.

℣   Bind all Christians more closely to yourself, their divine Head,

℟   lead them to proclaim your kingdom by the witness of their lives.

℣   Grant peace to the world,

℟   let every land flourish in justice and security.

℣   Grant to the dead the glory of resurrection,

℟   and give us a share in their happiness.

The Lord's Prayer
Our Father… [See prayer on back flap]

Prayer

Father of all that is good,
keep us faithful in serving you,
for to serve you is our lasting joy.
We ask this through our Lord Jesus Christ,
  your Son,
who lives and reigns with you
  and the Holy Spirit,
one God, for ever and ever. Amen.

Closing Rite Or Dismissal

[See Closing Rite on Back Flap]

CHRIST THE KING
Solemnity

Hymn

♦ Crown him with many crowns,
The lamb upon his throne;
Hark! how the heav'nly anthem drowns
All music but its own:
Awake, my soul, and sing
Of him who died for thee,
And hail him as thy matchless King
Through all eternity.

♦ Crown him the Lord of lords,
Who over all doth reign,
Who once on earth, the incarnate Word,
For ransomed sinners slain,
Now lives in realms of light,
Where saints with angels sing
Their songs before Him day and night
Their God, Redeemer, King.

♦ Crown Him the Lord of heav'n,
Enthroned in worlds above;
Crown Him the King, to whom is giv'n
The wondrous name of Love.
Crown Him with many crowns,
As thrones before him fall,
Crown him, ye kings, with many crowns,
For He is King of all.

Text: Matthew Bridges, 1800-1894; Godfrey Thring, 1823-1903

Psalmody

Ant. 1   He shall sit upon the throne of David and rule
over his kingdom for ever, alleluia.

Book 5: Psalm 110: 1-5, 7
The Messiah, king and priest

[SIT]   ♦ The Lord's revelation to my Master:
"Sit on my right:
your foes I will put beneath your feet."

♦ The Lord will wield from Zion
your scepter of power:
rule in the midst of all your foes.

♦ A prince from the day of your birth
on the holy mountains;
from the womb before the dawn I begot you.

♦ The Lord has sworn an oath he will not change.
"You are a priest for ever,
a priest like Melchizedek of old."

♦ The Master standing at your right hand
will shatter kings in the day of his great wrath.

♦ He shall drink from the stream by the wayside
and therefore he shall lift up his head.

[BOW]   ♦ Glory to the Father…

Ant.   He shall sit upon the throne of David and rule
over his kingdom for ever, alleluia.

Ant. 2   Your kingdom shall be an everlasting kingdom,
and you shall rule from generation to generation.

Book 5: Psalm 145: 1-13
'Praise' of God's majesty

♦ I will give you glory, O God my King,
I will bless your name for ever.

♦ I will bless you day after day
and praise your name for ever.
The Lord is great, highly to be praised,
his greatness cannot be measured.

♦ Age to age shall proclaim your works,
shall declare your mighty deeds,
shall speak of your splendor and glory,
tell the tale of your wonderful works.

♦ They will speak of your terrible deeds,
recount your greatness and might.
They will recall your abundant goodness;
age to age shall ring out your justice.

♦ The Lord is kind and full of compassion,
slow to anger, abounding in love.
How good is the Lord to all,
compassionate to all his creatures.

♦ All your creatures shall thank you, O Lord,
and your friends shall repeat their blessing.
They shall speak of the glory of your reign
and declare your might, O God,

♦ to make known to men your mighty deeds
and the glorious splendor of your reign.
Yours is an everlasting kingdom;
your rule lasts from age to age.

[BOW]   ♦ Glory to the Father…

Ant.   Your kingdom shall be an everlasting kingdom,
and you shall rule from generation to generation.

Ant. 3   On his cloak and on his thigh a name was written:
King of kings, and Lord of lords. To him be glory
and power for ever.

Canticle based on Revelation 19: 1-7
The wedding of the Lamb

✦ Alleluia.
Salvation, glory, and power to our God:
(℟ Alleluia.)
his judgments are honest and true.
℟ Alleluia (alleluia).

✦ Alleluia.
Sing praise to our God, all you his servants,
(℟ Alleluia.)
all who worship him reverently, great and small.
℟ Alleluia (alleluia).

✦ Alleluia.
The Lord our all-powerful God is King;
(℟ Alleluia.)
let us rejoice, sing praise, and give him glory.
℟ Alleluia (alleluia).

✦ Alleluia.
The wedding feast of the Lamb has begun,
(℟ Alleluia.)
and his bride is prepared to welcome him.
℟ Alleluia (alleluia).

[Bow] ✦ Glory to the Father...

Ant. On his cloak and on his thigh a name was written: King of kings, and Lord of lords. To him be glory and power for ever.

Reading: 1 Corinthians 15: 25-28

Christ must reign until God has put all enemies under his feet, and the last enemy to be destroyed is death. Scripture reads that God "has placed all things under his feet." But when it says that everything has been made subject, it is clear that he who has made everything subject to Christ is excluded. When, finally, all has been subjected to the Son, he will then subject himself to the One who made all things subject to him, so that God may be all in all.

Responsory

℣ Your throne, O God, shall stand for ever.
℟ Your throne, O God, shall stand for ever.
℣ The scepter of your kingdom is a scepter of justice.
℟ It shall stand for ever.
[Bow] ℣ Glory to the Father, and to the Son, and to the Holy Spirit.
℟ Your throne, O God, shall stand for ever.

Canticle Of Mary

Ant. All authority in heaven and on earth has been
[Stand] given to me, says the Lord.

Magnificat: Luke 1: 46-55
My soul ✠ proclaims the... [See Prayer On Back.]

Intercessions

Introductory Formula
Let us pray to Christ the King. He is the firstborn of all creation; all things exist in him.
℟ May your kingdom come, O Lord.

Petitions
℣ Christ, our king and shepherd, gather your sheep from every land,
℟ give them pasture in green and fertile meadows.
℣ Christ, our leader and savior, form all men into your own people, heal the sick, seek out the lost, guard the strong,
℟ call back those who have wandered far away, strengthen those who waver, gather all your sheep into one flock.
℣ Judge of all ages, when you hand over your kingdom to your Father, place us at your right hand,
℟ so that we may inherit the kingdom prepared for us from the beginning of the world.
℣ Prince of peace, break the weapons of war,
℟ and inspire the nations with your peace.
℣ Christ, heir of all nations, gather humanity and all the good things of your creation into the kingdom of your Church which your Father bestowed on you,
℟ so that the whole body of your people, united in the Holy Spirit, may acknowledge you as their head.
℣ Christ, firstborn of the dead and firstfruits of those who have fallen asleep in death,
℟ bring all who have died to the glory of the resurrection.

The Lord's Prayer
Our Father... [See prayer on back flap]

Prayer

Almighty and merciful God,
you break the power of evil
and make all things new
in your Son Jesus Christ, the King of the
  universe.
May all in heaven and earth acclaim your glory
and never cease to praise you.
We ask this through our Lord Jesus Christ,
  your Son,
who lives and reigns with you
  and the Holy Spirit,
one God, for ever and ever. Amen.

Closing Rite Or Dismissal [See Back Flap.]

SUPPLEMENTAL MATERIAL

LITURGICAL CALENDAR

This calendar will guide you in determining what feast to pray on any given Sunday. However, it is not a definitive guide, since the celebration of certain feasts may vary from diocese to diocese. When there are two likely feasts for a given day, the page numbers for both feasts are given.

To find the feast you need to pray, first find the current year; next, the month and date (which have a background shading); and finally the page number for that feast, which falls directly below the date.

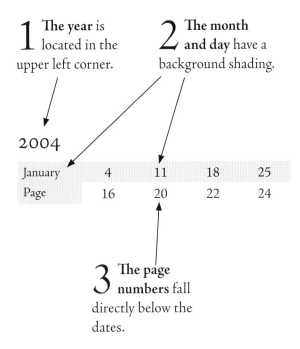

1 **The year** is located in the upper left corner.

2 **The month and day** have a background shading.

2004

January	4	11	18	25
Page	16	20	22	24

3 **The page numbers** fall directly below the dates.

Liturgical Calendar

2004

January	4	11	18	25	
Page	16	20	22	24	
February	1	8	15	22	29
	26	30	32	34	40
March	7	14	21	28	
	42	44	46	48	
April	4	11	18	25	
	50	52	54	56	
May	2	9	16	23	30
	58	60	62	64 or 66	68
June	6	13	20	27	
	70	72 or 80	82	86	
July	4	11	18	25	
	90	92	94	96	
August	1	8	15	22	29
	98	102	106	108	110
September	5	12	19	26	
	112	114	118	120	
October	3	10	17	24	31
	122	124	126	128	130
November	7	14	21	28	
	136	140	142	2	
December	5	12	19	26	
	4	6	8	12	

2005

January	2	9	16	23	30
Page	16	20	22	24	26
February	6	13	20	27	
	30	40	42	44	
March	6	13	20	27	
	46	48	50	52	
April	3	10	17	24	
	54	56	58	60	
May	1	8	15	22	29
	62	64 or 66	68	70	72 or 76
June	5	12	19	26	
	78	80	82	86	
July	3	10	17	24	31
	90	92	94	96	98
August	7	14	21	28	
	102	104	108	110	
September	4	11	18	25	
	112	114	118	120	
October	2	9	16	23	30
	122	124	126	128	130
November	6	13	20	27	
	136	140	142	2	
December	4	11	18	25	
	4	6	8	10	

Liturgical Calendar

<table>
<tr><td colspan="6">**2006**</td><td colspan="6">**2007**</td></tr>
<tr><td>January</td><td>1</td><td>8</td><td>15</td><td>22</td><td>29</td><td>January</td><td>7</td><td>14</td><td>21</td><td>28</td><td></td></tr>
<tr><td>Page</td><td>14</td><td>20</td><td>22</td><td>24</td><td>26</td><td>Page</td><td>20</td><td>22</td><td>24</td><td>26</td><td></td></tr>
<tr><td>February</td><td>5</td><td>12</td><td>19</td><td>26</td><td></td><td>February</td><td>4</td><td>11</td><td>18</td><td>25</td><td></td></tr>
<tr><td></td><td>30</td><td>32</td><td>34</td><td>36</td><td></td><td></td><td>30</td><td>32</td><td>34</td><td>40</td><td></td></tr>
<tr><td>March</td><td>5</td><td>12</td><td>19</td><td>26</td><td></td><td>March</td><td>4</td><td>11</td><td>18</td><td>25</td><td></td></tr>
<tr><td></td><td>40</td><td>42</td><td>44</td><td>46</td><td></td><td></td><td>42</td><td>44</td><td>46</td><td>48</td><td></td></tr>
<tr><td>April</td><td>2</td><td>9</td><td>16</td><td>23</td><td>30</td><td>April</td><td>1</td><td>8</td><td>15</td><td>22</td><td>29</td></tr>
<tr><td></td><td>48</td><td>50</td><td>52</td><td>54</td><td>56</td><td></td><td>50</td><td>52</td><td>54</td><td>56</td><td>58</td></tr>
<tr><td>May</td><td>7</td><td>14</td><td>21</td><td>28</td><td></td><td>May</td><td>6</td><td>13</td><td>20</td><td>27</td><td></td></tr>
<tr><td></td><td>58</td><td>60</td><td>62</td><td>64 or 66</td><td></td><td></td><td>60</td><td>62</td><td>64 or 66</td><td>68</td><td></td></tr>
<tr><td>June</td><td>4</td><td>11</td><td>18</td><td>25</td><td></td><td>June</td><td>3</td><td>10</td><td>17</td><td>24</td><td></td></tr>
<tr><td></td><td>68</td><td>70</td><td>72 or 80</td><td>82</td><td></td><td></td><td>70</td><td>72 or 78</td><td>80</td><td>82 or 84</td><td></td></tr>
<tr><td>July</td><td>2</td><td>9</td><td>16</td><td>23</td><td>30</td><td>July</td><td>1</td><td>8</td><td>15</td><td>22</td><td>29</td></tr>
<tr><td></td><td>86</td><td>90</td><td>92</td><td>94</td><td>96</td><td></td><td>86</td><td>90</td><td>92</td><td>94</td><td>96</td></tr>
<tr><td>August</td><td>6</td><td>13</td><td>20</td><td>27</td><td></td><td>August</td><td>5</td><td>12</td><td>19</td><td>26</td><td></td></tr>
<tr><td></td><td>100</td><td>102</td><td>104</td><td>108</td><td></td><td></td><td>98</td><td>102</td><td>104</td><td>108</td><td></td></tr>
<tr><td>September</td><td>3</td><td>10</td><td>17</td><td>24</td><td></td><td>September</td><td>2</td><td>9</td><td>16</td><td>23</td><td>30</td></tr>
<tr><td></td><td>110</td><td>112</td><td>114</td><td>118</td><td></td><td></td><td>110</td><td>112</td><td>114</td><td>118</td><td>120</td></tr>
<tr><td>October</td><td>1</td><td>8</td><td>15</td><td>22</td><td>29</td><td>October</td><td>7</td><td>14</td><td>21</td><td>28</td><td></td></tr>
<tr><td></td><td>120</td><td>122</td><td>124</td><td>126</td><td>128</td><td></td><td>122</td><td>124</td><td>126</td><td>128</td><td></td></tr>
<tr><td>November</td><td>5</td><td>12</td><td>19</td><td>26</td><td></td><td>November</td><td>4</td><td>11</td><td>18</td><td>25</td><td></td></tr>
<tr><td></td><td>130</td><td>136</td><td>140</td><td>142</td><td></td><td></td><td>130</td><td>136</td><td>140</td><td>142</td><td></td></tr>
<tr><td>December</td><td>3</td><td>10</td><td>17</td><td>24</td><td>31</td><td>December</td><td>2</td><td>9</td><td>16</td><td>23</td><td>30</td></tr>
<tr><td></td><td>2</td><td>4</td><td>6</td><td>8</td><td>12</td><td></td><td>2</td><td>4</td><td>6</td><td>8</td><td>12</td></tr>
</table>

Liturgical Calendar

2008

January Page	6	13	20	27	
	18	20	22	24	

February	3	10	17	24	
	26	40	42	44	

March	2	9	16	23	30
	46	48	50	52	54

April	6	13	20	27	
	56	58	60	62	

May	7	11	18	25	
	64 or 66	68	70	72 or 74	

June	1	8	15	22	29
	76	78	80	82	86 or 88

July	6	13	20	27	
	90	92	94	96	

August	3	10	17	24	31
	98	102	104	108	110

September	7	14	21	28	
	112	116	118	120	

October	5	12	19	26	
	122	124	126	128	

November	2	9	16	23	30
	134	136 or 138	140	142	2

December	7	14	21	28	
	4	6	8	12	

2009

January Page	4	11	18	25	
	16	20	22	24	

February	1	8	15	22	
	26	30	32	34	

March	1	8	15	22	29
	40	42	44	46	48

April	5	12	19	26	
	50	52	54	56	

May	3	10	17	24	31
	58	60	62	64 or 66	68

June	7	14	21	28	
	70	72 or 80	82	86	

July	5	12	19	26	
	90	92	94	96	

August	2	9	16	23	30
	98	102	104	108	110

September	6	13	20	27	
	112	114	118	120	

October	4	11	18	25	
	122	124	126	128	

November	1	8	15	22	29
	132	136	140	142	2

December	6	13	20	27	
	4	6	8	12	

LITURGICAL CALENDAR

2010

January	3	10	17	24	31
Page	16	20	22	24	26

February	7	14	21	24	
	30	32	40	42	

March	7	14	21	28	
	44	46	48	50	

April	4	11	18	25	
	52	54	56	58	

May	2	9	16	23	30
	60	62	64 or 66	68	70

June	6	13	20	27	
	72 or 78	80	82	86	

July	4	11	18	25	
	90	92	94	96	

August	1	8	15	22	29
	98	102	106	108	110

September	5	12	19	26	
	112	114	118	120	

October	3	10	17	24	31
	122	124	126	128	130

November	7	14	21	28	
	136	140	142	2	

December	5	13	19	26	
	4	6	8	12	

2011

January	2	9	16	23	30
Page	16	20	22	24	26

February	6	13	20	27	
	30	32	34	36	

March	6	13	20	27	
	38	40	42	44	

April	3	10	17	24	
	46	48	50	52	

May	1	8	15	22	29
	54	56	58	60	62

June	5	12	19	26	
	64 or 66	68	70	72 or 86	

July	3	10	16	24	31
	90	92	94	96	98

August	7	14	21	28	
	102	104	108	110	

September	4	11	18	25	
	112	114	118	120	

October	2	9	16	23	30
	122	124	126	128	130

November	6	13	20	27	
	136	140	142	2	

December	4	11	18	25	
	4	6	8	10	

Hymn References

Creator of the Stars of Night. Melody: *Creator alme siderum.* L.M.; Music: Sarum plainsong, Mode IV; Text: Anon., 7th Century; Translator: J. M. Neale et al., alt.

Behold a Rose of Judah. Melody: *Es Ist Ein' Ros* 76.76.676; Music: Traditional Melody from Alte catholische geistliche; Kirchengesang, Cologne, 1599; Text: Es ist ein' Ros entsprungen, 15th cent.; Translator: Composite.

What Child Is This. Melody: Greensleeves 87.87.68.67; Music: 16th Century English Melody; Text: William Chatterton Dix, 1837-1898.

Sing of Mary, Pure and Lowly. Melody: Pleading Mother 87.87.D; Music: Joshua Leavitt's The Christian Lyre, 1830–1831; Text: Roland F. Palmer, 1938, based on a 1914 poem.

Virgin-Born, We Bow Before You. Melody: *Mon Dieu, Prete Moi L'Oreille* 88.77.D; Music: Genevan Psalter, 1543; Text: Reginald Heber, 1783-1826, alt.

As with Gladness Men of Old. Melody: *Dix* 77.77.77; Music: Adapted by William H. Monk, 1823-1889 from a chorale by Conrad Kocher, 1786–1872; Text: Chatterton Dix, 1837–1898.

Sing Praise to Our Creator. Melody: *Gott Vater! Sei Gepriesen* 76.76 with Refrain; Music: Mainz Gesangbuch, 1833; Text: Omer Westendorf, 1961.

Love Divine, All Love Excelling. Melody: *Hyfrydol* 87.87.D; Music: Rowland H. Prichard, 1811–1877; Text: Charles Wesley, 1707–1788, adapted by C.T. Andrew, 1968.

O Christ, You Are the Light and Day. Melody: Saint Anne C.M.; Music: William Croft, 1708; Text: *Christe qui Lux es et Dies*; Translator: Rev. M. Quinn, O.P. et al., 1965.

When Mary Brought Her Treasure. Melody: *Allons, Suivons Les Mages* 76.76.676; Music: Traditional French Carol; Text: Jan Struther 1901–.

This Is Our Accepted Time. Melody: Weimar 76.76.D; Music: Melchior Vulpius, 1609; Text: Michael Gannon, alt.

When I Survey the Wondrous Cross. Melody: Rockingham L.M.; Music: Adap. By E. Miller, 1731-1807 from A. Williams' A Second Supplement to Psalmody in Miniature, Oxford, c. 1780; Text: Isaac Watts, 1674-1748, slightly adapted.

Lord, Who Throughout These Forty Days. Melody: Saint Flavian C.M.; Music: Adapted from Psalm 132, John Day's Psalter 1562; Text: Claudia Hernaman, 1838-1898, alt.

Draw Near, O Lord. Melody: *Attende Domine* 11.11.11; Music: Paris Processional, 1824; Text: Attende Domine; Translator: Melvin Farrell, S.S.

O Sacred Head, Surrounded. Melody: Passion Chorale 76.76.D; Music: Hans Leo Hassler, 1601; Text: St. 1, Sir W. H. Baker, 1821-1877, alt., st. 2, Melvin Farrell, S.S., 1961.

At the Lamb's High Feast. Melody: Salzburg 77.77.D; Music: Jakob Hintze, 1622-1702; Text: *Ad regias Agni dapes*; Translator: Robert Campbell, 1814-1868, adapted by Geoffey Laycock.

Christ Jesus Lay in Death's Strong Bandsl. Melody: *Christ Lag In Todesbanden* 87.87.87.74 with Alleluia; Music: Walther's Gesangbuchlein, 1524; Text: based on Victimae Paschali laudes; Translator: Richard Massie, 1800-1897 ad. by Anthony G. Petti.

Alleluia! The Strife Is O'er. Melody: Victory 8.8.8. with Alleluias; Music: G.P. da Palestrina 1588, ad. with alleluias by W. H.; Monk, 1861; Text: Symphonia Sirenum Selectarum, Congne, 1695; Translator: Francis Pott, 1861, alt.

The Head That Once Was Crowned with Thorns. Melody: Saint Magnus (Nottingham) C.M.; Music: Attributed to Jeremiah Clarke, c. 1659-1707; Text: Thomas Kelly, 1789-1854, slightly adapted.

Come, Holy Ghost, Creator, Come. Melody: Tallis' Ordinal C.M.; Music: Thomas Tallis, c. 1510-1585; Text: Attributed to Rabanus Maurus, 766-856; Translator: Anon., Hymns for the Year, 1876.

Come, Thou Almighty King. Melody: Italian Hymn; Music: Felice de Giardini, 1716-1796; Text: Anon., c. 1757, alt.

Father, We Thank Thee. Melody: *Rendez a Dieu* 98.98.D; Music: Louis Bourgeois, 1543; Text: Didache, c. 110; Translator: F. Bland Tucker, 1941.

The Great Forerunner of the Morn. Melody: Sedulius L.M.; Music: Nurnbergisches Gesangbuch, 1676; Text: The Venerable Bede, 673-735; Translator: J. M. Neale, 1818.

The Eternal Gifts of Christ the King. Melody: *Deo Gratias* L.M.; Music: English Melody, 15th Century; Text: Saint Ambrose, d. c. 397; Translator: John Mason Neale, 1818-1866 and compilers of Hymns Ancient and Modern.

'Tis Good, Lord, To Be Here. Melody: Narenza S.M.; Music: Melody in Leisentritt's *Catholicum Hymnologium Germanicum*, 1584, adapted by W. H. Havergal, 1814-1878; Text: J.A. Robinson, 1858-1933.

Hail, Holy Queen. Melody: Hail Holy Queen; Music: Lucien Deiss, C.S.Sp.; Text: Lucien Deiss, C.S.Sp.

Hail, Redeemer, King Divine. Melody: Hail Redeemer, St. George's Windsor 77.77.D; Music: George J. Elvey, 1816-1895; Text: Patrick Brennan, C.SS.R., alt.

For All the Saints. Melody: *Sine Nomine,* 10.10.10 with Alleluias; Music: Ralph Vaughan1872-1958; Text: William W. How, 1823-1897

May flights of Angels. Melody: *Unde et Memores,* 10.10.10.10.10.10; Music: William H. Monk, 1875, alt.; Text: James Quinn, S.J., 1969.

Christ Is Made Our Sure Foundation. Melody: Belville (Westminster Abbey) 87.87.87; Music: Adapted by Ernest Hawkins, 1802-1868, from an Anthem by H. Purcell, 1659-1695; Text: Urbs beata Jerusalem, c. 7th century; Translator: John Mason Neale, 1818-1866, adapted by Anthony G. Petti.

Crown Him with Many Crowns. Melody: Diademata S.M.D.; Music: George J. Elvey 1816-1893; Text: st. 1, Matthew Bridges, 1800-1894, sts. 2 & 3, Godfrey; Thring, 1823-1903.

A Guide to Using the Book of Christian Prayer

As you become more familiar with praying Sunday Evening Prayer, you may want to add more Liturgy of the Hours to your prayer life. The book of *Christian Prayer* makes it possible for you to pray almost all of the Liturgy of the Hours. It includes all of the Hours except for the Office of Readings. To help you make this transition to the book of *Christian Prayer*, we have included a brief tutorial below, which explains the various parts of the book. Catholic Book Publishing Company publishes a yearly guide for the Liturgical Year. However, once one sees how the various sections of the Prayer Book are used together with the Four-Week Psalter, finding the right page is not difficult. Perseverance is the key and help is available.

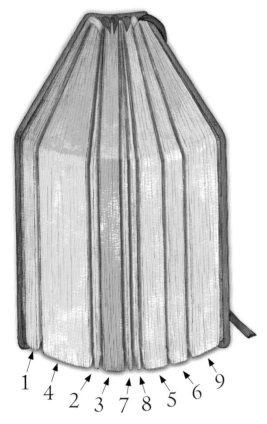

1 Pages 7-37: **General Instructions** and principles governing the praying of the Hours including a format of the Offices.

2 Pages 685-618: **The Ordinary** lays out in detail the proper procedures for the celebration of the two principal Hours, Morning and Evening Prayer.

3 Pages 699-993: **The Four-Week Psalter** is the "heart" of the Hours, containing the Psalms for Morning and Evening Prayer on a four-week cycle throughout the entire Liturgical year. The section also contains the balance of the prayer (reading, responsory, etc.) used in Ordinary time.

4 Pages 39-683: **The Proper of Seasons** contains the antiphons, readings, responsories, intercessions and concluding prayers "proper" to the particular Liturgical seasons, Sundays, and Solemnities throughout the year, beginning with the first Sunday of Advent. Unless included in this section, the psalms are taken from the four-week Psalter and under the title for each Sunday is listed which week of the psalms is to be used for each particular week.

5 Pages 1059-1353: **The Proper of Saints** follows the General Roman Calendar for the calendar year and contains information and prayers "proper" to each particular saint. These prayers are also used together with the prayers from the Four-Week Psalter.

6 Pages 1355-1500: **The Commons** contains readings, responsaries, antiphons, and intercessions "common" to particular categories of saints that are celebrated by the Church. (The Blessed Virgin, Apostles, Martyrs, etc.) These prayers are used together with the prayers from the Proper of Saints and the Four-Week Psalter.

7 Pages 994-1033: **Day Prayer** is the weekly cycle of prayer used in mid-morning, mid-day, and mid-afternoon.

8 Pages 1034-1051: **Night Prayer** is also a weekly cycle of prayer with the psalms, readings, etc. all contained in this one section.

9 Pages 1501-2079: **Hymns, readings from the Church Fathers, Psalms from the Office of Readings**, etc.

Cross Reference to the Book of Christian Prayer

The following is a reference guide showing the feasts of the year, the page where the feast is found in this *Evening Prayerbook*, and the page where the same feast is found in the single-volume book of *Christian Prayer*. Since this *Evening Prayerbook* is meant to be your entrance into the Liturgy of the Hours, the reference guide below may serve to you help you relate this book to the single-volume book of *Christian Prayer*, should you decide to advance to that book. You will notice if you use the book of *Christian Prayer* that the page numbers refer to Evening Prayer II. This is because Evening Prayer I for a given Sunday is prayed the night *before* the feast (on Saturday evening). Evening Prayer II is prayed on Sunday evening.

Feast	Psalter Week	Evening Prayerbook	Christian Prayer
First Sunday of Advent	I	2	45
Second Sunday of Advent	II	4	68
Third Sunday of Advent	III	6	91
Fourth Sunday of Advent	IV	8	114
Christmas		10	147
The Holy Family		12	156
Mary, Mother of God		14	178
Second Sunday after Christmas	II	16	185
Epiphany		18	214
Baptism of the Lord		20	242
Second Sunday in Ordinary Time	II	22	246
Third Sunday in Ordinary Time	III	24	247
Fourth Sunday in Ordinary Time	IV	26	248
Presentation of the Lord		28	1082
Fifth Sunday in Ordinary Time	I	30	249
Sixth Sunday in Ordinary Time	II	32	251
Seventh Sunday in Ordinary Time	III	34	252
Eighth Sunday in Ordinary Time	IV	36	253
Ninth Sunday in Ordinary Time	I	38	254
First Sunday of Lent	I	40	270
Second Sunday of Lent	II	42	294
Third Sunday of Lent	III	44	318
Fourth Sunday of Lent	IV	46	342
Fifth Sunday of Lent	I	48	366
Palm Sunday	II	50	390
Easter Sunday		52	429
Second Sunday of Easter		54	455
Third Sunday of Easter	III	56	478
Fourth Sunday of Easter	IV	58	500
Fifth Sunday of Easter	I	60	523

Feast	Psalter Week	Evening Prayerbook	Christian Prayer
Sixth Sunday of Easter	II	62	545
Ascension of the Lord		64	565
Seventh Sunday of Easter	III	66	581
Pentecost		68	605
Trinity Sunday		70	648
Corpus Christi		72	658
Eighth Sunday in Ordinary Time	IV	74	612
Ninth Sunday in Ordinary Time	I	76	613
Tenth Sunday in Ordinary Time	II	78	614
Eleventh Sunday in Ordinary Time	III	80	615
Twelfth Sunday in Ordinary Time	IV	82	616
Birth of John the Baptist		84	1176
Thirteenth Sunday in Ordinary Time	I	86	617
Sts. Peter and Paul		88	1183
Fourteenth Sunday in Ordinary Time	II	90	619
Fifteenth Sunday in Ordinary Time	III	92	620
Sixteenth Sunday in Ordinary Time	IV	94	621
Seventeenth Sunday in Ordinary Time	I	96	622
Eighteenth Sunday in Ordinary Time	II	98	623
Transfiguration		100	1215
Nineteenth Sunday in Ordinary Time	III	102	624
Twentieth Sunday in Ordinary Time	IV	104	625
Assumption of Blessed Virgin Mary		106	1229
Twenty-First Sunday in Ordinary Time	I	108	627
Twenty-Second Sunday in Ordinary Time	II	110	628
Twenty-Third Sunday in Ordinary Time	III	112	629
Twenty-Fourth Sunday in Ordinary Time	IV	114	630
Triumph of the Holy Cross		116	1256
Twenty-Fifth Sunday in Ordinary Time	I	118	631
Twenty-Sixth Sunday in Ordinary Time	II	120	632
Twenty-Seventh Sunday in Ordinary Time	III	122	633
Twenty-Eighth Sunday in Ordinary Time	IV	124	635
Twenty-Ninth Sunday in Ordinary Time	I	126	636
Thirtieth Sunday in Ordinary Time	II	128	637
Thirty-First Sunday in Ordinary Time	III	130	638
All Saints		132	1306
Commemoration of the Faithful Departed		134	1310
Thirty-Second Sunday in Ordinary Time	IV	136	639
Dedication of St. John Lateran		138	1312
Thirty-Third Sunday in Ordinary Time	I	140	640
Christ the King		142	679

ABOUT THE ST. THOMAS MORE HOUSE OF PRAYER

The Saint Thomas More House of Prayer was founded for the purpose of praying and promoting the Liturgy of the Hours among the laity. The House of Prayer is hidden away in the little village of Van, Pennsylvania. At the House, all of the Hours are prayed throughout the day, rooms are available for overnight retreats and the Blessed Sacrament is present in the chapel all for the spiritual edification of the faithful. A separate apartment is available for priests who would like to come for retreat and to assist in the mission of the House. For more information call 814-676-1910 or visit our website at www.liturgyofthehours.org.

As part of its efforts to promote the Liturgy of the Hours, the St. Thomas More House of Prayer has teamed up with Patmos, a newly-formed publishing group led by Anthony Mioni of Shohola, Pennsylvania, to create this unique book on Sunday Evening Prayer. Other helpful products may be found on the Patmos website at www.patmos.us.

The St. Thomas More House of Prayer • 814-676-1910 • www.liturgyofthehours.org